The Culture of the Quake

MICHIGAN MONOGRAPH SERIES IN JAPANESE STUDIES
NUMBER 78

CENTER FOR JAPANESE STUDIES
THE UNIVERSITY OF MICHIGAN

The Culture of the Quake

The Great Kanto Earthquake and Taishō Japan

ALEX BATES

CENTER FOR JAPANESE STUDIES
THE UNIVERSITY OF MICHIGAN
ANN ARBOR 2015

Published by the Center for Japanese Studies,
The University of Michigan
1007 E. Huron St.
Ann Arbor, MI 48104-1690

Library of Congress Cataloging-in-Publication Data

Names: Bates, Alex, 1974-
Title: The culture of the quake : the great Kanto Earthquake and Taishō Japan / Alex Bates.
Description: Ann Arbor : Center for Japanese Studies/The University of Michigan, 2015. | Series: Michigan monograph series in Japanese studies ; number 78 | Includes bibliographical references and index.
Identifiers: LCCN 2015035085 | ISBN 9781929280865 (pbk. : alk. paper)
Subjects: LCSH: Japanese literature--Taishō period, 1912-1926--History and criticism. | Kanto Earthquake, Japan, 1923, in literature. | Kanto Earthquake, Japan, 1923, in motion pictures. | Kanto Earthquake, Japan, 1923--Personal narratives. | Motion pictures--Japan--History--20th century.
Classification: LCC PL726.63.K356 B38 2015 | DDC 895.609/0044--dc23
LC record available at http://lccn.loc.gov/2015035085

This book was set in Times New Roman.

This publication meets the ANSI/NISO Standards for Permanence of Paper for Publications and Documents in Libraries and Archives (Z39.48—1992).

Printed in the United States of America

Contents

Illustrations

Acknowledgments

This book would not have been possible without the support of several mentors, friends, and family members. Most of all, I would like to thank Ken Ito, whose guidance and support helped me through all stages of its development. Other mentors at Michigan included Esperanza Ramirez-Christensen and Markus Nornes, and both provided valuable feedback. Nakagawa Shigemi guided me during my initial research in Japan and has provided me an academic home at Ritsumeikan University on multiple occasions. Van Gessel was the inspiration to start this journey while I was an undergraduate student at Brigham Young University, and he has provided useful insights in every interaction since.

I was lucky to have supportive friends and classmates during my graduate student days. Timothy Van Compernolle and Mimi Plauche were valued *sempai*, and I can't imagine getting through without David Henry, Jan Leuchtenberger, Hoyt Long, Bob Rama, Jeremy Robinson, Kristina Vassil, Shawn Walker, and Jason Herlands. While I was at Ritsumeikan, Naitō Yoshitada, Tomoda Yoshiyuki, and other students provided me with friendship and support. I am particularly indebted to Murata Hirokazu, whose friendship and conversation over the years has proved invaluable. My colleagues at Dickinson College have provided me with comments on several chapters. Shannon Egan, Nicoletta Marini-Maio, John MacCormick, and Walter Chromiak were part of a writing group that helped me think through chapter six. I would particularly like to thank Shawn Bender and David Strand for their insight and advice at multiple stages. I also appreciate the anonymous reviewers for their insightful comments.

The Fulbright Scholar Program, administered by the Institute for International Education, supported the initial research for this project. A subsequent fellowship from the Japan Foundation helped to further my work and to bring the book to completion. I am extremely grateful for their support.

Teri Bates, John and Natalie Bates, and Victoria Scott helped with the editing process, and the prose is much better for their help. Bruce Willoughby, at the University of Michigan Center for Japanese Studies Publications Program, has ably guided me through the process of turning the manuscript into a book.

Finally, I would like to thank Amy Bates for sticking with me throughout. It is to you this book is dedicated.

Needless to say, all shortcomings herein are entirely my own.

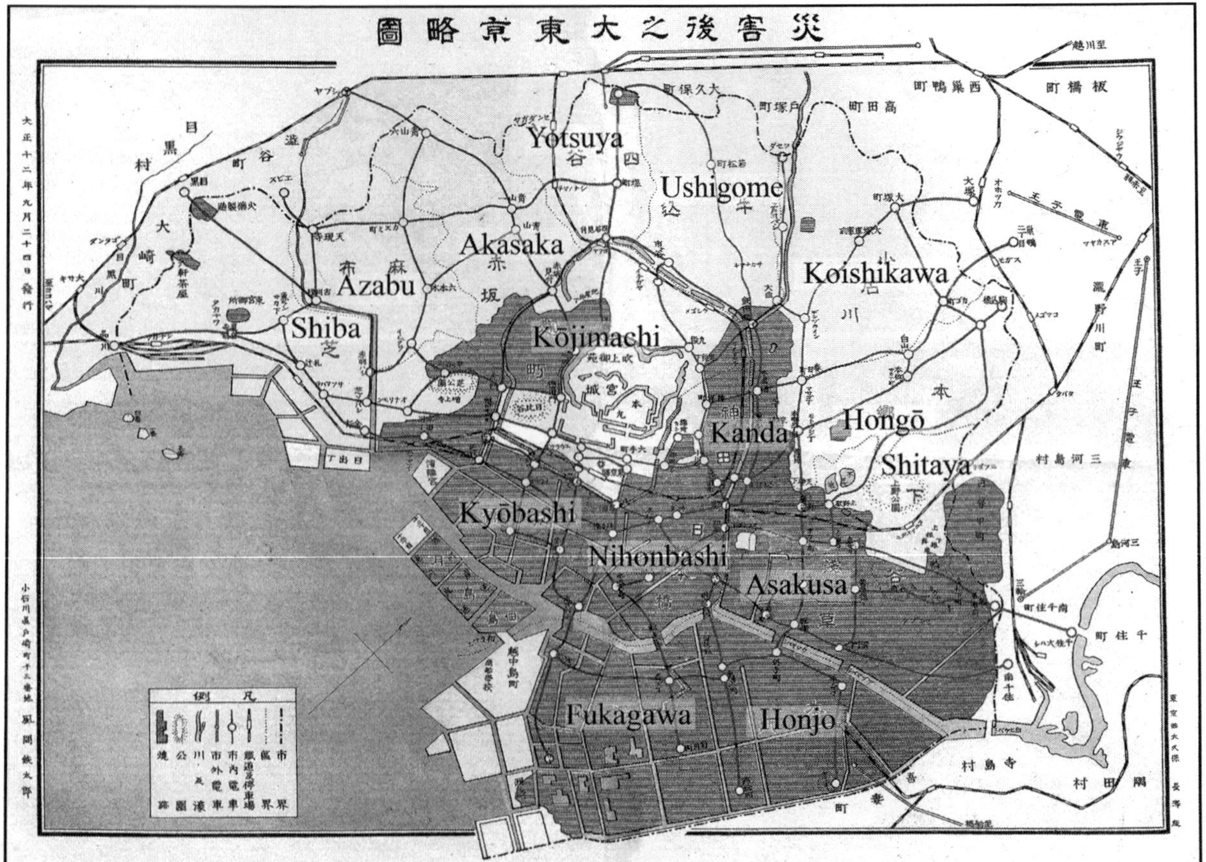

Fig. 1. Contemporary map of the area destroyed by the fires. Tetsutarō Kazama, *Saigo no Dai Tōkyō no ryakuzu* (Nagasawa Printing, 1923).

Introduction

Just before noon on the first day of September in the twelfth year of Taishō (1923), the author Tayama Katai (1872–1930) was at his house in the western suburbs of Tokyo. At that moment, tectonic plates shifted beneath the Sagami Bay, about 80 kilometers away. When the first tremors struck, he and his family dashed into their garden, sheltering under the plum and persimmon trees. They sat outside drinking tea and eating grapes for a few hours, until the larger aftershocks had subsided. Together the family set about cleaning up the damage, stacking roof tiles that had fallen, returning books to bookshelves, and sweeping the floor. According to Katai's *Record of the Tokyo Earthquake* (*Tōkyō shinsaiki*, 1924), in the midst of this picture-perfect domestic scene someone remarked, "If this is all it is, I guess it wasn't such a large earthquake after all." It was not until later that they noticed the huge clouds of smoke rising from the other half of the city. As Katai wrote, "At that moment, the terrible conflagration had begun in the city. The fearsome whirlwinds churned, and no matter where one turned, the flames provided no possibility of escape. The numbers of those burned to death climbed into the tens of thousands in this horrific tragedy."[1]

Though the initial shocks were severe, estimated at a magnitude of about 7.9 to 8.3, the fires Katai mentions caused most of the damage.[2] In Tokyo there were about one hundred initial fires, most of which burned out of control and spread across the city for over three days. Neighboring Yokohama fared no better. Once the fires had died down and the damage was surveyed, most of Yokohama and almost half of Tokyo lay smoldering in ruins. Across the greater Kanto area, over one hundred thousand people were listed as dead or missing and four hundred and fifty thousand houses were destroyed, leaving

1. Tayama Katai, *Tōkyō shinsaiki* (Hakubunkan, 1924), 18–19.
2. Takemura Masayuki, *Kantō daishinsai: Dai Tōkyō ken no yure wo shiru* (Kajima Shuppankai, 2003), 44.

about two and a half million people homeless.[3] It was indeed a "horrific tragedy," and a disaster of immense proportions: the Great Kanto Earthquake (*Kantō daishinsai*).

The most grisly site of death and destruction was the *hifukushō*, the location of a recently demolished military clothing depot in the industrial Tokyo ward of Honjo. The growing urbanization during preceding decades had transformed Honjo into a crowded mass of small wooden homes and tenements. In contrast to the many parks and open spaces in Katai's neighborhood (including family gardens), the *hifukushō* was the only place of refuge available for residents of Honjo. The lot was soon crowded with people who had had nowhere else to run when flames closed in on them from all sides. In a collection of earthquake-related stories, an anonymous author wrote about the experience of a man and his brother who were among the few to survive the *hifukushō* inferno: "The sound of wood blazing surrounded him from all sides and reverberated in his ears like the rumblings of the earth. He could not open his eyes. He was pouring water, pouring mud on himself and praying to the gods and buddhas unceasingly, knowing if he were to stop pouring water for one minute he would be dead. Forgetting that he was hungry, forgetting that he was tired, forgetting that he was scared, without any sensations, he was mechanically pouring the muddy water over himself."[4] Both brothers found themselves buried in bodies when the fires subsided, but they had lived. Most of the almost forty thousand people who had taken refuge at the *hifukushō* were killed. The loss of life in the *hifukushō* was so great that it inscribed the location with a particular connection to the disaster. It became, in the words of Narita Ryūichi, a "topos symbolizing the earthquake" as a whole.[5]

Despite the initial assessment in Katai's *Record of the Tokyo Earthquake*, the Great Kanto Earthquake was a major catastrophe that became a defining moment in the lives of all Japanese at the time, not only those who lived within its sphere of destruction. It was accounts such as those of Katai and the brothers in the *hifukushō* that enabled the disaster to become a part of Japan's collective memory. The earthquake dominated media for months afterward, resulting in a massive number of works in a variety of different formats. Individual experiences and

3. Tokyo and Yokohama were hit the hardest, but damage was reported across Kanagawa, Chiba, Saitama, Shizuoka, Yamanashi, and Ibaraki prefectures (listed in decreasing order of damage). Fujisawa Morihiko and Bureau of Social Affairs Home Office, *The Great Earthquake of 1923 in Japan* (Naimushō-Shakaikyoku, 1926), 40–51, 87. Recent research suggests that the initial estimate of 142,000 was too high and that the actual number was closer to 105,000. Moroi Takafumi and Takemura Masayuki, "Kantō jishin (1923–9–1) ni yoru higai yoin betsu shisha sū suitei," *Nihon jishin kōgakkai ronbun hōkoku shū* 4, no. 4 (September 2004): 21–45.

4. Dai Nihon Yūbenkai Kōdansha, ed., *Taishō daishinsai daikasai* (Kōdansha, 1923), 176–77.

5. Narita Ryūichi, "Kantō daishinsai no metahisutori no tame ni: hōdō, aiwa, bidan," *Shisō* 866 (August 1996): 68. The *hifukushō* was later designated the official site of earthquake remembrance, and even today houses the Earthquake Memorial Hall designed by Itō Chūta.

perceptions of the disaster were translated and combined into visual and linguistic forms that could be shared with others. In other words, the disaster was brought into the realm of representation.[6]

The body of work produced for public consumption in the aftermath of the 1923 earthquake has only recently begun to be explored. Charles Schencking has mined magazines, newspapers, and political documents for his historical study, and Gennifer Weisenfeld has written about the visual culture of the earthquake in her monograph focusing on documentary images and film from the disaster.[7] My study, in contrast, focuses on fictional approaches to the disaster in literature and film, while situating them amid the myriad nonfictional works that surrounded them. I interpret these representations around three different nodes that are linked to the disaster itself, but also to the development of Taishō-era culture.[8] The first has to do with the high literature of the time, which was inordinately centered on the lives of individual authors. Though narrowly focused narratives continued for some years after the quake, their dominance was challenged by new movements that looked to the outside world for inspiration.[9] This transition was in part shaped by a disaster that forced authors to confront the world.

The second node is centered on popular representations of the earthquake. This study moves beyond high literature to explore the moral issues surrounding the earthquake that are revealed in popular melodramatic narratives in fiction and film. In some ways, the excesses of melodrama were appropriate to depict the excesses of the disaster. Nevertheless, while the attention to the lives of everyday people and their suffering in these popular works is a welcome change from the narrower focus of some high literature on the quake, many of these melodramas support simplistic moralities that reaffirm conservative values.

The third node is shaped by the class and ethnic divisions apparent in the aftermath of the earthquake. The unequal distribution of damage by socio-economic status and the subsequent targeting of Koreans as scapegoats challenged state

6. Stuart Hall has defined representation as "the production of the meaning of the concepts in our minds through language [broadly defined]." It is in this sense that I am using the word. Stuart Hall, "The Work of Representation," in *Representation: Cultural Representations and Signifying Practices*, ed. Stuart Hall (London; Thousand Oaks, CA: Sage, 1997), 17.

7. J. Charles Schencking, *The Great Kanto Earthquake and the Chimera of National Reconstruction in Japan* (New York: Columbia University Press, 2013); Gennifer Weisenfeld, *Imaging Disaster: Tokyo and the Visual Culture of Japan's Great Earthquake of 1923* (Berkeley, CA: University of California Press, 2012).

8. By representations of the earthquake, I mean cultural products such as short stories, novels, photos, and films that specifically depict, interpret, or give shape to the very real earthquake disaster, its damage, or the experiences of people in its midst.

9. This is Seiji Lippet's argument about modernism, but the same could be said for the proletarian literary movement. See Seiji M. Lippit, *Topographies of Japanese Modernism* (New York: Columbia University Press, 2002), 32–33.

notions of national homogeneity. Some works ignore these divisions, while others attempt to confront them to varying effect.

These texts all share an attempt to deal in some meaningful way with a disaster that cost a hundred thousand lives and brought countless hardships. The earthquake left an indelible mark on the physical world, but its impact in the realm of representation was equally dramatic. It is the latter that we can explore through personal accounts of well-known authors, anonymous tales of personal suffering, melodramatic films, and proletarian dramatic theater. In these representations—examples of what I term "earthquake culture"—we can see how people responded to a disaster of this magnitude, and also to the social realities laid bare by the disaster.

THE EARTHQUAKE AND THE VULNERABLE

The stark contrast between Katai's experience of the earthquake and that of the two brothers in the *hifukushō* shows that not everyone within an affected area experiences disaster in the same way, and that these differences are the result not of the disaster itself but of a complex interaction between the natural destructive force and the built environment. This interaction is what we label a "disaster," here defined as the combination of a vulnerable population and a destructive force that results in large-scale disruption of society.[10] In this case, the population was that of the developed Kantō plain, and the force was the movement of tectonic plates.[11] This definition emphasizes the fact that the community at risk is in a "condition of vulnerability" resulting in part from social and economic factors external to the risk. That is, the way the population is organized, the way it is *structured*, makes it (and individual segments of that population) more or less vulnerable to the destructive force. The fact that Katai lived in one area of Tokyo and that those who took refuge in the *hifukushō* lived in another was a major determining factor in their experiences and their chances of survival.

Broad statistics that group the stricken area into one entity conceal the unequal distribution of damage across socio-economic class, seen clearly in the difference between Katai's experience and that of the brothers in the *hifukushō*.[12] Geographical segregation along class lines is a social reality. Therefore, mapping

10. Susannah M. Hoffman and Anthony Oliver-Smith, eds., *Catastrophe & Culture: The Anthropology of Disaster* (Santa Fe, NM; Oxford: School of American Research Press, 2002), 4.

11. Though the effects of the earthquake were felt across the globe, for my purposes the affected area is that in which damage from the event itself was recorded. This means the prefectures of Tokyo, Kanagawa, Chiba, Saitama, Shizuoka, Yamanashi, and Ibaraki. As Tokyo was where most authors and filmmakers were living at the time, I also focus primarily on Tokyo. Fujisawa Morihiko and Bureau of Social Affairs Home Office, *Great Earthquake of 1923*, 40–41.

12. For example, reporting that five hundred deaths resulted from the 1995 Chicago Heat Wave hides the fact that almost all of those heat-related deaths were among the city's poor. See Eric Klinenberg's fascinating study, *Heat Wave: A Social Autopsy of Disaster in Chicago* (University of

class and destruction onto geographical space provides a detailed analysis of disaster statistics that brings social divisions into focus. Contemporary maps of the damage and detailed statistics show areas that were hardest hit and thus more vulnerable. By linking those areas to the class and cultural background of their inhabitants, we can see how the earthquake exposed both the social structure of the city and its structure of power.[13]

Even today, Tokyo is often broadly divided into the *shitamachi*, the reclaimed tidal marshland to the south and east of the imperial palace, and the *yamanote*, the hilly region to the north and west of the palace. The *yamanote* and the *shitamachi* are neither clearly defined areas nor internally homogenous, nor are they historically stable, but the terms do reflect some general class-based cultural divisions in Taishō-era Tokyo.[14] The division is most well known in English-language scholarship in the title to Edward Seidensticker's book *Low City, High City*. Seidensticker identifies the *shitamachi* (low city) as the more plebeian half of the city.[15] Other

---

Chicago Press, 2003). This disparity was particularly evident to the American public in the aftermath of Hurricane Katrina in 2005. See Jeremy I. Levitt and Matthew C. Whitaker, *Hurricane Katrina: America's Unnatural Disaster* (Lincoln, NE: University of Nebraska Press, 2009); Michael Dyson, *Come Hell or High Water: Hurricane Katrina and the Color of Disaster* (New York: Basic Civitas, 2006); and Havidán Rodríguez and Russell Dynes, "Finding and Framing Katrina: The Social Construction of Disaster," http://understandingkatrina.ssrc.org/Dynes_Rodriguez/ (accessed November 15, 2010). The March 11, 2011 Tohoku Kanto Earthquake and subsequent tsunami disproportionally affected the elderly, but perhaps there is a similar economic disparity as well that will become more apparent as research continues.

13. I contend that various groups across the city can be differentiated not only by class but also by cultural background. The people in the *shitamachi,* especially the *Edokko* born and raised in Tokyo, have a distinct culture valorized in the Tora-san series of films of the postwar era. Even in the Taishō era, differences in cultural background could be seen among the *Edokko,* white-collar educated workers who came from wealthy rural samurai families, laborers from impoverished farms, and Korean workers.

14. At the time, the *shitamachi* was generally considered to have included the wards of Honjo, Fukagawa, Asakusa, Shitaya, Kanda, Nihonbashi, Kyōbashi, and Shiba. The *yamanote* consisted of Hongō, Koshikawa, Ushigome, Yotsuya, Akasaka, and Azabu. The central ward of Kōjimachi, which housed the imperial palace, spanned the two. As Takie Sugiyama Lebra has claimed, despite being founded in Tokyo topography, "these designations [of *yamanote* and *shitamachi*] are strongly symbolic of class divisions more than denotative of geography." See Lebra, *Above the Clouds: Status Culture of the Modern Japanese Nobility* (Berkeley, CA: University of California Press, 1993), 149. Paul Waley has explored the historical changes in the meaning of the *shitamachi* in particular in his article "Moving the Margins of Tokyo," *Urban Studies* 39 (August 2002): 1539–50.

15. Edward Seidensticker, *Low City, High City: Tokyo from Edo to the Earthquake* (New York: Knopf, 1983), 8. There are problems with Seidensticker's conception of the Edo-period history of the divide, but Henry Smith agrees that the association of the expanded *shitamachi* with "plebeian" does hold true in the late Meiji and Taishō eras. See his review article "Review: Low City, High City: Tokyo from Edo to the Earthquake," *Monumenta Nipponica* 39, no. 2 (1984–07–01): 208, and his chapter "The Edo-Tokyo Transition: in Search of Common Ground," in *Japan in Transition, from Tokugawa to Meiji*, ed. Marius B Jansen and Gilbert Rozman (Princeton, NJ: Princeton University Press, 1986), 370–74.

more rigorously academic studies support his assertion, noting the cultural and linguistic differences continuing through the twentieth century.[16] In 1923 these class divisions were primarily between the "new" middle class centered in the *yamanote* and western suburbs, and the "old" middle class and the working class centered in the *shitamachi*. Perhaps warranting yet another division, laborers were especially concentrated in the newly annexed eastern wards of Honjo and Fukagawa, but they, too, were considered part of the *shitamachi*. Of all 23 districts in the city, the *shitamachi* areas of Honjo and Fukagawa were the most industrial and the poorest.[17]

The new middle class was comprised primarily of those Meiji-era newcomers to the city who worked in the "white-collar" management and bureaucratic occupations. In terms of income this group may not have differed greatly from the "old" middle class of shopkeepers, but their occupations, and especially their mobilization of cultural and educational capital, set them apart.[18] This "new" middle class preferred homes in the *yamanote* region of Tokyo, especially the wards of Shiba, Kojimachi, Azabu, and Akasaka, leaving the *shitamachi* as a less desirable area that was home mostly to the "old" middle class.[19] Additionally,

16. Theodore Bestor's chapter "Tokyo's 'Traditional' Urbanism," in *The Cultural Meaning of Urban Space*, ed. Robert Rotenberg and Gary McDonogh (Westport, CT: Bergin & Garvey, 1993), especially p. 51, provides a good overview. For a linguistic exploration of the divide, see Junko Hibiya's chapter, "Variationist Sociolinguistics," in *The Handbook of Japanese Linguistics*, ed. Natsuko Tsujimura (Malden, MA: Blackwell Publishers, 1999). For a late 1970s to early 1980s look at the cultural differences, see Dorinne Kondo's *Crafting Selves: Power, Gender, and Discourses of Identity in a Japanese Workplace* (University of Chicago Press, 1990), 49–75.
17. See Sally A. Hastings, *Neighborhood and Nation in Tokyo, 1905-1937* (Pittsburgh, PA: University of Pittsburgh Press, 1995) for a detailed history of this area from 1905–37, and Andrew Gordon, *Labor and Imperial Democracy in Prewar Japan* (Berkeley, CA: University of California Press, 1991), for a look at labor issues in Honjo, Fukagawa, and the industrial suburbs of Minami Katsushika County over a similar time frame.
18. See, for example, Hiromichi Ishizuka, "The Slum Dwellings and the Urban Renewal Scheme in Tokyo, 1868-1923," *The Developing Economies* 19, no. 2 (1981): 187; Pierre Bourdieu, "The Forms of Capital," in *Education: Culture, Economy, and Society*, ed. A. H. Halsey, Hugh Lauder, Phillip Brown, and Amy Stuart Wells (Oxford; New York: Oxford University Press, 1997); Jordan Sand, *House and Home in Modern Japan: Architecture, Domestic Space, and Bourgeois Culture, 1880-1930* (Cambridge, MA: Harvard University Asia Center, 2005–09–06), 12–13; and David Ambaras, "Social Knowledge, Cultural Capital, and the New Middle Class in Japan, 1895-1912," *Journal of Japanese Studies* 24, no. 1 (Winter 1998): 1.
19. In their analysis of a 1922 "Who's Who" of office managers (*Marunouchi benran*), Fujioka Hiroyasu and Imafuji Akira show that white-collar workers had a clear preference for homes in the *yamanote* area and in the western suburbs, such as Shinjuku and Shibuya. When they narrowed their analysis to upper-level management, most lived in the *yamanote* "upper-class residential areas" of Shiba, Kōjimachi, Azabu, and Akasaka. See "'Marunouchi shinshiroku' Taishō 11 nenban, Taishō 15 nenban, Shōwa 6 nenban ni keisai sareta kōkyū shain no kyojūchi bunpu ni mirareru tokuchō: Taishō makki kara Shōwa shoki ni okeru Tōkyō no chūsan kaikyū no kyojūchi ni kansuru kenkyū," *Nihon kenchiku gakkai keikakukei ronbunshū* 470 (1995): 235–42. Takie Sugiyama Lebra similarly locates prewar aristocratic residences as centered in Akasaka and Azabu in *Above the Clouds*, 150.

almost all of the Tokyo writers listed in the 1923 literature yearbook had homes in the *yamanote* districts.

The most visible clue to the unequal distribution of damage is the extent of the fires. Maps of earthquake and fire damage were ubiquitous in the months after the tragedy, and clearly show that the area most affected by the fires was the *shitamachi* (see fig. 1 across from the beginning of this chapter). The areas of the city destroyed by the fires were also where most of the deaths occurred (see figs. 2 and 3). A full 20 percent of the Honjo population, over 50,000 people, died in the quake (most in the *hifukushō*). Those living in the *yamanote* area and beyond in the suburbs were comparatively unscathed. Though about one third of the Tokyo population resided in the *yamanote* at the time, less than 5 percent of the total deaths were from the *yamanote* region, and no *yamanote* ward lost more than 1 percent of its population to the disaster. In extreme contrast to Honjo, the western city ward of Yotsuya reported seven people killed or missing out of a population of 68,000 (0.01 percent of its population).[20]

The causes of this inequality in the impact of the earthquake are numerous. Fortunately for those living there, the *yamanote* region is built on firm bedrock, resulting in weaker seismic shocks.[21] Most of the temples in the city, with their vast grounds, were also in these hills, as were the larger public parks. The villas of aristocrats and wealthy businessmen in prestigious *yamanote* neighborhoods were spacious, with large gardens surrounding them. Even more modest homes, such as those of many writers, had some sort of garden. These wider spaces provided places of refuge for those who lived there, helped prevent the fires from spreading, and made fighting the fires easier.

The *shitamachi*, in contrast, was built on the unstable flood plain, resulting in a greater impact of the seismic waves (see fig. 4).[22] The rapid urbanization in the previous decades made the *shitamachi* especially crowded, with small wooden homes packed into small blocks with no green space. Overcrowding was especially apparent in the industrial areas of Honjo and Fukagawa. The only place of refuge available for residents of Honjo was the fateful *hifukushō*, undeveloped only because the military clothing depot that had occupied the space had recently been torn down. People in these regions suffered more because of their location, and class was the primary determinant of residence. As the proletarian critic Aono

20. While none would deny the economic disparity in the destruction, Daniel Aldrich has argued that the speed of recovery across the city differed not based on economics, but on the social cohesion of the affected communities. Daniel P. Aldrich, *Building Resilience: Social Capital in Post-Disaster Recovery* (Chicago: University of Chicago Press, 2012): 54–73.

21. The Bernal Heights area in San Francisco was similarly spared during the 1906 earthquake.

22. For a look at estimates of the shaking across Tokyo, see Moroi Takafumi and Takemura Masayuki, "Kantō jishin (1923–9–1) ni yoru higai yoin betsu shisha sū suitei," and Takemura Masayuki, *Kantō daishinsai: Dai Tōkyō ken no yure wo shiru*.

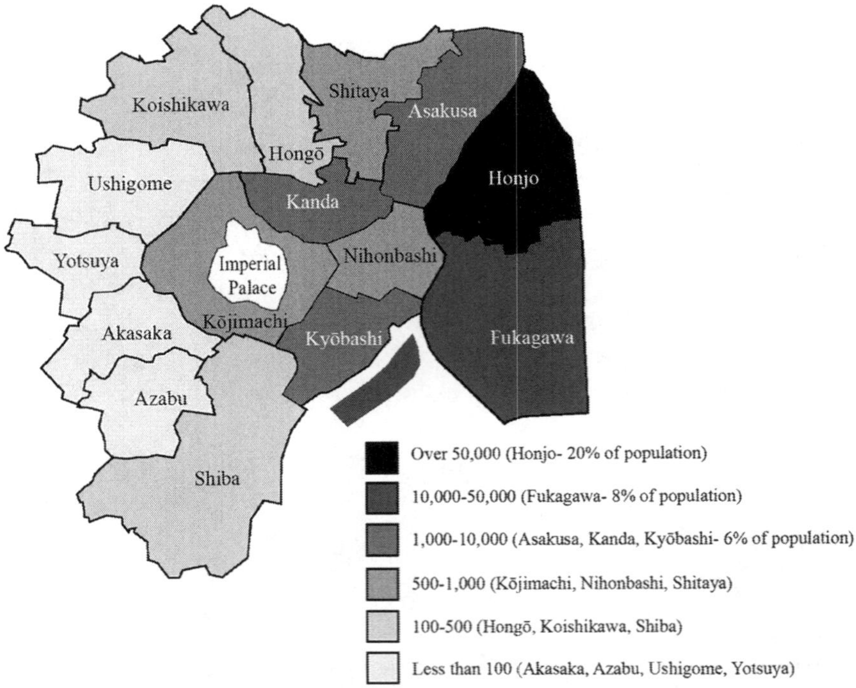

Fig. 2. Map showing dead and missing by city ward. Data taken from Fujisawa Morihiko, ed., *The Great Earthquake of 1923 in Japan* (Naimushō-Shakaikyoku, 1926).

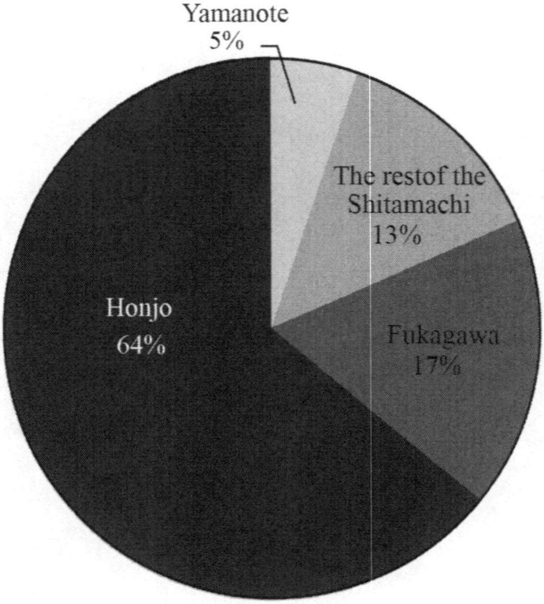

Fig. 3. Chart showing percentage of total dead and missing by area. The wards of Honjo and Fukagawa account for over three-fourths of the deaths. Data taken from Fujisawa Morihiko, ed., *The Great Earthquake of 1923 in Japan* (Naimushō-Shakaikyoku, 1926).

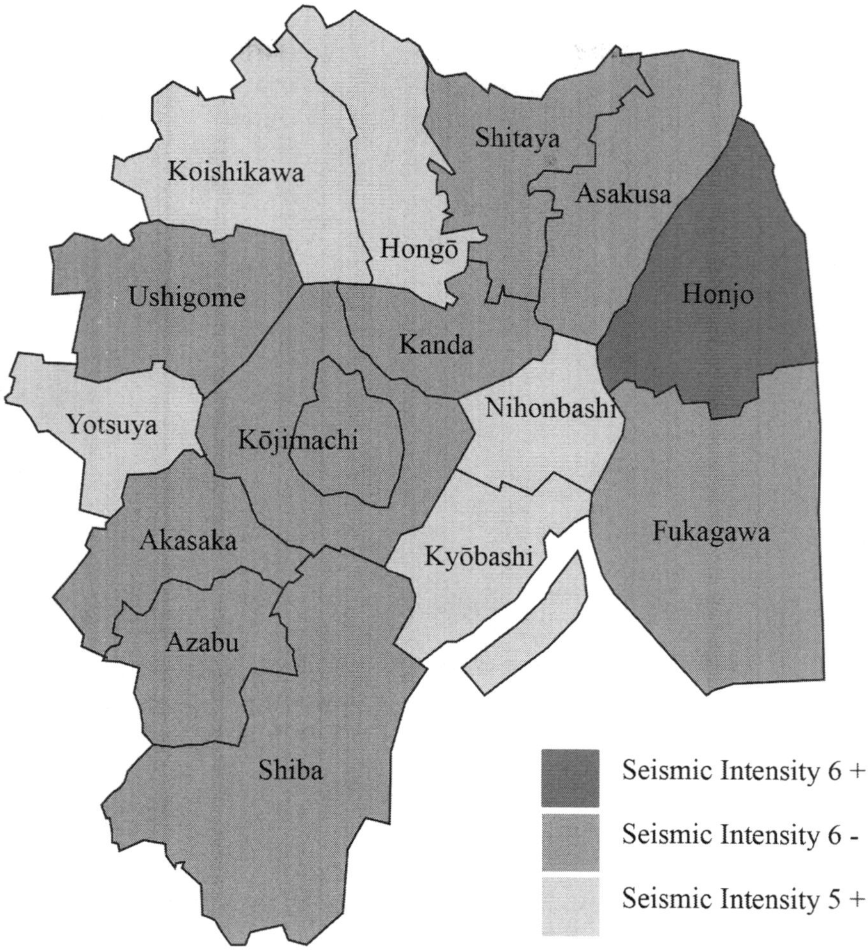

Fig. 4. Map showing difference in seismic intensity between the city wards (average intensity over ward area). Redrawn from page 114 of Takemura Masayuki, *Kantō daishinsai: Dai Tōkyō ken no yure wo shiru* (Kajima Shuppankai, 2003).

Suekichi (1890–1961) wrote, "The earthquake and the fires may not have recognized class distinctions, but the calamity that befell people was certainly based on class."[23]

Other segments of the population were also at risk, not as a result of where they lived but because of their ethnicity or ideology. Rumors spread almost as quickly as the fires, the most malicious of which attributed the fires to "unruly

23. Aono Suekichi, "Shakai no genjitsu to shisō to," *Shinkō* 1:1 (February 1924), quoted in Kūm Pyōng-dong, *Chōsenjin gyakusatsu ni kansuru chishikijin no hannō*, vol. 2 (Ryokuin Shobō, 1996), 9.

Koreans" (*futei Senjin*) and socialists, or claimed that Koreans were massing for an attack to take advantage of the confusion.[24] In his earthquake memoir, Katai described a conversation he had with his wife about rumors that a hundred of "those people" (understood to be Koreans or Communists) were approaching from a nearby neighborhood.[25] These unconfirmed reports also turned official. Proletarian writer Ema Shū (1889–1975) records seeing a warning posted on an electric pole claiming that three hundred Koreans were rallying to attack.[26] The origins of the rumors remain uncertain, but they were clearly widespread and were disseminated in part by official and semi-official representatives of the government.[27] In certain neighborhoods across Tokyo, "self-protection" groups (*jikeidan*) created makeshift checkpoints and patrolled streets looking for Koreans. Their unchecked actions, in conjunction with rogue police and military groups, led to a massacre. Though exact numbers are hard to pinpoint, most scholars agree that thousands of Koreans were killed.[28]

Koreans were not the only group targeted as scapegoats. In response to rumors suggesting that socialist activists were inciting the Koreans and planning a revolution, police rounded up radical workers and labor officials across the city. The day of the earthquake, Hirasawa Keishichi (1889–1923), a poet, playwright, and labor activist in the radical Nankatsu labor union, was put into the Kameido prison with nine others. At some point after the first night, all were killed and several were beheaded, in what later became known as the Kameido Incident.[29] Over

24. For an overview of the Korean Massacre in English, see Sonia Ryang, "The Great Kanto Earthquake and the Massacre of Koreans in 1923: Notes on Japan's Modern National Sovereignty," *Anthropological Quarterly* 76, no. 4 (2003): 731–48, Jinhee Lee, "Instability of Empire: Earthquake, Rumor, and the Massacre of Koreans in the Japanese Empire" (Ph.D. dissertation, University of Illinois, 2004); and Jinhee Lee, "The Enemy Within: Earthquake, Rumours and Massacre in the Japanese Empire," in *Violence: Mercurial Gestalt*, ed. Tobe Levin (Amsterdam & New York: Rodopi, 2008).
25. Tayama Katai, *Tōkyō shinsaiki*, 49. The actual mention of the term "Korean" was often censored at the time.
26. Ema Shū, *Hitsuji no ikaru toki* (Shūhōkaku, 1925), 154. There are several other recorded examples of official notices of Korean attacks. See Kūm Pyōng-dong, *Chōsenjin gyakusatsu ni kansuru chishikijin no hannō*, vol. 1 (Ryokuin Shobō, 1996a).
27. Some clearly blame the government for having instigated the rumors, but the evidence is not conclusive. For an example of this line of thought in English, see Yoshiaki Ishiguro, "A Japanese National Crime: The Korean Massacre after the Great Kantō Earthquake of 1923," *Korea Journal* 38, no. 4 (Winter 1998): 331–54. In Japanese, Kang Tōk-sang is the most outspoken proponent of this idea. See Kang Tōk-sang, *Kantō daishinsai* (Chūō Kōron-sha, 1975). See also Matsuo Takayoshi's critique in "Kantō daishinsai ka no Chōsenjin gyakusatsu 1," *Shisō* 471 (1963): 45–46.
28. Yamada Shōji analyzes the various surveys and numbers, and their strengths and weaknesses. See his *Kantō daishinsaiji no chōsenjin gyakusatsu* (Sōshisha, 2003), 164–211. His conclusion is that the number will never be known but is probably in the thousands, though less than the 6,600 suggested by some.
29. For more information, see Fujita Fujio and Ōwada Shigeru, *Hyōden Hirasawa Keishichi: Kameido Jiken de gisei to natta rōdō engeki, seikyō, rōkin no senkusha* (Kōbunsha, 1996).

two weeks after the earthquake, Ōsugi Sakae (1885–1923), a prominent anarchist critic of the Taishō period, was murdered by army lieutenant Amakasu Masahiko (1891–1945).[30] Ōsugi, his lover Itō Noe (1895–1923), and his young nephew, Tachibana Sōichi (age 7), were taking a walk when they were accosted by Amakasu and his squad. They were killed sometime on the sixteenth of September and their bodies thrown down a well. In contrast to those responsible for Hirasawa's death, Amakasu was tried and convicted for his role in the deaths, though he received a relatively light sentence.[31]

The attacks on labor activists and on Ōsugi were an extreme manifestation of the fear among officials that disgruntled masses would violently erupt to protest a lack of governmental aid. People displaced from the devastated *shitamachi* suffered shortages of food, shelter, and medical attention for several days. Immediately following the earthquake, the head of police, Akaike Atsushi (1879–1945), saw the masses of refugees gathered on the grounds in front of the imperial palace and feared their anger would be directed at the government. Following his visit, Akaike recorded in his diary: "I was anxious this would generate some unforeseen incident. . . . There is the fear that the entire capital will fall into a great riot. Thus, at this point we should muster the strength of not just the police force but also the entire nation to preserve the peace. I feel we must take action with haste. . . . I spoke to the home minister about the need to put the city under martial law."[32] Akaike's fears of the dispossessed crowds gathered on the grounds of the imperial palace were manifest in his suggestion that military and police action would be necessary to keep the masses in check. Martial law was instituted shortly thereafter. Coupled with the martial law was an ideological campaign stressing unity in the face of the national disaster.

THE RESPONSE OF THE STATE

In 1923, Japan was a sophisticated nation-state with spheres of control that had greatly expanded over the previous half century. When the earthquake hit, it did

30. Oftentimes these are called the "three atrocities," referring to the murder of Ōsugi Sakae, the Kameido Incident, and the Korean Massacre. Kang Tŏk-sang has argued persuasively against this reference because of the vast differences between the Korean Massacre and the other two in *Kantō daishinsai*, 192–93.

31. Amakasu was given a sentence of ten years, but served only three. For a more detailed examination of the Amakasu Incident, as the murder of Ōsugi came to be called, see chapter 11 in Thomas Stanley, *Ōsugi Sakae, Anarchist in Taishō Japan: The Creativity of the Ego* (Cambridge, MA: Council on East Asian Studies; Harvard University Press, 1982). Some newspapers praised Amakasu for killing Ōsugi, but were censored. On the censorship of articles praising Amakasu, see Matsuo Shōichi et al., *Kantō daishinsai seifu, riku-kaigun kankei shiryō* (Nihon Keizai Hyōronsha, 1997), 272.

32. Kūm Pyōng-dong, *Chōsenjin gyakusatsu ni kansuru chishikijin no hannō*, 11.

not merely destroy a handful of cities but struck the political, economic, and cultural heart of an empire. Its repercussions were felt beyond the reach of its destruction. In response to the chaos generated by the earthquake, the government marshaled its ideological resources to mask divisions in the national homeland that had been brought to the forefront by the disaster. Two imperial rescripts issued in the months after the quake endeavored to interpret the earthquake in the national interest. Both were printed in the newspapers, along with commentary so that the public could understand their archaic language.[33] The first appeared two weeks after the quake, and the second two months later. Chief among the goals of these two rescripts was to absolve the government of blame and to mobilize the national community toward reconstruction.

The first official rescript, the "Imperial Edict on Reconstruction," begins with a narrative of national advancement, overseen by a continuous imperial lineage and culminating in the Meiji Restoration and the current emperor. In the midst of this account, the earthquake strikes: "Now, without forewarning and suddenly, there has occurred the terrible earthquake of September 1." The implication is that the emperor will see the nation through this new trial, as he has done earlier and as previous emperors did before him. However, the rescript also stresses the "naturalness" of the disaster, lest the populace think that imperial control over the nation extends to control over the damage of the earthquake.[34] Though this was a terrible event, the rescript explicitly states, "It is beyond human will or effort to prevent the inexorable convulsions of nature (*tensaijihen*)."[35]

Both rescripts concentrate on reconstruction rather than the disaster itself and particularly on the national responsibility to return Japan to prosperity. The conclusion to the first rescript gives a direct imperial order to work for the benefit of the nation: "The people of the nation (*kokumin*) are ordered to assist in the realization of government's undertakings and earnestly to fulfil their duty to the public, thereby strengthening the foundations of our Empire."[36] This order univer-

33. The Tokyo *Asahi shinbun* printed the rescript on September 12, as a special edition on the first day it resumed printing after the quake. It appeared with commentary in the September 13 edition of the Osaka *Asahi shinbun* and in the September 14 editions of the Tokyo *Asahi shinbun* and the *Yomiuri shinbun*.
34. This was probably to counter ideas that natural disasters show corruption in government. This idea the government corruption was linked to earthquakes had appeared as recently as the Ansei earthquake in 1854. See, for example, Hiroi Osamu, *Saigai to Nihonjin: kyodai jishin no shakai shinri* (Jiji Tsūshinsha, 1986). For more on the connection between government and disaster, and the idea of heavenly punishment, see Chapter 7.
35. Fujisawa Morihiko and Bureau of Social Affairs Home Office, *Great Earthquake of 1923*, frontispiece. Unless otherwise noted, the translations are as they appeared in the English language version, cited here.
36. Fujisawa Morihiko and Naimushō-Shakaikyoku, *Taishō shinsaishi* (Iwanami, 1926) and Fujisawa Morihiko and Bureau of Social Affairs Home Office, *Great Earthquake of 1923*, frontispiece, slightly modified to translate *kokumin* as "the people of the nation" instead of "the general nation."

salizes the responsibility by using the term *kokumin*: all Japanese nationals, and not just those in the disaster area, are encouraged to do their part in overcoming this national disaster.

The second imperial rescript, the "Rescript on Strengthening the National Spirit,"[37] is more explicit in its call for national unity. It deals not only with reconstruction but also with the moral responsibility of the people to strengthen Japan in the wake of a disaster of this magnitude: "It may not be possible to hope for the restoration of national culture and prosperity unless the determined will of the whole nation is aroused. This is the time when the people must be one in their courageous endeavor for the prosperity and expansion of the country."[38] Here the goals of the nation are clear: the "prosperity and expansion of the country." And the perils of doing nothing are stagnation and even regression.

The narratives invoked by the rescripts are *national* histories, and the earthquake is represented as a stumbling block on the *national* path toward prosperity and progress. Furthermore, in addressing the people, the rescripts use terms such as *kokumin*, or "nationals," rather than terms that focus on the survivors. In so doing, the rescripts draw upon the imagined community of the nation. Thus they encourage those beyond the scope of the disaster to feel an urgency not only to help those in the disaster zone (seemingly a secondary concern) but to reemerge energized to work for the "continued prosperity and expansion" of the nation.[39] These rescripts attempt to subsume the various differences within the nation into a grand, unified identity equal to the nation-state. The rescripts worked to subsume the disaster into a narrative of national history, and thus to mobilize it for national purposes. As Prasenjit Duara wrote in another context, "National history secures for the contested and contingent nation the false unity of a self-same, national subject evolving through time."[40] But "national history" was only one voice in the aftermath of the quake.

EARTHQUAKE CULTURE

Popular writers, members of the literary establishment, and filmmakers each had their own interpretations of the disaster. The official discourse surrounding the

37. This is my translation of the rescript title "Kokumin seishin no sakkō no shōsho." In the English version the title is "Imperial Edict Enjoining Sincere and Strenuous Life." The Japanese version and my translation emphasize the national aspect of the rescript.
38. Fujisawa Morihiko and Bureau of Social Affairs Home Office, *Great Earthquake of 1923*, frontispiece.
39. Efforts to encourage people throughout Japan and its colonies to help meet the specific needs of those who were harmed directly were successful. Donations poured in from all over Japan and the colonies. People of Japanese descent contributed a full 20 percent of aid coming from the United States, the largest foreign donor. Though the Japanese-American community was well established by the time of the earthquake, and there could be several causes behind this astonishing percentage, it is likely that these donors saw themselves as part of the national community affected by the disaster despite their physical separation. Ibid., 379.
40. Prasenjit Duara, *Rescuing History from the Nation* (University of Chicago, 1995), 4.

earthquake, of which the rescripts form only one part, illustrates the stakes for representing the earthquake, namely, the national community. Some of the texts produced in the aftermath of the quake aligned with state discourse, whereas others took a more oppositional approach. At the same time, the state was not the ultimate foil for cultural products, but one thread, albeit a powerful one, in the discursive fabric created in the aftermath of the earthquake.

Despite being largely incapacitated at first, the print and film industries soon emerged from the ashes, bringing the disaster into the realm of discourse. First to emerge were newspapers and picture postcards, followed shortly thereafter by magazines, books, and films. These cultural products catered to the needs of audiences searching to know more about the disaster, and the demand for these products in turn helped the cultural industries rebuild. In this book, the plethora of cultural products and practices that take the earthquake and its destruction as their object are subsumed under the term "earthquake culture."

Earthquake culture spans audiences, literary schools, media, and genres. There were fictional stories by famous authors in high-culture journals and true stories of miraculous survival published in newspapers anonymously. Essays, stories, plays, and poems appeared in magazines and book-length collections marketed to an array of audiences. A mere month after the earthquake, people were lining up to see films of raw disaster footage as well as fictional melodramas set during the catastrophe. Chapter 1 provides an overview of the kinds of cultural products available in the aftermath and the impact of the quake on Japan's cultural industry. In these texts of "earthquake culture" we can see the effects of the disaster on a cultural industry already in a state of transition.

Many of the changes seen in Japanese culture following the earthquake were set in motion beforehand. Audiences were expanding for both print and film. Total numbers of magazines and books sold went from approximately 100 million in 1916 to 175 million in 1926.[41] Film viewership more than doubled, from a monthly average of 750,000 in 1918 to 1,747,000 in 1924.[42] Newcomers sensing opportunities in the growing markets began to challenge the old guard. Kikuchi Kan's (1888–1948) literary magazine *Bungei shunjū* (*Literary Annals*) began publication in 1923. Though it started small, it was already showcasing young talent and starting on the path to being the arbiter of taste it later became. Noma Seiji (1878–1938), the founder of Kōdansha, was deep into planning his mass-circulation general-interest magazine *King,* which, delayed by the earthquake,

41. Edward Mack, *Manufacturing Modern Japanese Literature: Publishing, Prizes, and the Ascription of Literary Value*, Asia-Pacific: Culture, Politics, and Society (Durham, NC: Duke University Press, 2010), 64.

42. From data available in Iwamoto Keiji and Makino Mamoru, eds., *Eiga nenkan Shōwa hen*, vol. 1 (Nihon Tosho Sentā, 1994), 33.

made a spectacular debut the next year. Though not perhaps as large a market force as the others, the landmark proletarian-literature magazine *Tanemaku hito* (*The Sower*), launched in 1921, was making waves in intellectual circles. In film the newcomer Shōchiku, which challenged the cinematic norm with new international film techniques, threatened the virtual monopoly of the Nikkatsu studio.

Japanese literature was having an identity crisis in the midst of this growth. Two major schools of writing had dominated high-culture Japanese letters in the 1910s: Naturalists such as Tayama Katai and Shimazaki Tōson (1872–1943), and the Shirakaba group, including Shiga Naoya (1883–1971), Arishima Takeo (1878–1923), and Satomi Ton (1888–1983).[43] The primary output of both groups consisted of narrowly focalized narratives revolving around a persona closely resembling the author himself, a form of fiction later named the I-novel, or *shishōsetsu*. By 1923 the solid position held by these writers was beset on several fronts. Socially conscious literature from the burgeoning proletarian movement suggested an alternative to the narrow focus on the self. The rising demands of a literate public and the growth of the print industry suggested that literature written and read by an elite few could not remain insulated for long. Finally, new trends toward modernist experimentation questioned the limits of realist fiction.

Happening as it did in the midst of these trends, the earthquake was inevitably seen as symbolizing a break. As Miyoshi Yukio writes, "The Great Kanto Earthquake had a great impact on the metropolitan literature of the time and made more insistent its self-doubt and instability. Thus the shaking of the earth held a type of symbolic meaning to a literary world caught at a time of transition."[44] Though Miyoshi sees the earthquake only as symbolic, it played a role in forcing writers outside themselves to see larger forces at work in the world. Following the overview of the industry in Chapter 1, Chapter 2 outlines the impact of the earthquake on the literary elite (the *bundan*). This chapter focuses on how *bundan* critics responded to the earthquake and concludes with a famous literary debate between Kikuchi Kan and Satomi Ton. This debate recast earlier debates in light of the disaster. Whereas Satomi Ton argued for the persistence and purity of art, Kikuchi Kan asserted that art had to take into account the disaster and the masses.

Chapter 3 explores the best-known work on the earthquake by a high-culture writer, namely, Tayama Katai's *Record of the Tokyo Earthquake*. Though the title implies that it is a comprehensive look at the earthquake, and advertisements

43. The Shirakaba group refers to writers and critics who published regularly in the magazine *Shirakaba*. They were primarily from aristocratic backgrounds and adhered to a humanistic and individualistic philosophy. The Shirakaba group is discussed in greater detail in Chapter 2.

44. Miyoshi Yukio, "Jishin to bungaku- Kantō daishinsai wo megutte," in *Jishin,* ed. Hayashi Kentarō (Tōkyō University Press, 1976), 301.

stressed its literary aspect, this text is a narrowly focused memoir recounting Katai's experiences and thoughts in the aftermath of the disaster. This chapter shows how Katai's earlier work had positioned him as a high-culture observer of the earthquake, a disaster *flâneur*. Katai's objective style and literary philosophy distance him from the suffering and focus on the self, thus providing an example of the interiority characteristic of Meiji and early Taishō literature. Nevertheless, this book also includes a melodramatic story of suffering in one of its final chapters. This story shows a move outward not only in subject matter but also in audience, and further highlights the porous boundary between high and low, even in an author as respected as Katai.

Melodrama was the common mode of representation for popular works that depicted the earthquake. Chapter 4 covers spectacular emotional tales of suffering in print and fictional films. After a survey of factual stories about the earthquake, called *jitsuwa*, it focuses on examples of fictional melodramas in print and film, namely, Nagata Mikihiko's "Wild Geese" ("Kari," 1923) and the Shōchiku film *Facing Death* (*Shi ni men shite*, 1923). As is the case with Western melodrama, these stories often reinforce a particular moral code. This morality is often in line with imperial rescripts; they praise acts of loyalty and sacrifice, and condemn earthquake opportunism.

There was some backlash against the commodification of earthquake suffering in popular melodrama and in postcards and films. Chapter 5 explores the response to the spectacle of suffering in popular literature, particularly in one high-culture work, Masamune Hakuchō's (1879–1962) "The Suffering of Another" ("Tanin no saigai," 1924). In this short story Hakuchō rejects the spectacle to focus on individual suffering, particularly in a middle-class setting. This story effectively critiques those who commodify suffering as spectacle and those who consume suffering through these commodities but also through disaster tourism, a staple of post-earthquake Tokyo.

Disaster tourism involved traveling from a relatively safe zone into the most devastated areas of town, the *shitamachi*. It was a rare subject, but a few writers explored the unequal distribution of earthquake damage implied by this sightseeing. Chapter 6 covers the anxiety these authors felt when confronted with this incongruity, centered on one text, Nagata Mikihiko's (1887–1964) "Wild Dance of the Flames" (Honoo no ranbu," 1923). Though this work shies away from social criticism, it reveals the middle-class narrator's anxiety over his relative comfort when faced with the suffering of those who just barely survived the flames. At the same time, there is a tension between the particular suffering of the protagonist and the more universalizing discourses of sufferers in general and the nation.

Chapter 7 explores the varying ways "heavenly punishment," or *tenken*, appears in culture. The idea of *tenken*, first proposed by industrialist Shibusawa

Ei'ichi (1840–1931), suggested that the quake was punishment for Japan's decadence and laxity toward Confucian morality. Other writers, including the Christian thinker Uchimura Kanzō (1861–1930) and author Chikamatsu Shūkō (1876–1944), soon echoed his pronouncement. Several films from the era, especially the Nikkatsu films produced in the later months of 1923, resonated with *tenken* discourse. One film, *The Earth Shakes* (*Daichi wa yuragu,* 1923), clearly identified the wealthy as targets of criticism. Though authors such as Chikamatsu sided with Shibusawa, others, such as Kikuchi Kan and Akutagawa Ryūnosuke, argued that inflecting the disaster with conservative morality was a dangerous abstraction that threatened to demonize innocent victims.

Chapters 8 and 9 explore the frenzy over the rumors of Korean unrest following the earthquake and the subsequent Korean Massacre. Chapter 8 provides an overview of how the massacre was represented at the time and illustrates how some works fanned the flames whereas others worked to critique the systems that brought about the tragedy. Chapter 9 is focused on the work of proletarian and leftist writers, who most often wrote about the massacre. Some of these writers used the massacre as a way to further their ideas about the class struggle, while others used their writing to emphasize the plight of the resident Koreans in Japan.

The shaking of the earth triggered a series of destructive events embedded in a particular social and cultural landscape, resulting in a disaster of immense proportions. Since that time, the earthquake disaster of September 1, 1923 has been known by various names: as the "Great Taishō Earthquake," the "Great Tokyo Earthquake," and its lasting moniker, the "Great Kanto Earthquake" (*Kantō daishinsai*). For a disaster to be a disaster, it must be so named by the community impacted. As Tanaka Jun wrote in 1923 in the journal *Bungei shunjū*, "It was not until we went out into the streets, saw the collapsed houses, the crying parents, and the bodies being dug out of the wreckage that we began to see this as a disaster (*saigai*)."[45]

It is not the destructive force alone but human consciousness that makes a disaster. In other words, although the destruction and death are real, "disaster" is a name given to the perceived social disruption by humanity. The impact of the fault movement under Sagami Bay in 1923 on those living in the area was almost immediately brought into the realm of discourse and given the name *daishinsai*, or great earthquake disaster. Human culture both creates the conditions of vulnerability and gives the resulting damage a name; in this way disaster is, at least in part, socially and culturally constructed both before the calamitous event strikes and in its aftermath.

45. Tanaka Jun, "Yurareteiru toki," *Bungei shunjū* 1, no. 11 (November 1923): 61–63.

* * * * *

Though the shifting in the earth's crust was caused by natural geological forces, the Great Kanto Earthquake of 1923 was a multilayered disaster that cannot be completely described as "natural." For example, the overcrowding in the poorer districts made those areas more susceptible to the fires, and newspaper fear-mongering made resident Koreans and socialists targets of suspicion. This book recognizes both the pre-quake production of vulnerability and the post-quake discursive construction of the earthquake as a catastrophe. It focuses on the post-disaster "earthquake culture," the body of texts that represent the earthquake: high-culture texts and popular writings depicting the earthquake, and proletarian texts depicting the massacre of Koreans perpetrated in the aftermath. These texts show how various preexisting discourses were affected by the earthquake, how various actors represented the earthquake, and thus how they attempted to interpret the disaster. Societal fissures, such as those of class and ethnicity, were laid bare in the disaster, and how those fissures were articulated or ignored in cultural products reveals much about their creators and the time in which they were created. Within these texts we see the ideal of the national community contested, as fractures appear in the illusion of a unified and homogenous Japan.

Chapter 1

Earthquake Culture

By 1923 Tokyo was the unchallenged center of a vibrant print culture. Japan was one of the world's largest producers of books, and almost five times as many books were being published in Tokyo as in Osaka and Kyoto combined.[1] The physical infrastructure for the print industry was concentrated in Tokyo, and so were the writers who produced the words for the pages. Prior to the earthquake, the industry produced about three hundred books and more than six hundred different magazines in Tokyo each month.[2] The impact of the earthquake was felt immediately, dealing a major blow to the industry, from production to storage to distribution. Though most companies bore some damage, few suffered as much as the book publisher Iwanami Shoten, which was hit across the chain of production. It lost its offices in Kanda, a printing facility, three warehouses, and two bookstores.[3] Of the six hundred some magazines in print before the disaster, only seventy were able to produce an October edition. In December 1923, only forty-five books were published.[4]

Despite the severity of the initial damage, the industry quickly regained its position and even expanded its audience base considerably. Estimates of the sale of books and magazines increased 15 percent between 1921 and 1926,

1. Edward Mack shows that in 1922, 8,856 book titles were published in Tokyo and only 1,812 in Osaka and Kyoto combined. These figures, combined with information from other municipalities, suggest that over 17,000 books were published in Japan in 1922. Edward Mack, *Manufacturing Modern Japanese Literature*, 63. Exact numbers are difficult, but this figure makes Japan one of the world's largest producers of books at the time.

2. Ibid., 72, and Odagiri Susumu, "Kindai bungaku to Kanto daishinsai," in *Nihon kindai bungaku daijiten*, vol. 4 (1977): 81–82.

3. Edward Mack, *Manufacturing Modern Japanese Literature*, 72.

4. Ibid., 70; Edward Mack, "The Value of Literature: Cultural Authority in Interwar Japan" (Ph.D. dissertation, Harvard University, 2002), 122, and Odagiri Susumu, "Kindai bungaku to Kanto daishinsai."

notwithstanding the effects of the quake.[5] One factor in the rapid recovery of the industry was the considerable boost in post-quake sales, driven by a large public demand for information, images, and narratives of the earthquake. The explosion of texts that emerged in the wake of the disaster reflects an industry struggling to meet that demand. The few publishers able to do so distributed their magazines and books dealing with the earthquake to readers across the country within a month. The earthquake dominated the media for the remainder of the year and well into 1924.

Writers were, of course, instrumental in this rebuilding effort as they produced the raw material—the words—for the publishers to print and sell. In fact, the human cost of the disaster to the publishing industry was relatively slight. The *bundan*, or literary and publishing elite, lost very few people to the disaster. At the same time, these authors struggled to represent the sheer scope of the catastrophe. This chapter explores the print culture following the disaster and the authors who contributed to it.

EARTHQUAKE PRINT CULTURE

Printed works served a variety of purposes following the disaster. Newspapers brought much-needed information (along with harmful misinformation) to the far reaches of the empire.[6] Magazines provided information as well, but digested that information to convey more detailed analysis of the disaster in collections of articles and essays. Books ranged from magazine-like collections of essays to more specialized works centered on certain aspects of the disaster or the experiences of people who had lived through it. Books also had an advantage over magazines in that they provided a more permanent and thus collectable commemorative object. What these various media share is that they all made it possible for people beyond the Kantō area to understand what happened in the disaster and its aftermath. Furthermore, though information and analysis were important, a key component was often stories of personal survival and sorrow, allowing people in the far reaches of the nation to sympathize with those who suffered the most.

The most affordable and readily available form of written media following the earthquake was the newspaper. As early as four o'clock on the day of the earth-

5. As Mack has shown, this recovery was due to the amassed capital held by these companies and the fortunate survival of some key elements of the infrastructure. The central offices of several companies survived, but more importantly, a few major printing presses remained operational or repairable. Shūei-sha (which printed the magazine *Kaizō*), Nisshin Insatsu, and Hakubunkan's state-of-the-art printing facility in Koishikawa were located in the *yamanote* region and survived with minimum damage. The survivors were based primarily in the *yamanote*, for example, Kōdansha in Hongō, Chūō Kōron-sha in Kōjimachi, and Shinchōsha in Ushigome. Edward Mack, *Manufacturing Modern Japanese Literature*, 65–66, 82.

6. Newspapers were printed locally but often borrowed information from other regions.

quake, the *Hōchi shinbun* was able to print a simple extra edition with basic information about the disaster. *Hōchi* was able to continue printing two- or four-page hand-printed papers until September 5, when larger-scale operations began again, but they were one of the few newspapers that was able to do so. The *Tokyo Nichinichi* resumed printing on September 6, but the *Tokyo Asahi* and *Yomiuri* papers were unable to restart operations for more than two weeks after the disaster.[7] All these papers struggled with a lack of raw materials, electricity, and, most importantly, reliable information. As a result, many of the rumors circulating around the city were spread across the country in the authoritative voice of newspaper headlines.

In an attempt to stem the tide of rumors, and to avoid the publication of damning material, the government censored newspapers, but information often found its way to the public despite government intervention. In his fictionalized account of experiencing the earthquake from afar, Tokuda Shūsei (1871–1943) wrote of seeing soldiers confiscate an extra edition: "When Toki [Shūsei's alter ego] approached them, the soldiers took the papers and left. His heart raced and he thought that he could probably find someone who had bought one before they were seized. . . . Before long he saw a crowd of people gathered around a paper near the entrance and went to see."[8] The story refrains from mentioning the item that drew the attention of the soldiers, but many of the censored articles were about Koreans.

Though other rumors were spread, those about Koreans were the most damaging. Stories about Koreans poisoning wells or starting fires ran in newspapers from Hokkaido to Kyushu. The government forbade publication of anything to do with the Koreans soon after the earthquake, but this was only sporadically enforced. This directive was presumably designed to prevent further spread of the rumors, but the result was that news of the massacre was also suppressed.[9] It

7. Ibid., 78.

8. Tokuda Shūsei, "Fuan no naka ni," in *Shūsei zenshū*, vol. 6 (1991): 188–89.

9. The result of this suppression has been a persistent belief in the rumors. In fact, misperceptions about what happened to Koreans after the earthquake remain even today. A friend told me of an encounter she had with an elderly Japanese woman who, upon hearing that my friend was studying Koreans, told her, "The Koreans started fires and poisoned wells after the Kanto earthquake, you know." More publicly, the governor of Tokyo, Ishihara Shintarō, said in 2000: "When we look at Tokyo today, lots of illegal thirdies [*sangokujin*, a derogatory word for people from places such as Korea, China, and other non Euro-American nations] foreigners are repeatedly involved in brutal crimes. Crimes in Tokyo aren't like they used to be. If we look at this situation, when a major disaster strikes there'll probably be a great big riot. This is something we can assume given this state of affairs" (*Sankei shinbun*, April 13, 2000). Ishihara later clarified his position, without making things any better: "It's a pity that many Koreans were killed due to demagoguery at the time of the Great Kanto Earthquake, but I'm afraid they will be killing us Japanese when the next big earthquake hits Tokyo" (*Seiron*, April 2000). He continued to put his foot in his mouth when he called the March 11, 2011 earthquake a "punishment from heaven." For more on this topic, see Chapter 7.

was not until late October that the ban was lifted and newspapers retracted some of their stories or reported the events of the massacre. Many rumors remained uncorrected even after restrictions were loosened. On October 21, several newspapers reported on official Justice Department documents about Korean violence, many of which were based on hearsay. For example, the *Nichinichi* reported on several "true" accounts of Korean violence, including many instances of "unknown Koreans" perpetrating violence against "unknown victims." One case was an allegation that four or five unknown Koreans raped and killed an unknown girl 16 or 17 years old and then threw her body into the Arakawa river.[10] Nothing substantiated these accounts. A few days later the *Nichinichi* ran a general correction: "The various reports of the Korean uprising at the time of the earthquake that ran in newspapers recently seem to have contained a great deal of misinformation."[11] The article went on to suggest that newspapers merely passed along the reports of the government without undertaking sufficient investigation.

One staple of post-quake newspapers was the *jitsuwa* (literally, "true story"). These short vignettes were focused on the personal experiences of people in the disaster zone, and were published alongside overarching discussions of the damage and political and economic ramifications of the earthquake. The title of the genre makes claims to authenticity, but many examples drew on conventions of fiction and are not clearly documented. For about a week after it resumed publication, the *Tokyo Asahi shinbun* ran a column featuring tales of sadness, improbable survival, and the strange. Some of the titles in the series were "The Sad Tears of an Orphaned Boy," "The Miraculous Reuniting of Three Sisters," and "Two Young Women Clutching Severed Heads."[12] These stories gave a degree of personal emotion to the reporting on the disaster and later appeared in magazines and book collections.

In addition to these anonymous tales, there were also accounts of famous people who lived through the quake, including updates on members of the imperial family, aristocrats, and authors. On September 6, the *Osaka Asahi shinbun* ran an article explaining what happened to many authors in the earthquake. Later, another article in the same paper focused on author Tanizaki Jun'ichirō (1886–1965) and his earthquake experience in Hakone. The paper subsequently followed his search for his family in Yokohama. A picture of the reunited family arriving in Kobe ran in the September 21 issue, along with Tanizaki's account of the adventure.

10. *Tōkyō Nichinichi shinbun,* October 21, 1923. Reproduced in Yamada Shōji, ed., *Chōsenjin gyakusatsu kanren shinbun hōdō shiryō*, vol. 1 (Ryokuin Shobō, 2004), 182–83.

11. *Tōkyō Nichinichi shinbun*, October 24, 1923. Reproduced in Kang Tŏk-sang and Kŭm Pyŏngdong, *Kantō daishinsai to Chōsenjin* (Misuzu Shobō, 1963), 203.

12. See, for example, *Tōkyō Asahi shinbun,* September 19, 1923, 2.

Though newspapers quickly provided information on the disaster sought by an eager public, magazines had the time to offer a more comprehensive look at the disaster from a variety of perspectives. The first magazines appeared at the beginning of October. Though some companies might have been able to produce issues earlier, the Tokyo Magazine Association, spurred in part by the leadership of Kōdansha's editor-in-chief Noma Seiji, agreed to wait until October so as to level the playing field.[13] This agreement gave even some of the more damaged publishers enough time to put together and print their October editions. These rules did not apply to the newspapers or regional magazines not included in the association. The Osaka branches of the *Mainichi* and *Asahi shinbun* published their weekly magazines, the *Sunday Mainichi* and the *Shūkan Asahi* (*Weekly Asahi*), on schedule, as early as September 9.

The magazines with larger circulations—general-interest magazines such as *Taiyō* (*The Sun*), *Chūō kōron* (*Central Review*), and *Kaizō* (*Reconstruction*), women's magazines such as *Josei* (*Woman*) and *Fujin kōron* (*Women's Review*), and literary magazines such as *Bunshō kurabu* (*Literary Club*)—were able to produce an earthquake edition for October. Some minor titles, such as author and publisher Kikuchi Kan's recent addition to the literary scene, *Bungei shunjū* (*Literary Annals*), had to wait until November. Kikuchi used the final paragraph of his essay in *Chūō kōron* to apologize to his readers for the delay.[14]

Other magazines ended circulation with the quake. The most famous example was *Shirakaba* (*White Birch*), the journal begun by writers such as Shiga Naoya, Arishima Takeo, and Satomi Ton. For *Shirakaba*, the earthquake followed Arishima Takeo's love suicide a few months before, and the combined blow proved impossible to withstand. The collapse of *Shirakaba* symbolized the end of an era. Though its writers continued to publish actively, its brand of individualist humanist art was no longer a force in Japanese letters. The proletarian literary magazine *Tanemaku hito* (*The Sower*) was a similar casualty of the disaster. It ended in January 1924, with a special issue on the Kameiido murder of labor activists. Unlike *Shirakaba*, those involved with *Tanemaku hito* returned in 1924 with the more ambitious journal *Bungei sensen* (*Literary Front*).

Magazines that produced an October 1923 issue had much in common. Those that could do so often included a series of photographs on the first few pages. They often contained essays on Tokyo's future, and general articles with conjectures on the effect of the disaster on government, business, and the arts. Many also included the earthquake experiences of popular authors and other public figures. The earthquake edition of the magazine *Kaizō*, for example, included essays on the challenges Japan faced as it rebuilt, analyses of the newly formed Yamamoto

13. Edward Mack, *Manufacturing Modern Japanese Literature*, 67.
14. Kikuchi Kan, "Saigo zakkan," *Chūō kōron* 38, no. 11 (October 1923): 119.

cabinet, and the earthquake experiences of sixteen authors.[15] Some of the same writers' names are found in the general-interest magazines *Chūō kōron* and *Shinchō*, not to mention more narrowly focused literary magazines such as *Bunshō kurabu*. Almost half of the post-quake issue of the women's magazine *Josei* was taken up by experiences of authors. This magazine included poems by the female poets Yosano Akiko (1878–1942) and Nakahara Ayako (1898–1969), in addition to the standard lineup of male authors.

In fact, so many magazines asked authors for accounts of their earthquake experiences that it was a financial windfall for many.[16] Akutagawa Ryūnosuke (1892–1927) noted in an essay for one magazine that several others had also approached him for earthquake-related material.[17] An article in the *Yomiuri* newspaper reported that Kume Masao (1891–1952) made 500–600 yen by sending in earthquake-related manuscripts to eight different journals. (For comparison, a reasonable middle-class monthly salary was about 60–80 yen.) According to the article, the next most productive authors were Akutagawa, Ogawa Mimei (1882–1961), Uno Kōji (1891–1961), and Satomi Ton (1888–1983), who wrote four articles each.[18] Not to be outdone, Masamune Hakuchō accepted fifteen commissions for the New Year issues of different magazines in January 1924.[19]

The eight journals that published the earthquake experiences of Kume Masao were those interested in literature and the lives of authors. Other magazines published material more closely directed at their readership. *Shōjo no tomo* (*Girl's Friend*) devoted most of its disaster issue to *jitsuwa*, several of which dealt with young girls.[20] The November issue of the magazine *Shōnen sekai* (*Boy's World*), for example, devoted some space to the earthquake among its detective stories. One fictional story depicted the heroism of a young boy who rescued the family canary from the flames.[21] Another story, explicitly labeled a *jitsuwa*, recounted the sad death of a young boy among the refugees.[22] The magazine *Shin-seinen* (*New Youth*), another magazine famous for its crime stories, had a series of personal accounts and reportage in its first post-quake issue, including several *jitsuwa* re-

15. The authors featured included Akutagawa Ryūnosuke (1892–1927), Uno Kōji (1891–1961), Chikamatsu Shūkō (1876–1944), Satō Haruo (1892–1964), Satomi Ton (1888–1983), Kikuchi Kan (1888–1948), Mushanokoji Saneatsu (1885–1976), Ogawa Mimei (1882–1961), Akita Ujaku (1883–1962), Fujimori Seikichi (1892–1977), and Kume Masao (1891–1952).
16. This has been pointed out by Inagaki Tatsurō, "Kantō daishinkasai to bundan," *Kokubungaku: kaishaku to kyōzai no kenkyū* 129 (1964): 45.
17. Akutagawa Ryūnosuke, "Daishin ni saiseru kansō," in *Akutagawa Ryūnosuke zenshū*, vol. 10 (1995a): 152. The magazine was the October 1923 issue of *Kaizō*.
18. "Bungei ran," *Yomiuri shinbun*, October 13, 1923.
19. "Shinnen no shōsetsu wo jūgohen mo hikiuketa," *Yomiuri shinbun*, December 10, 1923, 4.
20. *Shōjo no tomo* 16, no. 10 (October 1923).
21. Seki Tōfū, "Mōka wo okashite," *Shōnen sekai* 29, no. 11 (November 1923): 64–70.
22. Ito'o Kazumi, "Shōnen no nageki," *Shōnen sekai* 29, no. 11 (November 1923): 50–56.

corded by author Tanaka Kōtarō (1880–1941). The coverage of the earthquake continued into the next issue, which included eight moralistic *jitsuwa*. Though the Edogawa Ranpo (1894–1965) detective story featured in November was not about the earthquake directly, it did dwell heavily and gruesomely on death by fire.[23]

Newspapers provided recent information on the disaster, and magazines were able to explore issues in more depth, but their poor durability made them less desirable as permanent mementos of the earthquake. Postcards were an accessible commodity through which people could own a material record of the earthquake, and as such were immensely popular. In one telling anecdote, a postcard vendor made 60 yen in five days (probably a good deal more than his usual monthly salary).[24] It was a windfall for the printing companies as well. Mitsumura Printing Company, one of only two lithography printers lucky enough to escape damage, made enough from postcard sales to repay all debts and still have plenty of capital for expansion.[25] The popularity of earthquake postcards stemmed from the already established practice of postcard collection.

The Kanto earthquake postcards were part of a larger commercial trend in photojournalistic postcards that began with the Russo-Japanese War in 1904 and continued to cover major events, including natural disasters such as the earthquake in Shiga (1910), the Yoshiwara fire (1912), the volcanic eruption in Sakurajima (1914), and the Tokyo floods (1917). Many earthquake postcards focused on the destruction of famous landmarks. The dramatic remains of the twelve-storied Ryōunkaku, broken off at the eighth floor, were often featured (see fig. 5). Others focused on famous districts transformed into burnt wastelands without recognizable landmarks. Landscapes were not the only preoccupation of the photographers. Postcards also featured the "barrack" camps full of makeshift houses for refugees, the throngs of people fleeing the city, and, morbidly, corpses on the streets and at the *hifukushō* (see figs. 6–8). There was an underground market for images of dead bodies, despite an official prohibition.[26] One postcard

23. Edogawa Ranpo, "Osoroshiki sakugo," *Shin-seinen* 4, no. 13 (November 1923): 122–48.

24. Kimura Matsuo and Ishii Toshio, *Ehagaki ga kataru Kantō daishinsai* (Tsuge Shobō, 1990), 139. At this time a laborer in a railway factory reportedly earned 47 yen per month, and a salaried worker at a magazine company earned 60 yen per month. Nagamine Shigetoshi, *Modan toshi no dokusho kūkan* (Nihon Edita Skūru Shuppanbu, 2001), 165, 224.

25. Masuo Nobuyuki, *Mitsumura Risō den* (Mitsumura Genshokuban Insatsusho, 1964), 364. Indeed, this caused some resentment, and a few months later some people burned down their offices. Supposedly they did this because the Mitsumura company was profiting from earthquake postcards. Ironically, arson, unlike natural disaster, was covered by insurance.

26. There were several newspaper accounts of people illicitly selling postcards of the dead. See, for example, the *Kokumin shinbun* of October 21, 1923 as quoted in Hiroi Osamu, *Saigai to Nihonjin*, 11. In an interesting side note, even two years after the quake a man was arrested for selling postcards of the earthquake dead along with "sexual" postcards. *Yomiuri shinbun*, November 6, 1925, morning edition, 3.

Fig. 5. Postcard depicting the dramatic remains of the Ryōunkaku. Collection of the author.

Fig. 6. Postcard depicting the throngs of refugees leaving Tokyo at the Nippori station. Collection of the author.

Fig. 7. Postcard depicting the dead laid out on a bridge. Collection of the author.

Fig. 8. Postcard supposedly depicting the moments before the *hifukushō* inferno with the pile of bones left after the cremation of the bodies. Kimura Matsuo and Ishii Toshio, *Ehagaki ga kataru Kantō daishinsai* (Tsuge Shobō, 1990), 14.

dramatically shows the tragedy at the *hifukushō* without using the dead, by juxtaposing a photograph of those taking refuge before the inferno with one of the pile of bones and ash after they were cremated (fig. 8).[27]

Books similarly provided durable mementos of the disaster and often combined journalism, personal stories, and photographs. The first book published in Tokyo after the earthquake, Kōdansha's *The Great Taishō Earthquake and Conflagration* (*Taishō daishinsai daikasai*), appeared only after much difficulty. Though the Kōdansha company itself was relatively unscathed, to prepare the book for release by the end of September, the head editor Noma Seiji had to overcome obstacles such as lack of paper supply, breakdowns in the chain of distribution, difficulties obtaining financing, and lack of advertising outlets. The end result was a volume that, in both appearance and distribution technique, blurred the boundaries between a book and a special edition of a magazine. In fact some magazine publishers accused Kōdansha, perhaps justly, of printing a book so as to circumvent the rules delaying magazine publication until October.

The efforts of Noma and Kōdansha paid off. With no real competing publications, *The Great Taishō Earthquake and Conflagration* sold very well. It was the first comprehensive overview of the earthquake, the damage it caused, the known science behind it, and stories of people who lived through the disaster. Though a paperback, it had a striking cover showing the city in flames and included eighty pages of photographs, all for the price of 1.5 yen. Exact sales numbers are hard to come by, but Kōdansha estimates that about four hundred thousand copies were sold.[28]

Other books soon followed. Many adhered to the Kōdansha model, providing a variety of information about the earthquake generously sprinkled with *jitsuwa*, but there were also volumes devoted to photographs or poetry.[29] In early October the Tokyo publisher Yūhōdō Shoten released a book by journalist Shibuta Kōtō.[30]

27. Gennifer Weisenfeld discusses postcards in her *Imaging Disaster*, especially chapter 2.

28. Edward Mack, *Manufacturing Modern Japanese Literature*, 75. Mack recounts the fascinating story of the publication of this book on pages 73–77. See also the corresponding description in the Kōdansha company history. Kōdansha Shashi Hensan Iinkai, *Kōdansha no ayunda gojūnen* (Kōdansha, 1959), 540–80. Iwasaki Katsumi also examines the book in his article "Kaigenreika no besuto serā: *Taishō daishinsai daikasai* 70 nen go no shohyō," *Masukomi jyanarizumu ronshū* 4 (December 1995): 56–84. Some suggested that as many as 550,000 copies were sold, but Miyake Gaikotsu argued that even the 400,000 number was inflated. Miyake Gaikotsu, "Bandai fukyū rokuhen genryō: Kōdansha no shinsaiki," *Shinsai gahō* 5 (January 1924): 96.

29. For books of photography, see *Sangai shashin chō: kyū Tōkyō meisho to Kantō no daishinsai* (Naigai Shuppan Kyōkai, 1923); Kanagawa-ken, *Taishō jūninen kugatsu ichinichi daishinsai shashinchō* (Yokohama: Kanagawa Shinbun-sha, 1923); and Okada Kōyō, *Kantō daishin daika kinen shashin chō* (Tōkyō Zuan Insatsu, 1924). Poetry volumes included Araragi Hakkōsho, ed., *Kaijinshū: Taishō jūninen shinsai kashū* (Kokin Shoin, 1924); and Shiwakai, ed., *Saika no ue ni: shinsai shishū* (Shinchō-sha, 1923).

30. This is the pen name of Shibuta Tsunetarō.

This hardcover volume was printed in Osaka and went through four printings in two weeks. It is primarily a collection of Shibuta's articles for the *Yorozu chōhō* newspaper, with some recounted personal experiences and added commentary. Shibuta includes statistics about the damage as well as copies of all edicts and notices issued by the government at the time. One of the primary features is Shibuta's own survey of the disaster zone, based on several trips into the *shitamachi* as well as to the outer regions affected by the earthquake.

Most books about the quake dwelt heavily on the *jitsuwa* genre. By emphasizing the personal hardship and emotion of those who lived through the worst of the disaster, they were immensely popular with a public searching for an emotional connection to the tragedy. About one third of the Kōdansha book was devoted to *jitsuwa*, and several appear in Shibuta's book. Sadamura Seihyō (1891–?) published two volumes from Tadaya Shoten in Chiba, in October and November, respectively.[31] The first was devoted to his own experiences, and the second to various *jitsuwa* he had gathered. Seishindō published a two-volume collection of *jitsuwa* called *Earthquake Romance* (*Shinsai romansu)* in November 1923.[32] Even as late as March 1924, a collection of student quake experiences from a *shitamachi* vocational school went through at least four printings in the month after it was published, illustrating how even a narrowly focused book sold better than expected.[33]

Some earthquake collections were promoted through their affiliation with a popular author. The writer Tanaka Kōtarō contributed his name as well as his experiences and observations to a collection called *A History of Japan's Earthquake Disasters* (*Nihon daishinsai shi*). This expensive and nicely bound earthquake history was released by Yumei Shobō in January 1924.[34] Author Nagata Mikihiko's contribution, *The Earth Shakes* (*Daichi wa furū*), is primarily an account of Mikihiko's earthquake experiences combined with *jitsuwa* and fictional *jitsuwa*-like stories. Tanaka Kōtarō and Nagata Mikihiko were both well-known writers of popular fiction, but the most recognizable "high-culture" name associated with an earthquake collection is Tayama Katai. Katai's memoir *Record of the Tokyo Earthquake* was published by Hakubunkan in April 1924. It revisits the Tokyo of his 1917 memoir, *Thirty Years in Tokyo* (*Tōkyō no sanjūnen*), to explore what happened to his adopted city in the disaster.

In May 1924 the magazine publisher Kaizōsha released a book more impressive than all that had preceded it—*A Record of the Taishō Earthquake and*

31. Sadamura Seihyō, *Yume no miyako: Daishin daikasai sōnan jikki* (Chiba: Tadaya Shoten, 1923) and *Taishō jūninen kugatsu tsuitachi daijishin daikasai sōnan hyakuwa* (Chiba: Tadaya Shoten, 1923). Some sources have his name as Seihei.

32. Arano Kōhei, *Shinsai romansu* (Seishindō Shoten, 1923). The title uses the word "romance" in a broad sense, to mean emotional tales.

33. Chūō Shōgyō Gakkō, ed., *Kugatsu tsuitachi: risai gakusei shuki* (Sankōsha, 1924).

34. It was four times as expensive as Kōdansha's book.

Conflagration (*Taishō daishin kasai shi*).[35] This 15-yen leather-bound volume was designed to be the ultimate disaster collection. It contained over 120 photographs, a separate comprehensive map of the area, scientific explanations of the earthquake, details about the effects of the quake on various government offices and industries, descriptions of famous buildings and artifacts lost in the quake, a discussion of social issues related to the earthquake, actions of relief groups, and personal experiences written by established authors. This final category included writing by Shimazaki Tōson, Satomi Ton, Arishima Ikuma, Akita Ujaku, Uno Kōji, Kume Masao, Murō Saisei, and Akutagawa Ryūnosuke.

AUTHORS AND THE QUAKE

Many printed works published in the aftermath were not written by the famous authors of the day, but by writers who could produce copy quickly. For example, Niizuma Kan, a journalist for the *Tokyo Nichinichi* paper, has described working on Kōdansha's *The Great Taishō Earthquake and Conflagration* after his hours at the paper.[36] His contributions were anonymous. In contrast, the authors whose experiences were collected in Kaizōsha's *A Record of the Taishō Earthquake and Conflagration* represented the publishing elite, the *bundan*. Since Tokyo was the center of the publishing world, residence there was almost a necessity for anyone pursuing a career in writing. Although these authors did experience the quake, most were protected from the worst of the damage because they lived in the *yamanote* and the western suburbs.[37]

The first post-quake edition of *Bunshō kurabu* (*Literary Club*) noted that most members of the literati (the *bundan*) escaped harm because "luckily" they were living in areas that were not heavily damaged.[38] The *yamanote*/suburban area that most emblemized this concentration was Tabata, on the northern outskirts of the city. It was home to several writers who had followed Akutagawa Ryūnosuke's

35. *Taishō daishin kasai shi* (Kaizō-sha, 1924).

36. Quoted in Iwasaki Katsumi, "Kaigenreika no besuto serā," 66.

37. A survey of addresses in the 1923 *Bungei nenkan* shows that almost 300 out of the 360 authors whose addresses were provided lived in the greater Tokyo area: 150 lived in Tokyo proper, and 140 lived in the suburbs. Of the 150 in Tokyo proper, 12 lived in the *shitamachi*, while Ushigome (39), Koishikawa (31), and Hongo (26) alone were home to almost 100 authors. One year later, the 1924 *Bungei nenkan* shows approximately 350 out of 450 authors in the greater Tokyo area: 160 in Tokyo proper, and 190 in the suburbs. Only two lived in the *shitamachi*; Ushigome (43), Koishikawa (41), and Hongo (24) were again home to the greatest number. In the *Bunshō kurabu* survey of what happened to the authors, only two are mentioned as living in the *shitamachi*, though one author living in the central ward of Kojimachi also lost his home to the fires. "Kusai to bundan shoka shōsoku ki," *Bunshō kurabu* 8, no. 10 (October 1923): 95–105. Another survey of writers and their experiences can be found in Tsuchida Mitsufumi, "Bungakusha no mita kanto daishinsai," *Nihon kosho tsushin* August (1992): 2–5.

38. "Kusai to bundan," 95.

(1892–1927) move to the area in 1914. At the time of the earthquake, Murō Saisei, Nogami Yaeko, Kikuchi Kan, and a few others were living there, giving Tabata the contemporary label of "literati village" (*bunshi mura*). Another popular region was Ushigome in the western part of the city, housing more than a quarter of the 150 authors listed in the *Bungei nenkan* (*Literary Yearbook*) as residing in the city. Kataoka Teppei (1894–1944), author and journalist for the *Osaka Asahi shinbun*, was staying in Ushigome with author Hirotsu Kazuo (1891–1968) when the earthquake struck. Kataoka and Hirotsu ran outside to take refuge at a nearby shrine. Amid those gathered there, they encountered not one but two fellow authors, Naoki Sanjūgo (1891–1934) and Sasaki Mosaku (1894–1966).[39] These chance encounters further testify to the geographical concentration of authors at the time of the quake.

Tayama Katai's experience of the earthquake, recounted in the Introduction, is perhaps emblematic of that of many authors. He lived in Yoyogi, in what was then a western suburb of the city. For Katai, the quake itself was a relatively minor event. It was unsettling and toppled several bookshelves, but caused no permanent damage. The proletarian writer Ema Shū (1889–1975) weathered the quake at his home in Hatsudai, not far from Katai. In his account of the disaster, Ema describes his neighborhood as being built on rice paddies, implying that it was on recently developed land. There is little to differentiate his account from Katai's.

In contrast to Katai and Ema on the western outskirts of the city, author Uno Kōji (1891–1961) lived in Shitaya, near Ueno Park, and thus not far from the *shitamachi* and the devastation. He went to the Ryōdaishi temple in Ueno after the tremors and described what he saw: "I was literally dumbstruck by the sea of fire I saw below me. From that vantage point, the *shitamachi* was entirely engulfed by flames for as far as I could see."[40] Uno later took refuge in the park, but moved to his friend Murō Saisei's house in Tabata as the fires drew nearer. Though he thought it necessary to take these precautions, Uno's neighborhood proved to be safe from the flames, and his home weathered the quake without much damage.

Some writers were living in Kamakura, the popular seaside resort town southwest of Yokohama. Kamakura was closer to the epicenter of the earthquake and was affected by the subsequent tsunami. Communication was difficult in the aftermath of the quake, so information on authors living in Kamakura was difficult to come by. Early rumors proclaimed the deaths of Kume Masao and Satomi Ton, though both were found safe when representatives from the *bundan* sought them out.[41] Kasai Zenzō (1887–1928) writes of experiencing the quake in Kamakura in his short story "Wriggling Things" ("Ugomekumono," 1924). He felt

39. "Sono hi no bunshitachi," *Ōsaka Asahi shinbun,* September 6, 1923, 3.
40. Uno Kōji, "Shinsai bunshō," in *Uno Kōji zenshū*, vol. 12 (1969): 9.
41. "Kusai to bundan," 95.

the quake while shaving and, recognizing its severity, fled from the old temple he was staying in: "At that point I flew out of the entryway in bare feet, as if in a dream. After I had crawled about 2 *ken* [approximately 4 meters], I turned to look at the building, just in time to see the two-story thatched roof collapsing with a bang."[42] His descriptions are vivid, and the destruction was more severe than in the *yamanote*, but Kasai was safe.[43] The more rural setting of Kamakura did not have as much to fear from the fires that ravaged Tokyo and Yokohama, though the shaking and the tsunami caused great deal of damage.

The most famous story about an author and the earthquake revolves around Tanizaki Jun'ichirō, who permanently fled the more earthquake-prone Kantō region for western Japan, or Kansai after the disaster. The earthquake is often identified as a transition point between his fascination with the West, exemplified by his novel *Naomi* (*Chijin no ai*, 1924), and the return to Japanese aesthetics some see in his *Some Prefer Nettles* (*Tade kuu mushi*, 1928).[44] The shift in Tanizaki's literary production is more nuanced than such a simple explanation suggests, but he did credit the earthquake as the impetus for him to settle in Kansai.

Despite this dramatic move, Tanizaki's actual earthquake experience was far from extreme. He described his experiences for the *Osaka Asahi shinbun* and wrote of his escape and return to the devastated area in later essays.[45] He was riding a bus home from a vacation in Hakone when the quake struck: "I stayed awestruck in my seat, watching the treetops shaking as if being torn apart by giants. The forest and the cliffs were moving in unison and the crest of the road just ahead was moving up and down like a crane."[46] The bus rode out the shocks until they reached a section of road safe enough for the passengers to disembark. From there Tanizaki continued on foot out of the mountains, and then by various modes

42. Kasai Zenzō, "Ugomekumono," in *Kasai Zenzō zenshū*, vol. 2 (1974): 44.

43. Research has shown that while the shaking was mostly about a 5 on the Japanese seismic intensity scale in the *yamanote*, in Kamakura it was a 7, indicating severe shaking (several areas in Honjo and Fukagawa also reached a 7). Chūō bōsai kaigi saigai kyōkun no keishō ni kan suru senmon chōsakai, "1923 no Kantō dai jishin hōkokusho," http://www.bousai.go.jp/jishin/chubou/kyoukun/rep/1923--kantoDAISHINSAI/index.html (accessed November 16, 2011). See also Takemura Masayuki, *Kantō daishinsai: Dai Tōkyō ken no yure wo shiru*, 25.

44. Tanizaki began serializing *Naomi* in March 1924 in the *Osaka Asahi* newspaper, six months after the quake.

45. *Ōsaka Asahi shinbun*, September 21, 1923, 2. His most famous account of the quake is in the essay "Thoughts on Tokyo." See Tanizaki Jun'ichirō, "Tōkyō wo omofu," *Chūō kōron* 49, nos. 1–4 (January–April 1934), reprinted as Tanizaki Jun'ichirō, "Tōkyō wo omofu," in *Tanizaki Jun'ichirō zenshū*, vol. 21 (1983): 1–76. In this essay Tanizaki writes that his first concern was for his wife and daughter, but the possible loss of family members is pushed to the side by thoughts on the grand reconstruction of Tokyo into a modern city. See the partial translation and brief discussion in Edward Seidensticker, *Low City, High City*, 14–15.

46. Tanizaki Jun'ichirō, "'Kugatsu tsuitachi' zengo no koto," in *Tanizaki Jun'ichirō zenshū*, vol. 22 (1983): 218.

of transportation to Osaka. Because his family had left Hakone earlier, Tanizaki had no way of knowing what happened to them in the disaster. He managed to return to Yokohama by boat to look for his family, and finally found them safe at a relative's house in the *yamanote* area of Tokyo.[47] His house on the Yokohama bluff was damaged, and Tanizaki took his family back to Kansai, where they eventually settled permanently.

Like Tanizaki, many outside the disaster area were worried about relatives living in the Tokyo area and traveled to the disaster zone as soon as they could. The uncertainty and anxiety of waiting for news of loved ones was deftly described by Tokuda Shūsei in his semi-autobiographical "Amid the Uncertainty" ("Fuan no naka ni" 1924). In this short story, Tokuda describes the forced period of inaction as he waits in Kanazawa for news of his family. The updates from Tokyo were troubling. Shūsei describes his alter ego, Toki, imagining his wife in the newspaper descriptions:

> Amid the various reports, those that best depicted the real tragedies of the fires were the accounts of reporters who had seen the streets of Tokyo with their own eyes. Reading them, Toki was immediately overcome with vivid visions of the disaster. Women, the elderly, scores of children chased by the flames. Babies cast to the ground and trampled by the mob as it fled. The young with their strength could flee at will, but what about the old people with weak legs? He imagined his children pulling their mother, who was often ill and prone to fainting in less severe circumstances, sweating in the heat of the flames, being pushed along in the waves of people, stumbling over the dead bodies, eventually separating from each other, and finally, thankfully, surviving to cry out in suffering on the edge of life and death. As Toki read, the various scenes and situations he conjured only made his head hurt.[48]

Days go by as the protagonist waits in fear until the railroad is finally opened. The story ends before we find out what happened to them, but Tokuda's real-life family was unharmed. Though Tokuda did not experience the disaster directly, his story shows the degree to which people left outside the immediate disaster zone were affected by the quake, in ways more emotional than physical.

Though most writers were comfortably safe after the quake, a few lost their homes and people close to them. The poet Fukushi Kōjiro (1889–1946) returned to Aomori prefecture after his house in Fukagawa was destroyed.[49] Kubota Mantarō (1889–1963) was burnt out of his home in Asakusa.[50] He wrote a short story

47. The details of this trip were recorded in the *Ōsaka Asahi shinbun*, September 21, 1923, 2.

48. Tokuda Shūsei, "Fuan no naka ni," 190.

49. *Bungei nenkan*, vol. 2 (Bunsendō Shoten, 1974), 225.

50. "Kusai to bundan," 96. Kubota's house was also destroyed in the air raids in 1945, making a total of three times he was burned out of his home.

loosely related to the quake, called "The Townspeople" ("Shiseijin," 1950). In it a young writer refuses to return to Tokyo, having left his uncle and the family business (a Yoshiwara brothel) just before the disaster. The uncle was safe, but the brothel was reduced to ashes along with the rest of Yoshiwara. Though the story ends with the quake, the focus is on the drama leading up to it. Playwright Kawatake Shigetoshi (1889–1967) was burned out of his home in Honjo and lost his son to the disaster.[51] Another playwright, Yamazaki Shikō (1875–1939), lost his home and his daughter's family to the flames.[52] He wrote about his daughter and his grandchildren in the poignantly titled essay "Gathering Four Sets of Bones" ("Yonin no hone wo hirō")[53]: "Not long before that fateful day, my daughter brought her two children to celebrate the birthday of her youngest son, who would have turned one on September first. We ate the sweet red rice she brought, but she returned home before lunch. She must have bought a doll on the way home, because I found its brightly colored head, undamaged from the fires, not far from her bones. When I put the bones into the jar, I added that too."[54] Yamazaki was in his late forties at the time, and the blow ended his career in literature. Before the quake he was producing period dramas at the rate of more than one per year, but his last production was in June of 1922.

Hori Tatsuo (1904–53), who had not yet entered the *bundan* proper,[55] lost his mother in the disaster. They separated after taking refuge in the Sumida River in Honjo. Murō Saisei, Hori's mentor at the time, mentions this tragedy in his own earthquake record, saying that the young Hori, eighteen at the time, had aged about four years during those horrifying days.[56] Though his experiences were more extreme than those of almost any other writer, Hori rarely dealt with the quake in his writing. One exception is a brief appearance in a short work he produced ten years later, "Faces" ("Kao," 1933).[57] In that work, the protagonist, Rui, meets a young girl after he is separated from his parents. He feigns sleep

51. For Kawatake's story, see Kawatake Shigetoshi, "Honjo wo dasshutsu shite," *Josei* 4, no. 5 (November 1923): 110–18 and "Sōnan ki," in *Taishō daishin kasai shi* (Kaizō-sha, 1924). His story has also been told by Charles Schencking in *The Great Kanto Earthquake and the Chimera of National Reconstruction in Japan*, 23–24.

52. "Kusai to bundan," 96.

53. Yamazaki Shikō, "Yonin no hone wo hirō," *Fujin kōron* 8, no. 12 (1923): 57–64. There were a few others with significant losses. Araraki poet Takada Ryokichi lived in Honjo at the time. He spent the night in a canal and survived, but lost his mother and three sisters. For brief information on Takada and others, see Tsuchida Mitsufumi, "Bungakusha no mita kanto daishinsai."

54. Yamazaki Shikō, "Yonin no hone wo hirō," 63.

55. It was later in the 1920s that Hori Tatsuo emerged onto the literary scene, although he was recognized as a literary youth and had met several important authors by the time of the quake.

56. Murō Saisei, "Nichiroku," *Kaizō* 5, no. 10 (October 1923): 213.

57. Another story by Hori Tatsuo that deals with the earthquake and losing his mother is "Autumn" ("Aki," 1934). See Sasaki Kiichi and Tanida Shōhei, *Hori Tatsuo: sono shōgai to bungaku* (Kayōsha, 1983), 37.

next to her that night in a refugee camp, aroused by her warm body next to his. He meets up with his father the following day: "His father, slow to make his escape, had spent the night in the river. But his mother's whereabouts was still unknown. People eventually found her body in the river. Rui had no choice but to help drag his mother's corpse from the water. His expression as he performed this act suggested that it did not affect him one way or the other."[58] In contrast to the callousness of his protagonist, Hori memorialized his mother with a poem on her grave marker: "My mother gone, the pain at not knowing which one is her."[59] This short haiku lament conveys the emotional difficulty of searching for a loved one amid countless bodies.

Only one major figure closely connected to the *bundan* was killed in the disaster itself. Kuriyagawa Hakuson (1880–1923), a mentor to Kikuchi Kan and a well-respected literary scholar, was in Kamakura at the time of the quake. Kuriyagawa and his wife had successfully escaped the initial shock and the sparse fires, only to be caught by the subsequent tsunami waves. He lived for several hours after being pulled from the mud and debris, but did not survive the night. Several writers wrote memorials to Kuriyagawa, and his wife published accounts of his death in different magazines.[60] *Bunshō kurabu* had a memorial in its October issue, and in December the magazine *Geimon* (*Arts and Letters*) published a special issue on Kuriyagawa that included several reminiscences.

The deaths that truly shocked the *bundan* were not directly caused by the earthquake, the fires, or the tsunami, but can be indirectly attributed to the chaos afterward: namely, the murders of Hirasawa Keishichi, Ōsugi Sakae, and Itō Noe by police and military personnel (see Introduction). There were several eulogies for Ōsugi in the November edition of *Kaizō*, and the post-quake (and final) edition of the left-wing journal *Tanemaku hito* was dedicated to Hirasawa and the nine others killed with him. Though censorship forbade explicit condemnation of the police and the state as complicit in their deaths, the writing on their deaths stood as a testament to the violence.[61]

58. English translation by Donald Keene in *Dawn to the West: Japanese Literature of the Modern Era; Fiction* (New York: Columbia University Press, 1998), 687–88.

59. Sasaki Kiichi and Tanida Shōhei, *Hori Tatsuo: sono shōgai to bungaku*, 38.

60. See, for example, Kuriyagawa Chiyōko, "Kanashiki tsuikai—Kuriyagawa Hakuson hakase no shi," *Josei* 3, no. 6 (November 1923): 119–47 and "Kanashimi no tsuioku," *Josei Kaizō* 2, no. 11 (November 1923): 107–13. Kikuchi Kan's essay ran in *Josei Kaizō*; see "Kuriyagawa Hakuson-shi no omoide," *Josei Kaizō* 2, no. 11 (November 1923): 105–6. It is collected in volume 14 of the *Kikuchi Hiroshi zenshū* (Chūō Kōron-sha, 1937), 421–22.

61. Perhaps the testimony most critical of the state violence is the epitaph on the grave of Ōsugi's young nephew, Tachibana Sōichi, written by his father. The inscription on the back reads: "Sōichi, age 8, was killed by dogs on September 16, 1923 along with Ōsugi Sakae and Itō Noe after the Great Tokyo Earthquake while he was revisiting Japan."

Despite these tragic exceptions, the members of the Japanese literary elite escaped major harm. This was often attributed to their "good luck," but the defining reason for their escape was their location, which was linked to their socio-economic class. As Uno Kōji writes in "The Dream of Three-Hundred Years" ("Sanbyakunen no yume," 1923), "Thankfully, perhaps because something was just right in the earth or location of my neighborhood, I was able to escape the tremors and the fires quite comfortably."[62] Later in the essay, Uno gives a clue to the cultural status of those in his neighborhood, though without linking his escape from damage to his socio-economic position: "In general the neighborhood in which I lived seemed to be comprised of elegant people, whom some may say tended toward being self-righteous."[63] The very factors that made his neighborhood attractive to "elegant people" (in other words, upper-middle-class and upper-class people) also helped it weather the disaster—something *was* "just right" in the location of his neighborhood.

* * * * *

The *bundan* writers' experience of the quake was a fundamentally different experience from that of residents of the *shitamachi*. That difference allowed them the luxury to write. As Kikuchi Kan wrote in the first post-quake issue of the general-interest magazine *Chūō kōron*, "As long as one has a brush and paper, who's to say you can't write something good?"[64] Thus literary authors could provide the material for the publishers to print as soon as the presses were up and running. Their work, along with that of countless anonymous others, contributed to the swift availability of texts about the earthquake, and thus to the regeneration of the industry. But the texts produced by these *bundan* writers were different from much of the other print culture following the quake. They were literati, and what they wrote was not just something to read. It was "literature."

62. Uno Kōji, "Sanbyakunen no yume," *Shinchō* 39, no. 4 (October 1923): 20.
63. Ibid., 22. The word for "elegant" in this passage is *jōhin*.
64. Kikuchi Kan, "Saigo zakkan," 118.

Chapter 2

Literature after the Quake

After their immediate survival needs were met, the question for members of the literary elite (the *bundan*) soon became what to write: in other words, what effect would the earthquake have on literature? Prior to the earthquake, the most well-regarded works of fiction by *bundan* authors had been loosely fictionalized versions of their own lives. These works were personal and limited in scope. This genre, later labeled the "I-novel," or *shishōsetsu,* could not do justice to the magnitude and scope of the disaster, and there was also a question as to whether works that dealt with earthquake suffering could really be literary. Yet at the same time there was a struggle over how literature could respond to the disaster. This chapter discusses the dominance of the I-novel before the quake and how certain voices in the debates following the disaster called for a greater social awareness.

The *Bundan,* the I-Novel, and the Confines of the Literary before the Quake

At its loosest, the term *bundan* refers to anyone involved in publishing literature, but in his study of the I-novel Edward Fowler strictly limits the definition of the *bundan* to those striving for "pure" literature, as opposed to popular fiction.[1] His definition is useful, but best when supplemented by the observations of Edward Mack, who focuses on the way members of the *bundan* mobilized cultural authority to define their literary production as pure. As Mack puts it, the *bundan* is "the world of fiction that matters and the individuals with the power to determine what that is."[2] And the way they were able to control what

1. Edward Fowler, *The Rhetoric of Confession: Shishōsetsu in Early Twentieth-Century Japanese Fiction* (Berkeley, CA: University of California Press, 1988), 128–29.
2. Mack points out that the *bundan* was not aloof from issues of print capitalism, as implied in previous scholarship, but rather intricately tied to the publishing industry. In so doing he sets himself apart from people such as Fowler and the postwar Japanese literary scholar Itō Sei. Edward Mack, *Manufacturing Modern Japanese Literature*, 248, note 28. He delves into this topic in further detail in his dissertation, "The Value of Literature," 38–44.

mattered was through publication outlets. Major literary and general-interest journals bestowed cultural authority and determined literary value.[3] By acting as filters for literary value, these journals established the writers within them as "pure" artistic authors.

Writing was thus determined to be "pure" and "high-culture" based more on where it was published—and thus on who read it—than on who wrote it.[4] Nagamine Shigetoshi has analyzed the readership and the publication industry in the interwar period, and traces the emergence of the middle class as readers during this time period. Nagamine notes that the new class of salarymen were interested in the cultural capital offered by the literary world, and that this contributed to the success of literature-focused magazines such as *Bungei shunjū* and *Bunshō kurabu*. An ad for *Bungei shunjū* cited by Nagamine declares, "There is nothing more uncouth than being caught reading a low-class magazine on the trains."[5] Though both the middle and lower classes enjoyed the popular period fiction published in Kōdansha's mass-market magazine *Kingu*, it was the "artistic" work, found in the literary and general-interest magazines, that allowed those who could buy and appreciate it to adopt the cultural authority of the *bundan*.

Cultural capital in the publishing world was linked to fiction deemed "artistic" by the *bundan* and published in magazines they controlled. And the literary genre that dominated the high-culture magazines of the Taishō period was the I-novel, a form of semi-autobiographical fiction that was centered on the lives of the authors who wrote in this mode.[6] As Edward Fowler writes in his discussion of the genre, "The *shishōsetsu* so dominated the Taishō literary world that the phrase 'Taishō literature' now connotes its heyday."[7] Though it was certainly not the only genre available—the works of Tanizaki and Akutagawa, for example, are notable exceptions—the I-novel was the prototypical form of *bundan* literature in the Taishō era. In a roundtable discussion in the mid-1960s, Satō Haruo, Hirano Ken, and Itō Sei raised the question of the most representative Taishō writer. The contention was between the I-novelist Kasai Zenzō, whom they identified

3. The number of journals in which important "literary" works were being published was limited. Mack names the most important journals previous to the earthquake as being *Chūō kōron*, *Kaizō*, *Bungei shunjū*, *Shin-shōsetsu*, and a few others. Of these he singles out *Chūō kōron* as particularly important. See Mack, "The Value of Literature," 11–12, 80–84.
4. Many authors wrote both for the masses and for the journals that determined literary worth. A good example is Tayama Katai's *kikōbun* (travelogues) and travel guides.
5. Nagamine Shigetoshi, *Modan toshi no dokusho kūkan*, 116.
6. The I-novel was not named as a genre until 1924, but scholars place its origins well before the name. Though it is called an I-novel in English, many, if not most, examples of the genre were short episodic stories.
7. Edward Fowler, *Rhetoric of Confession*, 128.

as the quintessential *bundan* author, and Akutagawa Ryūnosuke, who did not fit the I-novel mold. Though each could be considered representative of the time in his own way, these scholars agreed that Kasai was the more mainstream figure because he wrote in the dominant form.[8]

The self as depicted in the Taishō-era I-novel was predominantly male and bourgeois. In her study of the genre, *Narrating the Self*, Tomi Suzuki traces the I-novel to changing notions of the self that emerged with the People's Rights movement, Meiji-era Christianity, and, ultimately, the political ideals associated with Taishō democracy.[9] Though the themes of the I-novel were anything but political, its focus on the bourgeois self emphasizes the autonomy and individualism central to the push toward political enfranchisement. In fact, novels and short stories in this mode often shared a stage with political essays. For example, during the Taishō era, political thinker Yoshino Sakuzō (1878–1933) was featured in almost every issue of the general-interest magazine *Chūō kōron,* a publication that also functioned as the key arbiter of literary merit.

As literacy began to rise and more people began reading, there was a perceived need to differentiate the tastes of the bourgeois readers from those of the working masses. *Bundan* "literary" writing appeared in publications aimed at bourgeois readers. Works that catered to the tastes of the masses were not considered worthy of attention. This is clear in a 1916 article by Akagi Kōhei (1891–1949) that criticized various writers for catering too much to popular tastes.[10] Later, during the critical debates over the I-novel, Kume Masao was also influential in defining the boundary between the high and the low in his 1924 essay "The I-Novel and the State-of-Mind Novel" ("Watakushi shōsetsu to shinkyō

8. Katsuyama Kō, *Taishō shishōsetsu kenkyū* (Meiji Shoin, 1980), 3–4.

9. Suzuki singles out Yoshino Sakuzō's "popular polity," Abe Jirō's (1883–1959) "Personalism," and the "Humanism" of the Shirakaba group, each of which emphasized the individual self. Suzuki labels the class involved in the Taishō democracy reforms the "urban working class." Tomi Suzuki, *Narrating the Self: Fictions of Japanese Modernity* (Stanford, CA: Stanford University Press, 1996), 52. Suzuki's choice of term here seems problematic, as it was primarily middle-class office-workers and bureaucrats who were most closely associated with the reforms of Taishō democracy. This is argued persuasively in David Ambaras, "Social Knowledge, Cultural Capital, and the New Middle Class in Japan." It is probably this middle class to which Suzuki refers. The "urban working class," meaning those employed in factories, were increasingly involved in labor unions, but that was a distinct social movement and not at all connected with the literary world of the I-novel.

10. Akagi's article, "Yūtō bungaku no bokumetsu," is collected in *Kindai bungaku hyōron taikei*, vol. 4 (1971): 260–66. The idea also comes into play in the later 1910s and early 1920s, especially in the criticism of Kikuchi Kan, discussed later in this chapter. See, for example, Kikuchi's essay "Bungei sakuhin no naiyōteki kachi" ("On the Content Value of Literary Works") and the subsequent debate. Reprinted as Kikuchi Kan, "Bungei sakuhin no naiyōteki kachi," in *Kindai bungaku hyōron taikei*, vol. 5 (1972): 269–72, and "Bungei sakuhin no naiyōteki kachi," in *Gendai Nihon bungaku ronsō shi*, ed. Hirano Ken, 49–52 (Miraisha, 1956).

shōsetsu," 1924). In so doing he retroactively placed the I-novel squarely on the side of the high.[11]

At the time of the earthquake, the genre of the I-novel was comfortable in its prestige, but its standard formula was shaken by the disaster. It was in 1924, significantly the year following the quake, that Nakamura Murao (1886–1949) began what Edward Fowler and Katsuyama Kō call the first period of critical debate on the genre.[12] One can see in the ensuing debates how the I-novel's position of dominance began to be challenged by the rise of modernism, proletarian literature, and popular literature.[13] Though there had been cracks in the armor of the I-novel before, the debates over the relationship between society and literature were given new fuel in the aftermath of the earthquake.

The Earthquake in Literary Criticism

There was a feeling after the earthquake that its impact on the physical landscape, on the print industry, and on the psyches of Japanese authors meant that something new was in store for literature and the arts. In its first post-quake issue, the magazine *Josei* (*Woman*) advertised a contest for new (post-quake) literature, implying that literature written after the disaster would somehow be substantially different from that produced before.[14] As Odagiri Susumu has shown, most critics also thought that the earthquake would inspire a new kind of literature.[15] Just exactly how literature would be different was debated in essays scattered throughout various magazines and newspapers. At one end of the spectrum, the critic Chiba Kameo (1878–1935) wrote in a November 1923 essay that the earthquake was an opportunity for new blood in the *bundan*: "What must emerge after the quake must be something dignified that spurs life and vitality, something that emphasizes a spirit of purpose."[16] At the other end was Katagami Noboru (1884–1928), who thought that the earthquake would push literature toward more

11. Kume Masao, "Watakushi shōsetsu to shinkyō shōsetsu," in *Kindai bungaku hyōron taikei*, vol. 6 (1973): 50–57. I have borrowed the translation "state-of-mind novel" from Tomi Suzuki. Kume and other I-novel critics were discussing more than just high literature versus low. The discourse on the I-novel also contrasted Western and Japanese fiction. In Kume's mind, the former, even if masterfully executed by the likes of Tolstoy, Dostoyevsky, and Flaubert, was somehow less authentic than the native I-novel and thus "mere entertainment."

12. Edward Fowler, *Rhetoric of Confession*, 44, and Katsuyama Kō, *Taishō shishōsetsu kenkyū*, 174–89. For Nakamura's essay, see "Honkaku shōsetsu to shikyō shōsetsu to," in *Kindai bungaku hyōron taikei*, vol. 6 (1973): 11–16.

13. *Bungei jidai*, the journal of the *Shinkankaku-ha* modernists, began publication in October 1924. The first issue of *Bungei sensen*, a major literary journal of the proletarian writers, had appeared in June of that year.

14. *Josei*, October 1923, unpaginated front matter.

15. Odagiri Susumu, *Shōwa bungaku no seiritsu* (Keisō Shobō, 1965), 40–46.

16. Chiba Kameo, "Shinsaigo-ha no shisō to bungei," *Kaizō* 5, no. 11 (November 1923): 257–64.

escapist entertainment: "Just as our post-disaster society will seek out the easy, the cheap, the effortless, the light, I foresee that literature will turn toward things that offer direct stimulation, things that tug on our hearts, and bright, showy, cheerful things that entertain us."[17] Chiba predicted that literature would move toward loftier values; Katagami believed showy melodrama would be the end result of the disaster.

Between the extremes of Chiba and Katagami, one trend clearly visible in the critical discourse was that literature would be more socially aware. The critic Nakamura Murao (1886–1949) is well known for starting the debate on the I-novel with his critique of the form, but it is rarely acknowledged that his famous essay on the I-novel was originally paired with a critique of the lack of social consciousness in Japanese letters. Indeed, Nakamura claimed that the impetus for the essay was his embarrassment at the lack of authors' engagement with society following the disaster. As he put it, "The characters and psychology taken up in the works of recent and contemporary Japanese authors are completely divorced from society."[18] Despite favoring Western examples, Nakamura did not believe that all Japanese literature was lacking; he found much of it "artistic." Rather, his essay expresses hope that literature after the quake would, while retaining its artistic qualities, "have the power to actively engage with society."[19] The essence of Nakamura's critique of the I-novel is embedded within his optimism about authors perhaps shifting their gaze outward following the quake.

The tension between art and society in Nakamura's essay informs the best-known debate over the arts in the post-quake *bundan*: that between Satomi Ton and Kikuchi Kan. Like Nakamura and Chiba, several members of the *bundan* wrote essays on the quake and literature, but Kikuchi Kan and Satomi Ton emerged in the discourse as polar opposites. Kikuchi Kan's essay "Post-Disaster Impressions" ("Saigo zakkan") asserts that literature is useless in the face of disaster, whereas Satomi Ton's essay "The Pearl Will Not Be Broken" ("Tama wa kudakezu") views art as an indestructible jewel that cannot be affected by external events. Their response to the earthquake is only meaningful within the context of their earlier criticism and prior interaction.

Satomi Ton was an author affiliated with the *Shirakaba* (*White Birch*) coterie journal and the group of writers, artists, and critics who appeared in it. Despite the difference in surname (Satomi Ton is a pen name), he was the younger brother of Arishima Takeo, who is more famously associated with the magazine and the

17. Katagami Noboru, "Shinsaikasai to bungaku," in *Shinkō bungaku zenshū*, vol. 9 (1930): 501; originally published in December 1923.

18. Nakamura Murao, "Bungei jihyō: bungakusha to shakai ishiki," *Shin-shōsetsu* 29, no. 1 (January 1924): 11.

19. Ibid., 14.

group surrounding it.[20] The brothers' father was a former samurai who had transitioned smoothly into the Meiji era by securing a position in the new government and later moved on to a career in the private sector. His wealth and position gave him the ability to send his children to the respected Peer's School, Gakushūin, along with other high-born children, including those of the imperial family. It was at Gakushūin that these brothers, along with the similarly privileged Mushanokoji Saneatsu and Shiga Naoya, gave birth to the *Shirakaba* magazine.

Shirakaba was not only a literary journal; it also showcased important Western art and philosophy. From their European philosophical, literary, and artistic influences, the Shirakaba group inherited a romantic concern for the exceptionalism of the "artist," along with an individualistic humanism. Satomi shared the concerns of his brothers and other Shirakaba colleagues. He, too, believed in "Art for art's sake" and shunned direct political engagement. In his discussion of Shiga Naoya, Francis Mathy notes that the Shirakaba writers' literary theory was focused on self-cultivation. "Society as such," Mathy claims "had little place in their theory."[21]

Mathy's assertion about Shirakaba writers in general is reinforced in Satomi's own literary criticism. In a series of essays published in *Kaizō* the year before the quake, "Humble Thoughts on Literature" ("Bungei kanken"), Satomi articulated his thoughts on literary art and what it meant to him. In one of these essays Satomi defined "Art" as "the art (*jutsu*) of taking something deep inside the individual and giving it a shape one can see with the eyes or hear with the ears."[22] "What was this something?" he asks rhetorically, then replies: "the 'spirit' of the artist." By the end of the essay he suggests that a more suitable Japanese word for art (*geijutsu* 藝術) might be *genreijutsu* (現霊術), or the "art of displaying the spirit."[23] In short, Satomi believed that art was the manifestation of individual genius.

The month after Satomi Ton wrote his essay on the spirit of art, Kikuchi Kan published a response in the June 1922 issue of the journal *Shinchō* entitled "The Content Value of Literary Works" ("Bungei sakuhin no naiyō-teki kachi").[24] This

20. Satomi Ton's legal name was Yamanouchi Hideo. Satomi was adopted into his mother's family at a young age. Another brother, the artist and writer Arishima Ikuma, was also part of the journal.

21. Francis Mathy, *Shiga Naoya* (New York: Twayne Publishers, 1974), 40. Although there was no clear place for society, with its messy inequalities and contradictions, in the Shirakaba literary theory, Mushanokoji Saneatsu, a key member of the group, was interested in social experimentation in utopianism and began a commune called New Village (Atarashiki Mura). In his postquake essay Kikuchi Kan cited Mushanokoji as an example of the "back to essentials" kind of life that would replace art after the disaster. Mathy's statement is certainly more true of Shiga Naoya, the subject of his study, and of Satomi Ton, than it is of Mushanokoji and others in the group including, famously, Arishima Takeo.

22. Satomi Ton, "Bungei kanken," in *Satomi Ton zenshū*, vol. 10 (Chikuma Shobō, 1979), 131; originally published in *Kaizō* in 1922.

23. Ibid., 133.

24. For the two reprints of Kikuchi Kan, "Bungei sakuhin no naiyōteki kachi," see note 10 above; it was originally published in the July 1922 issue of *Shinchō*.

became the first salvo in "The debate over the content value of literature" (Naiyōteki kachi ronsō). Though Satomi Ton was not mentioned specifically, Kikuchi wrote that he hated "esoteric theories of art that say things like 'spirit, blah, blah, soul, blah, blah.'"[25] Kikuchi explicitly stated that he saw no merit in a theory of art that dwelt heavily on the mystique of the "artist," a mystique that was central to the ideas of the Shirakaba writers and critics. Satomi Ton saw this as a direct attack against his position as he had explained it in the *Kaizō* series of essays, and rightly so. He soon responded in kind. The resulting debate over "content value" articulated the philosophical differences between these two critics and offers clues to their differing responses to the earthquake.

Although Kikuchi's "content value" essay was a response to Satomi's definition of art, it was also concerned with something very different—the need for art to engage with the world. Central to Kikuchi's argument was the fact that he had read things that affected him emotionally though aesthetically he was unimpressed by the form, as well as works that had impressed him aesthetically but left him unmoved. In short, he argued that there was a value in the "content" of fiction that was separate from the artistic value of the work. As he later clarified, this was not content as in the traditional divide between content and form within aesthetic theory, as Satomi Ton had mistakenly assumed.[26] Rather, what Kikuchi called "content value" was the moral or philosophical value in the work, the part of the work that directly benefited humanity. Fiction, he wrote, should concern itself with "life first, art second."[27] As Edward Mack puts it, for Kikuchi content value "is not a measure of artistic value but a measure of the value of art to society and mankind."[28] Thus, in contrast to Satomi Ton, Kikuchi was concerned not so much with what art is as with what art should be.[29] Art was personal for Satomi and social for Kikuchi. Satomi's interests lay with the artist, Kikuchi's with the audience.

The old wounds of the unresolved debate begun in 1922 were reopened with Kikuchi Kan's writings following the disaster. The first mention of Kikuchi's thoughts on literature after the earthquake comes from a quote from him that ap-

25. Kikuchi Kan, "Bungei sakuhin no naiyōteki kachi," in *Gendai Nihon bungaku ronsō shi*, ed. Hirano Ken, 50.

26. Satomi addresses the distinction between form and content in aesthetic theory in his essay series "Bungei kanken" and in his response to Kikuchi. Kikuchi corrected Satomi's mistaken interpretation of his essay in his second essay on the topic in September 1922; Kikuchi Kan, "Sairon bungei sakuhin no naiyōteki kachi," in *Gendai Nihon bungaku ronsō shi*, ed. Hirano Ken (Miraisha, 1956), 59–66.

27. Kikuchi Kan, "Bungei sakuhin no naiyōteki kachi," in *Gendai Nihon bungaku ronsō shi*, 52.

28. Edward Mack, *Manufacturing Modern Japanese Literature*, 150.

29. As Hirano Ken and others have pointed out, Kikuchi and Satomi argued at cross-purposes, highlighting a fundamental difference in how they viewed art. Hirano Ken, "Kaisetsu," in *Gendai Nihon bungaku ronsō shi* (Miraisha, 2006), 637.

peared in a September 25, 1923 article in the *Miyako shinbun*: "This disaster has made me feel that literature is mere luxury."[30] His more thorough explanation of this idea is found in "Post-Disaster Impressions" ("Saigo zakkan," 1923), an essay published a few weeks later, in the first post-quake edition of *Chūō kōron*. As its title implies, this essay is a loosely connected string of distinct "impressions" of the disaster, rather than a sustained argument.[31] Some sections describe Kikuchi's experiences, some his musings on earlier disasters, but the inflammatory statement for which the essay is best known appears near the introduction: "The first blow to us literati was the clear realization that, in the boundary between life and death, existence and extinction, this thing called literature, along with antique scrolls, is nothing more than useless luxury. Although we must have already known this, to have it shown with such clarity is truly depressing."[32] Kikuchi sees disaster as a liminal moment between life and death, and in that moment he sees no place for literature or the arts. Disaster reduces humanity to its basic needs for survival. He continues:

> In this last earthquake, we finally discovered what is most important in life. In the boundary between life and death, nothing is important besides sleeping and eating. Eating and sleeping. Sasaki Mosaku playfully suggested that we must establish an "eating-and-sleeping" literary movement.[33] In the four or five days following the earthquake, we did nothing but think of eating and sleeping. "Man shall not live by bread alone" is a luxury of safety.[34]
>
> Even among all business transactions, only those most important to human life remained. That is to say, only the food stores. Even fabric stores and sandal shops could not easily remain open. Galleries, photo shops, and antique shops will be in ruin for quite some time. A musical instrument store in my neighborhood is now selling *miso*. Such are the sorrows of art.
>
> Of course, this life of sleeping and eating is not the entirety of human existence, but it is the basic core of human existence. That ultimately art is a useless luxury in human life is, to us, an extremely troubling reality. That we have lost faith in our work is the first casualty.[35]

After the earthquake Kikuchi saw human necessities, "eating and sleeping," as

30. Anonymous, "Shinsaigo no shisōkai," in *Kikuchi Hiroshi zenshū*, vol. 2 (2002): 171.
31. This essay by Kikuchi is more closely aligned with the Japanese essay form of the *zuihitsu* or the essays of Montaigne than a standard argumentative essay.
32. Kikuchi Kan, "Saigo zakkan," *Chūō kōron* 38, no. 11 (October 1923): 116.
33. Sasaki Mosaku (1894–1966) was an author and editor active from the late 1910s. He was also a friend and colleague of Kikuchi Kan at the time of this article.
34. With this quotation from the Bible (in quotes and biblical language in the original, from Deuteronomy 8:3, Matthew 4:4, Luke 4:4), Kikuchi Kan is aligning religion with literature as another "useless luxury."
35. Kikuchi Kan, "Saigo zakkan," *Chūō kōron* 38, no. 11 (October 1923): 116–17.

the ultimate basis of existence, and therefore, along with the arts in general, literature had no meaning in the struggle to survive. As a poignant metaphor for this transformation, Kikuchi describes a local musical instrument shop owner who is forced to sell *miso* to survive.

Unable to remain idle as Kikuchi Kan began the old argument again, Satomi Ton soon responded with "The Pearl Will Not Be Broken" ("Tama wa kudakezu"), an essay reasserting the value of art and the centrality of the artist. As was the case with their prior debate, Satomi Ton wrote about something slightly different. He ignored Kikuchi's central dilemma, questioning—and outright denying—the value of art after disaster, in favor of arguing that art cannot be affected by a *mere* disaster. "The Pearl Will Not Be Broken" clearly asserts that the earthquake caused no "fissure in art, either visible or invisible."[36] Satomi was not so blind as to think that there will be no material effect on artists, but he believed that the effect would be they would have to move to the more popular forms of their craft to survive: "A painter might have to paint signs for food, . . . and the musician might have to become one part in a cinema orchestra . . . but as long as they are artists . . . art is safe."[37] Satomi acknowledges that artists will turn to menial labor and popular entertainment, but art resides within them nonetheless. Thus he concedes the fact that the instrument shop may have to sell *miso*, but holds that the effect on art itself is nonexistent.

Satomi's faith stems from his definition of art. "The Pearl Will Not Be Broken" begins by reasserting the importance of individual genius to the creation of art—no matter the scope: "Even in the case of architecture, which requires tens of thousands of hands to bring to fruition, or music requiring hundreds, the resulting art is the manifestation of the singular spirit of the leader or planner."[38] Furthermore, Satomi asserts that art, unlike government or business, exists whether or not it has an audience. In his words, "Art is not a commodity directed at others."[39] This is one reason Satomi does not regard the "popular" forms of art as being truly art. That the instrument shop sells *miso* has no bearing on the issue for Satomi; art exists beyond its commodified form. Later in the essay Satomi takes the idea of disaster farther and imagines a world where everything is destroyed except for a single artist. In Satomi's thought experiment, the artist would not stop producing art. Even if all is lost, as long as the "spirit of the artist remains," art is safe.

For Kikuchi, the audience is essential to art. Even as he laments the "uselessness" of literature in his essay, he shows a preference for the audience, consistent with his essays from the previous year. It is the audience that is struggling on

36. Satomi Ton, "Tama wa kudakezu," in *Satomi Ton zenshū*, vol. 10 (1979): 102.
37. Ibid., 103.
38. Ibid., 102.
39. Ibid., 103.

the boundary of life and death and that thus needs no art. The store selling *miso* does so because it lacks customers for its instruments. This point is particularly clear in later sections of Kikuchi's "Post-Disaster Impressions": "Some say that authors' subjectivity has been colored by the earthquake, and that literature will therefore turn to more serious subject matter. Perhaps it will be so. However, that is from the point of view of the literati. I have a feeling that we cannot write as we wish. Basically, . . . the literature demanded by the consumers will probably be different. Probably entertaining, mass-culture literature will be popular. I think the readers will want to flee from cruel reality and run to pleasurable literature. In that sense as well, the decline in literature will come."[40] Here Kikuchi questions those such as Chiba Kameo who wrote that the new post-quake literature would be "something dignified that spurs life and vitality, something that emphasizes a spirit of purpose."[41] Rather, he sees an end to seriousness and literary artistry as the audience seeks to escape the realities of the burnt-out wasteland. It is the audience demand for entertainment that will drive literature, but this demand itself is proof to Kikuchi that artistry will decline. Kikuchi does not view this as an ideal result, for he certainly appreciates literary artistry as much as Satomi Ton. Rather, he merely shows that literary artistry will die of irrelevance without audience demand.

Satomi Ton perceived no need for art to interact with the outside world, and hence saw nothing change in his conception of art following the earthquake. But because Kikuchi Kan was concerned with how literature related to society, he believed that art would be affected when society itself was at risk. To return to his famous statement: "In the boundary between life and death, existence and extinction, this thing called literature, . . . is nothing more than useless luxury."[42] Kikuchi believed that art was the "decoration" added to something of social value. He could see the value inherent in art itself, but that aesthetic value had little importance to society in a disaster. In Kikuchi's worldview, the Great Kanto Earthquake showed the ultimate insignificance of idealized "art" as theorized by Satomi Ton.

Kikuchi Kan and Satomi Ton were soon recognized as opposites in the discourse on art and literature following the earthquake, just as they had been in the earlier debate over "content value." Others took sides as well. After describing his feelings when facing death, Tsuda Kōzō (1892–1971) wrote in the new magazine *Gakan* (*Our Views*) that the power of nature was so awe-inspiring that, in comparison, human art was "like some simple farting trick."[43] The majority, however, argued against Kikuchi's "uselessness of art" theory. These included

40. Kikuchi Kan, "Saigo zakkan," *Chūō kōron* 38, no. 11 (October 1923): 118.
41. Chiba Kameo, "Shinsaigo-ha no shisō to bungei," 257–64.
42. Kikuchi Kan, "Saigo zakkan," *Chūō kōron* 38, no. 11 (October 1923): 116.
43. Tsuda Kōzō, "Daishin to geijutsu," *Gakan* 1, no. 1 (October 1923): 120.

Hirotsu Kazuo (1891–1968) and Kamitsukasa Shōken (1874–1947).[44]

The most thought-provoking assessment of the two sides in the debate appeared in "Frivolous Questions and Deluded Answers" ("Mōmon mōtō"),[45] a dialectical essay by Akutagawa Ryūnosuke published in *Kaizō* in November 1923. In the essay, written in the format of a dialogue between a master and a disciple, Akutagawa examines the stances of Kikuchi Kan and Satomi Ton and remains dissatisfied by both. The essay begins with the disciple asking what the master thought about Kikuchi Kan's theory. The master says, "If your head is on fire, you will not think of how to represent the flames," thus seeming to support Kikuchi.[46] But unlike Kikuchi, the master finds nothing depressing about that fact: "You forget about everything and everyone when you are left with nothing but your life. So of course you would forget about art. For me it's not just about giant earthquakes. When I have to piss I forget about Rembrandt and Goethe. That doesn't mean that I'm belittling art in any way."[47]

"And so," questions the disciple further, "do you suggest that our artistic impulses come to naught when confronted with a terrible event such as this?" "No, they do not disappear completely," the teacher continues, "take the stories of the refugees, for example. There is a surprisingly great deal of art to be found there."[48] Here the master suggests that art is to be found even in the lowly *jitsuwa*, the sentimental "true" stories of refugees and other survivors. This would suggest that art, or at least "unintentional artistic impulses," as he puts it, do not die in the flames. In response to this the disciple asks, "So therefore you think the 'pearl will not be broken'?" Yet the master is not willing to fully support Satomi: "The pearl? Hmmm. The pearl may be broken, but the rock won't be. Artists might be destroyed. But perhaps a bear might survive and be moved by unconscious artistic impulses, or perhaps a bee."[49]

In his humorous master/disciple exchange, Akutagawa ends up siding with neither author, or as, the master puts it, "I like to say that there are parts of both that I agree with. Even I don't want to be caught in the crossfire between the two rivals."[50] Though he agrees with Kikuchi that conscious artistic efforts at art disappear in people who simply need to survive, Akutagawa sees no need to decry the "uselessness" of art in instances where art is ignored. Yet, by suggesting

44. Hirotsu Kazuo, "Hinan to bengo," in *Hennentai Taishō bungaku zenshū*, vol. 12 (2002): 558–64.

45. Akutagawa Ryūnosuke, "Mōmon mōtō," *Kaizō* 5, no. 11 (November 1923): 282–84; reprinted in *Akutagawa Ryūnosuke zenshū*, vol. 10 (1995): 166–69. All citations are to the page numbers in the reprinted edition.

46. Akutagawa Ryūnosuke, "Mōmon mōtō," in *Akutagawa Ryūnosuke zenshū*, vol. 10 (1995): 166.

47. Ibid., 168.

48. Ibid., 166–67.

49. Ibid., 168.

50. Ibid.

that there is art in these *jitsuwa*, or even in the impulses of animals and insects, Akutagawa also rejects the elitism of Satomi's "art as genius" argument. Art for Akutagawa was not a precious pearl reserved for the privileged artist. He saw art as informing expression of any sort, enduring despite the devastation of cities and even the deaths of elite artists.

The post-quake debate over the future of art had largely disappeared by the end of 1923. The infrastructure was rebuilt and the prophesied decline of literature did not materialize. In fact, demand for information increased, spurring the rapid revival of the print industry. Beyond his "Pearl" essay, Satomi Ton did not continue to directly engage Kikuchi Kan as he had done more than a year earlier. Instead he wrote a work of fiction, "Camellia" ("Tsubaki," 1923). In this work, as Edward Seidensticker has pointed out, Satomi attempted to show by example that "formal beauty was possible" after the quake.[51] It is a simple story about an aunt and her niece who discuss the fall of a camellia blossom late at night. There is nothing except the ominous connection between the fallen blossom and death to link the work to the immediate aftermath of the quake. Uno Kōji, in a 1956 essay, praises "Camellia" for its formal qualities and artistic mastery, with no reference whatsoever to the context of publication.[52]

Kikuchi Kan continued to defend and elaborate on his "uselessness of literature" argument for the next few months, mostly in his own journal, *Bungei shunjū*. In a November 1923 essay, he bemoaned his inability to leave the literary world to do something more productive.[53] Early the next year, he published an amusing play, *After the Quake* (*Shinsai no ato*, 1924), mocking Satomi Ton and his "pearl." In it several creatures and objects are discussing the earthquake, one of who is an oyster shown incessantly checking his pearl to make sure it is not broken.[54] In one of his last essays on the subject, "Settling of Accounts" ("Seisan," 1924), Kikuchi took the opportunity to respond to various critics who had emerged in the months following his initial statement in the *Miyako shinbun*. He particularly castigated writers who had little experience with the disaster but nevertheless belittled the effects of the earthquake on the arts.[55] How could someone who had not experi-

51. Edward Seidensticker, "Translator's Notes," in *Modern Japanese Stories: An Anthology*, ed. Ivan. Morris (Rutland, VT, and Tokyo: Charles E. Tuttle Co., 1961), 138.

52. Collected in Uno Kōji, "Satomi Ton," in *Satomi Ton Kubota Mantarō shu* (Chikuma Shobō, 1972), 418–22.

53. Kikuchi Kan, "Saigo zakkan," *Bungei shunjū* 1, no. 11 (November 1923): 71–72. Kikuchi published three completely different essays with the title "Saigo zakkan," or "Post-Disaster Impressions" (see Bibliography). The *Chūō kōron* one is the most famous.

54. Anonymous (probably Kikuchi Kan), "Shinsai no ato," *Bungei shunjū* 2, no. 1 (January 1924): 38–39. The characters include a snail, a sake bottle, a paintbrush, a sword, a duck, and the oyster.

55. Kikuchi Kan, "Bungei tōzachō: seisan," *Bungei shunjū* 2, no. 1 (January 1924): 51–53; reprinted in *Kikuchi Hiroshi zenshū*, vol. 14 (1937): 339–41. Kikuchi particularly singled out Kamitsukasa Shōken.

enced the earthquake, he argued, understand the feelings of someone who had? This was a question he answered in a later, more optimistic view of literature.

Kikuchi Kan did not abandon literature after the disaster—far from it. He continued to write plays and popular fiction and to edit one of the most prestigious literary magazines of the time. Though he never recanted his belief that literature was ultimately a useless luxury, by 1925 Kikuchi had regained his confidence in literature and its relevance. In a later essay, "Literature and Life" ("Bungei to jinsei," 1926), he claimed that literature opened readers' minds to the lives of others, and ultimately asserted that "he who knows not literature is confined to nothing more than his own life."[56] Even in this impassioned defense, Kikuchi does not valorize literature as art, but as something with a social value beyond the aesthetic. Kikuchi found a humanistic connection between literature and life—literature told stories that connected people to each other. It was through literature that the extreme experiences of the earthquake could be conveyed to those who had not experienced it.

Despite this debate and the magnitude of the disaster, most writing about the earthquake by *bundan* authors remained focused on themselves. Not only were personal experiences of *bundan* writers a staple in the many magazines after the earthquake, but some took up the earthquake in I-novel form. Tokuda Shūsei's "Amid the Uncertainty" ("Fuan no naka ni") is limited to the point of view of the protagonist/author anxiously awaiting news from the devastated capital. Kasai Zenzō, the author postwar critics saw as the typical *bundan* writer, included a surreal description of the earthquake in the midst of his angst about his mistress and unborn child in the story "Wriggling Things" ("Ugomeku-mono").

Yet even among the I-novels there were some that hinted at a greater social engagement. Fujimori Seikichi wrote about his own experiences trying to help a family affected by the quake in the story "Among the Refugees" ("Nogaretaru hitobito," 1924). Social consciousness was present in his work before the earthquake, and it is manifest in this story with particular clarity. In a review of this story Kawabata Yasunari wrote that he could see in the work "the beauty of the author's life and character."[57] Kawabata was reading "Among the Refugees" like an I-novel in which the character of the author shines through. At the same time, it was the "content value" of the work that impressed him, for he found the style "lacking in novelistic charm."[58]

* * * * *

56. Kikuchi Kan, "Bungei to jinsei," in *Kikuchi Hiroshi zenshū*, vol. 14 (1937): 347.
57. Kawabata Yasunari, "Shinshun bundan no shūkaku," in *Kawabata Yasunari zenshū*, vol. 30 (1982): 93.
58. Ibid.

The earthquake did not immediately change literature, but Nakamura Murao's desire for social engagement in literature did begin to be realized more concretely afterward. The fading dominance of the I-novel is apparent in Nakamura's 1924 critique as well as in the defense of the form that followed it. There was no need to theorize the I-novel when it was safe from attack. Nor is it coincidental that the two literary movements that shaped the later 1920s, those of the *Shinkankaku-ha* (Neo-Perceptionists) and the proletarian writers, rose to prominence during the year that followed the disaster. These two movements saw a need to engage with the outside world in ways that shattered the narrow focus on the self. In the case of the *Shinkankaku-ha*, the world they attempted to represent was the chaos of the modern city that emerged from the ashes of the disaster; for the proletarian writers, it was the world of capitalist exploitation of the workers. Yet not every author who went out into the devastated city after the disaster tried to capture the social reality. The father of the I-novel, Tayama Katai, remained rooted in his detached objective style. It is to his work that we now turn.

Chapter 3

Tayama Katai, Earthquake *Flâneur*

In March 1924 Tayama Katai published a short work entitled "Burnt Remains" ("Yakeato"), describing his journey into the ruined city. Though the story is ostensibly about searching for the narrator's mistress, "Burnt Remains" contains detailed descriptions of the sights seen, along with reminiscences about the past glory of the city of Tokyo. In a review of the work, Sasaki Mitsuzō wrote that reading the story reminded him of "listening to my grandpa's old stories."[1] Sasaki's response situates Katai, then 52, as a grandfather figure in the literary establishment, the *bundan*.[2] Katai had been one of the central *bundan* authors in the late Meiji era and is often credited with inventing the I-novel itself. As a writer from the earlier generation, Katai remained aloof from and unaffected by the literary debates among younger writers, such as Kikuchi Kan and Akutagawa Ryūnosuke, who by the 1920s had begun to overshadow him.

Katai's memoir *Record of the Tokyo Earthquake* (*Tōkyō shinsaiki*, April 1924), which includes "Burnt Remains," is now seen as one of the most important literary works depicting the earthquake by an established author.[3] This work reveals that generic and literary conventions partially determined Katai's response to the disaster, as well as the responses of others working within the *bundan*; it also shows how Katai put his prior literary theories to use in describing the "reality" of the disaster. Katai's theorizations posit an ideal observer as narrator, one who is detached and objective, and when that observer heads outside, he resembles the *flâneur*.

The term *flâneur* (literally, "idler" or "lounger") is most commonly linked with the work of the poet Charles Baudelaire. In Baudelaire's essay "The Painter of Modern Life," the ur-text of the *flâneur*, the male *flâneur* (and it is gender specific) is a wandering urban artist or poet with a keen eye intent on capturing

1. Sasaki Mitsuzō, "Sōsaku hihyō-san gatsu," in *Bungei nenkan* (Nishodō Shoten, 1925), 134.
2. Tayama Katai's fiftieth birthday was celebrated by the *bundan* elite and discussed in newspapers the year before the quake.
3. Takematsu Yoshiaki, "Metsubō suru teito: bungakushijo no kantō daishinsai," in *Haikyo no kanōsei: gendai bungaku no tanjō*, ed. Kurihara Yukio, Bungakushi wo Yomikaeru (Inpakuto Shuppankai and Izara Shobō, 1997), 175.

"the ephemeral, the fugitive, the contingent" that is modernity. This *flâneur* "enters into the crowd as though it were an immense reservoir of electrical energy," allowing himself to be influenced by its ebbs and flows.[4] Walter Benjamin modifies Baudelaire's definition by highlighting the social and economic class of the figure. For Benjamin, the *flâneur* is inseparable from his bourgeois identity and thus keeps his distance from the crowd. The *flâneur* accomplishes this distance by claims of sensibility and sensitivity to the joys of urban existence—in other words, by asserting his own cultural capital. As Benjamin puts it, "There was the pedestrian who wedged himself into the crowd, but there was also the *flâneur* who demanded elbow room and was unwilling to forgo the life of a gentleman of leisure."[5]

The trope of the *flâneur* in its current theorization reveals less about the objects of his gaze (the city) than it does about the subjectivity of the observer.[6] As such, it provides insight into Katai's narratives of his journeys into the ruins of Tokyo, despite the vast difference in subject matter between a lively city and a devastated one. In either case, it is the attitude of the observer that matters most. Katai maintains the detachment that Benjamin sees as inherent in the social class of the leisure observer, and that detachment allows him to wax philosophical on the ruined city that surrounds him. Interpreting Tayama Katai as a *flâneur* emphasizes the implications of his observations for his subjectivity and the way he positions himself in a topography of class. The earthquake forces Katai to look outward, but that outward gaze into the city is ultimately reflected back onto the self. Though the Parisian *flâneur* sees himself as the very image of cosmopolitan *joie de vivre*, Katai sees himself, and only himself, in the ruins.

THE QUESTION OF THE LITERARY IN TAYAMA KATAI'S *RECORD OF THE TOKYO EARTHQUAKE*

Katai's *Record of the Tokyo Earthquake* begins with the advent of the quake and continues into the following year. With some notable exceptions, it is a first-

4. Charles Baudelaire, *The Painter of Modern Life, and Other Essays*, trans. Jonathan Mayne (London: Phaidon, 1964), 9–10.

5. Walter Benjamin, *Charles Baudelaire: A Lyric Poet in the Era of High Capitalism*, trans. Harry Zohn (London: NLB, 1973), 54, 129.

6. Though Benjamin sees the *flâneur* retreating to a panoptic view of the street from a window, it is important to emphasize the difference between the gazes of the panopticon and the *flâneur*, and specifically the ways in which these two paradigms have been operating within contemporary scholarship. In her tracing of the *flâneur* across modernism and postmodernism, Anne Friedberg described the difference: "The panoptic model emphasizes the subjective effects of the imagined scrutiny and 'permanent visibility' on the observed, but does not explore the subjectivity of the observer." See Anne Friedberg, *Window Shopping: Cinema and the Postmodern* (Berkeley, CA: University of California Press, 1993), 16.

person narration of the actions, observations, impressions, and conversations of the narrator/protagonist, ostensibly the author Katai, in the days and months following the earthquake.[7] Yet it goes beyond being a simple diary. Rather, *Record of the Tokyo Earthquake* is a hybrid text that brings together various kinds of writing into a single volume. As a whole, it shows a concern for the city of Tokyo that makes it an extended epilogue to Katai's memoir *Thirty Years in Tokyo* (*Tokyo no sanjūnen*, 1917).[8] *Record of the Tokyo Earthquake* revisits some of the locations described in *Thirty Years in Tokyo* to highlight the changes brought about by the earthquake, and it references the earlier work with both brief asides and extended quotations. But there are some aspects of the later work that give it a very different feel from the 1917 memoir.

Most scholarly descriptions of *Record of the Tokyo Earthquake* make it into a coherent whole, but it is useful to see it as at least three separate works—the whole and two parts—published for three different audiences: (1) The stand-alone volume, *Record of the Tokyo Earthquake*, was published by Hakubunkan in April 1924, and contains (2) the complete I-novel "Burnt Remains," which was published in the journal *Shin-shōsetsu* (*New Fiction*) in March of the same year;[9] also included is (3) the story "A Single Grain Adrift in the Sea" ("Taikai no ichizoku"), published in October 1923 in the popular weekly the *Sunday Mainichi* (*Sandē mainichi*).[10] In treating *Record of the Tokyo Earthquake* as a single text, most scholarship ignores its constituent parts and the original audiences for each. In so doing, scholars make the short "literary" chapters that comprise "Burnt Remains" stand in for the whole.[11] Nevertheless, to examine each text and its respective audience separately illuminates contemporary boundaries that differentiated the literary from the popular. Only the short story "Burnt Remains" was considered worthy of attention by the *bundan*, but the publishers of the stand-alone book mobilized the cultural capital of the author to help boost sales.

By the time *Record of the Tokyo Earthquake* was available as a stand-alone volume in April 1924—more than six months after the earthquake—Kōdansha's

7. The narrator is a writer living in Yoyogi, then a suburb of Tokyo, and all personal details of the narrator that appear in the book mirror those of the author. The preface, signed by "the author," states that the contents of the book are things he "saw and heard," and the focalization is limited to the point of view of the narrator/protagonist.

8. *Thirty Years in Tokyo* is a conscious attempt to mimic Alphose Daudet's *Thirty Years in Paris*, a similar memoir of literary life in the city. See Tayama Katai, *Literary Life in Tōkyō, 1885–1915: Tayama Katai's Memoirs "Thirty years in Tōkyō,"* trans. Kenneth G. Henshall (Leiden; New York: Brill, 1987).

9. Tayama Katai, "Yakeato," *Shin-shōsetsu* 29, no. 4 (March 1924): 68–80. This work is found in chapters 11–15 in the *Record of the Tokyo Earthquake*.

10. Tayama Katai, "Taikai no ichizoku," *Sandē Mainichi* 2, no. 46 (October 21, 1923): 3. This story appears in *Record of the Tokyo Earthquake* as chapter 49.

11. In discussing *Record of the Tokyo Earthquake*, scholars rarely cite passages outside those of the "Burnt Remains" chapters.

The Great Taishō Earthquake and Conflagration had been in print for several months, as had many other earthquake collections. To set Katai's work apart from those that had already appeared required a rhetorical appeal to his status as a literary figure. This is evident in the advertisement for the book published in the pages of Hakubunkan's largest general-interest magazine, *Taiyō* (*The Sun*): "Announcing the appearance of a brilliant work from the eye of a literary master. There have been countless works recounting last year's earthquake, an event that should be preserved for posterity. But they all resemble long newspaper or magazine articles; and if they are not completely disjointed, they are nothing more than mere descriptions. We pledge that this book alone has artistic representations that recreate the real scenery, feelings, and emotions of the earthquake and is the ultimate volume for your reference. We recommend one for your new bookcase."[12] Here, Hakubunkan marketers position *Record of the Tokyo Earthquake* against Kōdansha's *The Great Taishō Earthquake and Conflagration* and the plethora of other books like it. They argue that the earthquake must be remembered, and that *Record of the Tokyo Earthquake* is most suitable way to preserve that memory because of its artistic merits. The advertisement focuses on the literary qualities of the work to appeal to readers' desire for the cultural capital offered by literature. "If you are going to have a book on the earthquake, as you should," the advertisement seems to say, "make sure it is literary."

Despite being advertised as literary, there are indications that *Record of the Tokyo Earthquake* was not the high-culture tome it purported to be, at least not in the eyes of the *bundan*. First, all eighteen books advertised in the final pages of the stand-alone volume were for *kikōbun* (travelogues) and travel guides, many of them written by Katai himself—there were none for "pure" literary works by either Katai or his contemporaries. Second, there was little acknowledgement of *Record of the Tokyo Earthquake* by the *bundan* critics. The book was not reviewed or included in surveys of "literature" in newspapers or magazine and is absent from the 1924 *Year in Literature* (*Bungei nenkan*), a summary of the works published and commentary on the state of the literary industry.[13] "Burnt Remains," however, was included. The reasons for the inclusion of one and not the other can be attributed to the boundary of the "literary," as policed by the *bundan*.

Stylistically, there is little that separates the "Burnt Remains" chapters of *Record of the Tokyo Earthquake* from the rest of the volume. Both "Burnt Remains" and the stand-alone volume as a whole are narrowly focalized through the narrator "Katai," and they share this characteristic with other I-novels from the time.[14] *Re-*

12. *Taiyō* 30, no. 5 (May 1924), front matter advertisement.
13. *Bungei nenkan*. vol. 2, Fukokuban edition, Bunsendō Shoten, 1974.
14. For more on the style and focalization of the I-novel, see Edward Fowler, *Rhetoric of Confession*, xvi. See also Tomi Suzuki, *Narrating the Self*, 70–71.

cord of the Tokyo Earthquake describes several journeys into the city; the chapters that comprise "Burnt Remains" are part of the second excursion. There is no shift in the longer work to show where the short story begins or ends. Yet this excerpt warrants closer attention.

In the opening to "Burnt Remains," the narrator/protagonist, ostensibly Katai himself, endures a difficult journey across the city and finally reaches the site of his mistress's house in Mukōjima in Honjo. There he learns that she is alive and has taken refuge in a park. In *Record of the Tokyo Earthquake*, the author continues the story to describe their reunion and Katai's return home, whereas the short story "Burnt Remains" ends with the narrator/protagonist breaking down in tears at the sight of familiar household objects buried and broken in the ashes. The plot is relatively simple; there is a journey and a destination. The protagonist moves from point A to point B, encountering various obstacles on his journey. When he finally arrives at the destination, he discovers what he went to find and the story concludes. Nevertheless, "Burnt Remains" functioned within the generic and literary boundaries of the I-novel in ways that *Record of the Tokyo Earthquake* did not. Specifically, "Burnt Remains" was directed toward an audience already familiar with Katai's life, and, furthermore, it dealt with the themes of love and human weakness found in his previous work.

The audience of the literary journal in which "Burnt Remains" appeared, *Shin-shōsetsu,* would have been familiar with the characters in the short story through Katai's prior mixture of personal details and fiction. The mistress in "Burnt Remains" would have been understood to be Katai's mistress, Iida Yone, who had appeared in Katai's works from 1912 onward.[15] In his review in the *Yomiuri shinbun,* Tanaka Jun claimed that curiosity to find out what happened to "the woman at Mukōjima whom we have heard so much about" was a major factor in his interest in the story.[16] Tanaka could not have been the only one who sought out "Burnt Remains" to discover her situation, especially knowing that Mukōjima was one of the areas of Tokyo that had been hardest hit.

Readers' familiarity with his life meant that Katai needed to supply little background information in the story itself. Fellow I-novel writer Uno Kōji pointed out the lack of biographical detail in the story in a roundtable discussion published in the journal *Shinchō* the month after "Burnt Remains" appeared. In the discussion, Uno complained that the protagonist is given no identifiable characteristics, such as age or circumstances, or even his relationship to the woman he is seeking. In Uno's words, "without knowing the personal history of the author named 'Katai,'

15. See Tayama Katai, *The Quilt and Other Stories*, trans. Kenneth G. Henshall (University of Tokyo Press, 1981), 29. Iida Yone is not mentioned by name, even in *Record of the Tokyo Earthquake*, but it is much clearer in that work that the unnamed woman is Katai's mistress, especially in the scene of their reunion.

16. Tanaka Jun, "Bungei-ran," *Yomiuri shinbun* (March 15, 1924), 7.

it is indecipherable. . . . That is, it doesn't stand alone as a story."[17] Uno's criticism is accurate; "Burnt Remains" is clear only to those who have intimate knowledge of the author's private life from his other works.[18] This familiarity was central to I-novel readership. *Record of the Tokyo Earthquake*, in contrast, is explicitly linked to the experiences of the author in both the preface and the text itself, and includes details for those who might not have followed Katai's career.

More than the audience, it is the thematics of "Burnt Remains" that help it conform to the genre of the I-novel and thus make it particularly worthy of *bundan* attention. I-novels tended to reveal the less savory aspects of the narrator/protagonist's character, particularly regarding their love interests. The specific focus in "Burnt Remains," on the narrator's unabashed personal relationship with his mistress, resonates with many other I-novels, including other works by Katai, such as *Futon* (1907). The final scene of "Burnt Remains" echoes that of the earlier novel: "I stood for a while in the burnt remains. I tried kicking at the ashes. I saw a familiar bowl broken in half. I saw a charred and cracked copper bucket that I recalled using. I saw iron kettles and copper pots collapsed on the ground. But before long, I couldn't stand it anymore. I stopped kicking around in the ashes and stood still. Tears fell quietly on the ash."[19] In this scene, as in his earlier novella, the protagonist cries alone in a space that reminds him of the absent lover. In *Futon,* it is the bedroom of his young pupil who had just left him; here, it is Iida's destroyed house. This conclusion to "Burnt Remains" brazenly presents the protagonist's sentimentality at confronting the remnants of his prior life with his mistress. She is safe, but her home and the objects that were once so familiar to him are no more.

This focus on the mistress is possibly the reason "Burnt Remains" was seen as literary. Katai's personal relationships are absent from *Record of the Tokyo Earthquake* once he finds his mistress safe. This is in contrast to one of Katai's last works, a long I-novel entitled *One Hundred Nights* (*Momoyo*, 1927), which delves into Katai's post-quake relationship with Iida Yone in detail. *One Hundred Nights* includes the earthquake, but most of the narrative occurs after the protagonist establishes his mistress, called O-gin in the novel, in a nearby house in the suburbs. *One Hundred Nights,* like "Burnt Remains," is about Katai's relationship to his mistress, whereas *Record of the Tokyo Earthquake* is about the disaster.

The narrow focalization of "Burnt Remains," its link to the actual life of the author, and its thematics establish the work as an I-novel, but some critics nevertheless questioned the literary qualifications of the story. In the *Shinchō* roundtable

17. *Shinchō,* April 1924. Quoted Kobayashi Ichirō, *Tayama Katai kenkyū*, vol. 9 (Ōfūsha, 1984), 229.
18. In Edward Fowler's discussion of I-novel as a "discursive contract" between author and reader, he claims that in an I-novel, the audience would "recognize the authorial persona in any story regardless of the main character's (or narrator's) name or situation." Edward Fowler, *Rhetoric of Confession*, xxv.
19. Tayama Katai, "Yakeato," 80. Included in idem, *Tokyo shinsaiki*, also on page 80.

with Uno Kōji, Kume Masao situates the story not with other examples of the yet-to-be-named I-novel, but with a more popular form. Kume introduces the dialogue on "Burnt Remains" with an odd pronouncement: "This is surely a travelogue [*kikōbun*]."[20] By labeling "Burnt Remains" a *kikōbun*, Kume acknowledges Katai's status as a well-known author of travelogues and places this work in a long tradition of writing about one's travels, but doing so also questions its "literariness."[21]

By the Taishō era, *kikōbun* were seen as popular guides to the country, and in this respect, Kume's declaration can be seen as a dismissive critique. Nevertheless, Kume's critique is not unfounded. In many ways, "Burnt Remains" resembles a *kikōbun*. It does contain a detailed account of a journey, along with descriptions of the observations, conversations, and impressions of the first-person narrator, not unlike Katai's other *kikōbun*. An example is the detail and attention to location in the following passage from the beginning of "Burnt Remains":

> I went left from Taisōji in Shinjuku, through a narrow road, and came out in Nukebenten in Ōkubo. . . . From Nukebenten I went into Wakamatsu-chō and continued to Benten-chō. Enoki-chō Street was very crowded, so I went from alleyway to alleyway. Then I went into Yamabuki-chō, next to the house in Tenjin-chō where Kawakami Bizan committed suicide, and from there into Akagishita-machi and on to Kaitai-chō. It was pretty bad there. Houses had toppled onto houses. In the case of some houses, the second floor had collapsed onto the first. Others were just in complete shambles. I thought at the time that this must be the most damaged part of the whole *yamanote* area.[22]

With the specific references to places and details of location, this section of "Burnt Remains" repeats the precision of Katai's guides to the countryside. The detail gives an almost cartographic feel to some of the passages, and it is easy to trace Katai's path on contemporary maps. Though the narrator moves physically through the city-space on his journey to his mistress, there is little these descriptions offer to further the plot or theme of the work. The preponderance of such scenes detracts from the diegetic flow toward the mistress and reveals a focus on the journey rather than its end.

20. *Shinchō,* April 1924. Quoted in volume 9 of Kobayashi Ichirō, *Tayama Katai kenkyū*, 229.

21. By some estimates Katai wrote more than sixty *kikōbun*, with about forty appearing as separate volumes (*tankōbon*). See Goi Makoto, "Tetsudō, 'Nihon,' byōsha: Tayama Katai no kikōbun 'Kusa-makura' wo megutte," *Nishōgakusha* 43 (2000): 53–75; and Miyauchi Shunsuke, "Shoki Tayama Katai ron: kikōbun to shōsetsu to no tanima," *Geibun kenkyū* 36 (1977): 222–33. Furthermore, Hakubunkan had published a three-volume collection of Katai's *kikōbun* immediately before the *Shinchō* article. Thus Katai's status as a *kikōbun* writer was very much in the public eye at the time.

22. Tayama Katai, *Tōkyō shinsaiki*, 59–60. In *Record of the Tokyo Earthquake*, this is the narrator/protagonist's second excursion into the city.

Despite the prevalence of such passages and Katai's history as a *kikōbun* writer, there are enough difficulties with Kume's pronouncement to question his application of this generic category to "Burnt Remains." The most blatant disjunction is the fact that the narrator is traveling through a devastated city marred by death, rather than through a picturesque country scene. In calling "Burnt Remains" a *kikōbun*, Kume Masao is stretching the meaning of the genre almost beyond recognition. At the same time, the way Kume questions the generic categorization of "Burnt Remains" implies that there was some consternation over how to think about works that depicted the earthquake—namely, that there might not have been a clear and appropriate genre in which to place a work that provided a tour of the devastation. Perhaps by calling "Burnt Remains" a *kikōbun*, Kume was merely struggling to classify this strange hybrid text, for it certainly differs in crucial ways from much of the literary production that preceded it. It was an I-novel in which descriptions of travel overshadow the personal drama, and a *kikōbun* in which images of death and destruction substitute for natural beauty.

There was little precedent for either an I-novel or a *kikōbun* in which the protagonist/narrator ventured out into a ruined cityscape. The critic Tanaka Jun voiced the dual nature of the work with characteristic precision in a review of "Burnt Remains" published in the *Yomiuri shinbun* just after the story had appeared: "I've grown weary of 'earthquake pieces.' But I was in Kamakura during the quake and know little of post-quake Tokyo, so I read it as a record of observing (*kenbutsu-ki*). It was perfect for that sort of thing because the places were named in detail."[23] Tanaka refrains from calling "Burnt Remains" a *shōsetsu*, or work of fiction; instead, he uses the word *kenbutsu-ki,* or "record of observing," which is notably different from *kikōbun*. *Kikōbun* emphasizes travel (*kikō*), whereas *kenbutsu-ki* is specifically connected to observation.

After the quake, there was an explosion of images depicting the damage, as well as the "earthquake pieces" referred to in Tanaka Jun's quotation above. It is hard to imagine that objective descriptions of post-quake Tokyo interested Tanaka on the basis of the scenery alone (the objects of the gaze). Rather, Tanaka was interested in the fact that Katai's piece was a "record of observing" or a "record of the observer." The one thing other representations of the earthquake lacked, Tanaka seems to be saying, was the ability to portray the subjective experience of being a *flâneur* in post-disaster Tokyo.

Artistic Detachment and Representing the Surface of Things

The focus on observation in Tanaka's term *kenbutsu-ki* links the I-novel qualities of "Burnt Remains" with Katai's descriptions of the journey across Tokyo after

23. Tanaka Jun, "Bungei-ran," 7.

the earthquake. I-novels emerged by turning the "objective" authorial gaze of Naturalism toward the self. As a *kenbutsu-ki*, Katai's post-quake writing takes that gaze out into the world. In so doing, Katai retains the style he developed in his earlier work and reapplies it to the devastated city. "Burnt Remains" and *Record of the Tokyo Earthquake* not only show how Katai's prior literary theories are put to use in describing "reality," but also how his theorizations posit a detached observer, or *flâneur*, as the ideal narrator, despite the object of his gaze.

Tanaka's review in the *Yomiuri shinbun* makes an implicit distinction between Katai's work and other texts and images that were readily available. This was also done in the advertisements for *Record of the Tokyo Earthquake*, which are worth revisiting here: "[Prior works] resemble long newspaper or magazine articles; and if they are not completely disjointed, they are nothing more than *mere descriptions*. We pledge that this book alone has *artistic representations* that recreate the real scenery, feelings, and emotions of the earthquake" (emphasis added).[24] Tanaka is not so blatant to claim, as did the Hakubunkan advertisement, that the difference between Katai's work and other earthquake writing is artistic, but both he and the ad note that the interest in "Burnt Remains" lies not in the objects of the gaze, but rather in the subjective experience of gazing. The Hakubunkan advertisement also shifts the focus from the object of observation to the observer, stressing the "eye" of the artist and the quality of the work as an "artistic representation" (*geijutsuteki byōsha*) rather than "mere descriptions" (*kijutsu*). The advertisement maps the difference between Katai's work and other earthquake accounts as being the difference between ordinary objective descriptions of the damage itself and representation filtered through the sensibilities of an artist.

This distinction is drawn from Katai's own introduction to *Record of the Tokyo Earthquake*. This introduction continues his earlier theoretical musings on his craft, throughout which we see the careful cultivation of an observing persona detached from the world around him. The introduction to *Record of the Tokyo Earthquake* centers on what it is that makes Katai's writing different from others—namely, the difference between portrayals (*byōsha*) and descriptions (*kijutsu*): "Though this is called a 'record of the earthquake,' it is merely what I saw and heard, and by no means complete. If you want to know more in greater detail, you will need to look at other records in newspaper articles and the like. However, those are mostly descriptions (*kijutsu*) and explanations, they are not portrayals (or 'representations,' *byōsha*), so though you may know what happened, you will not understand the real scenery and the feel of the earthquake. I can't say that this is a perfect representation, but I tried to do the best I could."[25] The words used

24. *Taiyō* (May 1924), advertisement.
25. Tayama Katai, *Tōkyō shinsaiki*, introduction.

to emphasize the differences between this book and others, *kijutsu* and *byōsha,* may not appear at first glance to be important theoretical terms, but Katai had previously addressed them in his theories on style. There is a subtle difference between the words *kijutsu* and *byōsha*, both of which are often translated into English as "description." *Kijutsu* implies journalistic objectivity and explanation. *Byōsha* appears often in Katai's essays on style to mean specifically artistic representation. Oddly enough, Katai sees *byōsha* as even more objective and detached than *kijutsu*, but the reasons for this belief require a closer examination of the terms.

Byōsha and *kijutsu* are most lucidly compared in Katai's 1911 essay "On Representation" ("Byōsha-ron"), published in the journal *Waseda bungaku* (*Waseda Literature*): "Someone intending to describe something (*kijutsu*) does not . . . attempt to write so that the object appears lifelike, so that a reader would see the reality in the work. Rather, they try to describe what they see and hear by abstracting some sort of narrative, or condense it into a plot and attempt to convey that abstraction. . . . The goal of *byōsha* (representation) is not to convey the gist or plot of something. . . . It is to take the raw scenery that enters the brain through the eye and attempt to recreate that scene as it is on the surface of the page."[26] Katai trusts in the transparency of language and the ability of a writer to recreate the scene in its entirety for the reader through *byōsha*. According to Katai, it is important that the attempt to recreate does not extend into explanation, but is limited to *objectively* conveying the *subjective experience of observing the scene*. The focus is on the scene as filtered through the eye and the brain. *Kijutsu* presents the scene as filtered through the concealed mechanism of the writer's consciousness, but *byōsha* shows the workings of that consciousness for a fuller evocation of reality.

The nuances of these definitions become clearer as Katai illustrates the difference between *kijutsu* and *byōsha* with the sentences "The plum blossoms are in bloom" (*kijutsu*) and "I saw the plum blossoms" (*byōsha*). The first sentence ignores the presence of the necessary observing subject, whereas the latter objectively states what the narrator saw. In other words, as theorized by Katai, *byōsha* stresses the importance of the observing subject. Katai had earlier termed this ideal *heimen byōsha* (surface portrayal).

Heimen byōsha involves an objective portrayal of the subjective experience of the observer. In other words, by concentrating on the individual, *heimen byōsha* is twice removed from the "real world." Katai's oft-quoted explanation of *heimen byōsha* comes from a 1908 interview published in *Waseda bungaku*: "This means not only to withhold the author's subjectivity, but that we must not enter into objective phenomena or the minds of the characters. We must only depict things

26. Reprinted as Tayama Katai, "Byōsha-ron," in *Kindai bungaku hyōron taikei*, vol. 3 (1971): 370.

as we see them, hear them, or touch them. In other words, surface portrayal (*heimen byōsha*)—that is the goal. We must depict . . . the real experiences of oneself without adding even a little subjectivity, or internal explanation or dissection. If one tries to write like that, the result will naturally be impressionistic."[27] *Heimen byōsha* does not mean that the subject is absent. The goal is to depict things as they are "seen, heard, or touched" by a subject, not as they are independent of the subject.

Heimen byōsha is an objective portrayal of subjectivity detached from both the author and the phenomenal world. This detachment is crucial. Though Katai first explained his theories more than a decade before the earthquake, when he posited his work as *byōsha* rather than *kijutsu* after the quake, he was pointing out the artistic quality of the writing and its ability to recreate and call to mind the sights and experiences of the disaster. In this endeavor, Katai-the-author sought detachment from Katai-the-narrator, and also created in that narrator the same detachment from the world he himself observed. This *heimen byōsha* style allowed Katai, in the words of Edward Fowler, to "treat all events and characters [including the character based on himself] with the same degree of studied aloofness."[28]

In "Byōsha-ron," Katai further explains the need for detachment, that is, the need to maintain what he terms a "spectatorial attitude" (*bōkanteki taido*), which he sees as necessary to analyze something objectively. He describes the proper artistic attitude thus: "I think that we must maintain an attitude that can control the urge to act, an attitude born between patience and knowledge. . . . Such an attitude allows for analysis. . . . This kind of analytical attitude necessarily engenders feelings of indifference, disdain, and denial and allows one to look at the world with detached irony."[29] The distance that Katai sought as a writer is characterized by his spectatorial attitude. He seeks total control without letting himself fall prey to the desire to comment. He claims that such detachment is necessary for analysis, but this quote also calls attention to the hierarchy inherent in Katai's brand of spectatorship. The detached irony he foregrounds is dependent on a position above the objects of observation, thus engendering feelings of "indifference" and "disdain." In "Burnt Remains" and *Record of the Tokyo Earthquake*, the narrator maintains a similar attitude of indifference with respect to his observations of the devastation surrounding him.

At the same time that Katai was striving for an objective look at the narrator/protagonist, he was creating that narrator as an ideal observer of the

27. Reprinted as Tayama Katai, "Sei ni okeru kokoromi," in *Kindai bungaku hyōron taikei* vol. 3 (1971): 448. Soma Tsuneo's explanation of *heimen byōsha* is useful in understanding the concept throughout Katai's oeuvre, in all its complicated iterations. See Soma Tsueno, "Tayama Katai no 'heimen byōsha,'" in *Nihon shizen shugi ron* (Yagi Shoten, 1970).

28. Edward Fowler, *Rhetoric of Confession*, 123.

29. Tayama Katai, "Byōsha-ron," 373.

world that surrounded him. One of the striking elements of "Burnt Remains," and also of *Record of the Tokyo Earthquake* as a whole, is the degree to which Katai successfully maintains the style of *heimen byōsha*, devoid of emotional commentary. The narrator treats the objects of his gaze with a cool indifference. Katai's descriptive style serves to distance the narrator from the objects he is observing, a technique that extends to his portrayal of the dead: "There I saw half-burnt houses and garments spread all over. I saw lots of metal from dressers, cans, and knobs in heaps. They said that most of the dead should have been cleared away by this point, but here and there I saw bodies with arms raised or legs in the air, tragically lying where they had died. I saw three or four horses collapsed and displaying their bloated stomachs. The stench of things burnt or rotting hung suspended in the bright dirty yellow air, so that there was no one who could pass without covering their noses."[30] In this passage, the human dead are merely one part of the scenery, along with metal debris and horses. The distance between the narrator and the objects of his gaze is formed by the extremely narrow focalization in the first-person narration, and the verb "I saw" is used repetitively to convey the subjective experience of seeing.[31] Throughout most of *Record of the Tokyo Earthquake*, the reader is denied insight into any other character, let alone the crowds of people in the streets. The practiced indifference and narrow focalization are emblematic of the *heimen byōsha* style, and serve to increase the distance between the narrating self and the objects of his gaze, thus precluding any opportunity for sympathetic identification with the suffering crowd.

The "Man of Leisure" and the Crowd

Like Walter Benjamin's "gentleman of leisure," the wandering "I" of *Record of the Tokyo Earthquake* desires distance from the crowd. Katai's narrator tries to stand apart, but at times finds himself sucked into the throng. Once the trains begin to run, they are too crowded to accommodate him, and the hordes of people disrupt his smooth passage to his destination. These other people become merely part of the landscape, like the bodies of the dead, or obstacles to overcome in his journey: "Even though I wanted to walk on the cooler, shaded side of the street, I couldn't. No matter how hot, or whether the sun was shining from the front, there was nothing I could do but walk on the left side of the street, carried along by the people and the carts."[32] The narrator is being carried by the ebb and flow of the

30. Tayama Katai, *Tōkyō shinsaiki*, 73.

31. Nevertheless, even Katai recognizes the repetitive nature of prose limited to subjective "I saw" sentences, and the most vivid sentence, the last sentence of the extract, is descriptive without being filtered through his senses. The final scene of "Yakeato," discussed above, also includes a repetition of "I saw," along with the tears.

32. Ibid., 61.

crowd, but rather than take pleasure in the experience, as the *flâneur* of Baudelaire is wont to do, he is annoyed that he is unable to walk freely where he feels entitled to do so. It becomes apparent that the narrator, like Benjamin's *flâneur*, demands "elbow room." Though he craves the detachment offered by his social class, as an actual physical body he is subject to the motions of the crowd. The narrator, however, responds by keeping his distance in other ways, namely, by maintaining his focus on the self.

The spectatorial attitude of the narrator toward the crowd is made possible both by his physical distance from the destroyed areas of Tokyo and by his separation from the sufferers in terms of social class. At the time of the earthquake, Katai lived in the quiet suburbs of Yoyogi and weathered the tremors without injury to home or family. This is in great contrast to the ward in which his mistress lived, Honjo, which was almost entirely destroyed by the fires. This difference in class and earthquake experience is the unspoken foundation for the studied detachment apparent in the work.

As a "man of leisure," like Benjamin's *flâneur*, Katai had the ability to wander in the ruins and observe freely without concern for rebuilding his home or workplace. The practice of *yakeato kenbutsu* (touring the devastation) presupposes a privileged position in the suburbs and underscores class differences.[33] It was also presumably his social class that allowed him to pass through barriers set up by self-protection groups (*jikeidan*) to prevent looting (and in some cases to persecute Koreans). Movement was very much limited in the aftermath of the earthquake, and status equaled mobility.

On the narrator's first trip to the city ruins in *Record of the Tokyo Earthquake*, he and a friend observe a group of refugees in the Yasukuni shrine district, just north of the imperial palace. Their gaze focuses on a group of people who appear to have taken refuge there from Fujimi-chō, a lesser-known pleasure district:

> A vivacious yukata-clad girl with her hair done up in the *onēsan* style, a gaudy kimono covered in mud hanging on a bamboo pole to dry, a long grill looking surprisingly polished, a beautiful young girl holding what could be utensils for the tea ceremony and standing with the knot of her summer obi toward us. An older geisha was sitting with poise and seemed to be reminding the young girl that she must maintain her appearance even in circumstances such as these. A man who must

33. At the same time, *yakeato kenbutsu* (touring the devastation) emphasizes the difference between the writers of the *bundan* (or the *flâneur*) and the "regular" middle-class audience. The latter had to work toward rebuilding while the former could wander in the ruins and scavenge for literary material. Following Walter Benjamin, scholars exploring the idea of the *flâneur*, such as Keith Tester and Anne Friedberg, often note the detachment of the *flâneur* from his own social class because of this ability to freely go into the city, and desire to do so. Keith Tester, *The Flâneur* (London; New York: Routledge, 1994), and Anne Friedberg, *Window Shopping*.

> have been a cooper shuffled here and there incessantly. We observed these colorful scenes spread out amusingly across the landscape. Even in a disaster such as this, we could not overlook the beautiful picture extending out before us, lit up by the afternoon sun cascading through the leaves of the cherry trees. "What an ideal place for refuge!" we said as we passed.[34]

In this passage, the narrator aestheticizes a scene of suffering. Although it is not a scene of the abject suffering of the burnt districts or the wails of people crying over loved ones in Honjo, these are people displaced by the quake and subsequent fires. The scene is an empty image to be filled by his aesthetic imagination. The narrator invents a dialogue between the older geisha and her young trainee, emphasizing his ability to control the representation of their interaction. The narrator and his friend observe the scene from a distance, and that distance enables them to maintain the illusion of beauty amid disaster.

As a *kenbutsu-ki,* Katai's *Record of the Tokyo Earthquake* reveals little about the destruction or the crowds of sufferers—the objects of the gaze—but rather retains its focus on the subjectivity of the observer, the *flâneur*. Katai creates the ideal observer, as posited in his theorizations, by focusing on the narrator's ability to remain distant from the objects of his gaze. This distance, visible in the style that is employed in the text, is also linked to a hierarchy of class between the viewer and the viewed. For Katai, the ruined city becomes the focal point of philosophical ruminations, and forms the basis for both the narrator's ideas of modernity and his conception of the self. Although for Baudelaire the crowd is the source of the *flâneur's* identity, it is the city itself and the changes that have befallen it that reflect the subjectivity of *Record of the Tokyo Earthquake*'s narrator.

THE RUINED CITY, THE RUINED SELF

As he surveys the wasteland that was once his lover's neighborhood in Honjo, Katai-the-narrator muses, "I felt I saw in the large ruins of Tokyo the smaller-scale personal ruin within myself."[35] There is an odd contradiction in the dialectic of distance and intimacy discernible in this passage: the large-scale view of a desolate expanse and the intimate view of the self. What exactly does the narrator see in the ruins, and what was the personal ruin within himself? This passage can only be understood within the context of Katai's philosophy on "the ruin," a concept that first emerges as a theme in his essays in the late 1910s.

In Katai's brand of Naturalism, different from that of his European counterparts, there is a fundamental distinction between nature and society, with hu-

34. Tayama Katai, *Tōkyō shinsaiki*, 36.
35. Ibid., 78.

manity falling on the side of nature. This idea appears in Katai's oeuvre as the opposition between the individual, coded as "natural," and the requirements of society. For example, the conflict in Katai's *Futon* revolves around the protagonist's "natural" yearnings for his pupil and his inability to act on that desire because of propriety. This binary is also inextricably connected to Katai's ideas of writing. The subjectivity that Katai fears will pollute his *heimen byōsha* style is the voice of society; he is interested in displaying the narrator at his most "natural." Katai's statement about the ruin within himself should be understood in terms of this opposition between nature and society.[36] In the physical ruin, Katai sees the natural overtaking the monuments of society, its very structures.

The sociologist Georg Simmel, a contemporary of Walter Benjamin, was also interested in the concept of "the ruin." In an essay by that name, Simmel discusses the attraction of architectural ruins, which he believes stems from the internal tension between the competing drives of nature and spirit—by which he means human creation, or culture. Although for Katai humanity is nature, for Simmel the spirit is that which distinguishes humanity from nature. Therefore Simmel makes a distinction between the noble melancholy of the architectural ruin and the degeneracy of human "ruins": "The aesthetically satisfying impression, which is associated with the tragedy . . . of destruction, is so often lacking when a person is described as a 'ruin.'"[37] For Simmel, the fall of humans into ruin is degeneration because the negative drives of the body destroy the mind and spirit. The result is a ruin without the nobility of tragedy; it is merely "sad."

For Katai, there is no philosophical difference between architectural ruins and human ruins. When the narrator of *Record of the Tokyo Earthquake* sees himself in the ruin, he sees himself as nature emerging from its confines. This is not the negative degeneration that Simmel detects in human "ruins." It is, rather, a ruin that promises new life, just as a glorious modern city will emerge from the ashes of Tokyo. In a reworking of this recurring theme, Katai likens the ruin of the city to the ruin of the person: "Do not ruins continuously repeat themselves within the human heart? Do they not reveal themselves within human debauchery, ennui, indulgences, and fatigue? And from within that 'ruin' there emerges a new sprout.

36. Most scholars read *Record of the Tokyo Earthquake* through the lens of Katai's philosophy on "the ruin." See, for example, Takematsu Yoshiaki, "Metsubō suru teito," 175, and Sawa Toyohiko, "Kisei sakka no daishinsai: Tayama Katai to Nagata Mikihiko no ba'ai," *Shakai bungaku* 8 (July 1994): 69–72. The other common thread treats *Record of the Tokyo Earthquake* as a nostalgic elegy for lost Edo, as mentioned earlier. See, for example, Haruno Ogasawara, "Living with Natural Disasters: Narratives of the Great Kanto and Great Hanshin Earthquakes" (Ph.D. dissertation, Northwestern University, 1999), 81–82. Nostalgia is certainly present as a theme of the text, but that nostalgia is part of a larger concern with modernity.

37. Georg Simmel, "The Ruin," in *Essays on Sociology, Philosophy, and Aesthetics*, ed. Kurt Wolff (New York: Harper and Row, 1965), 263.

A new love is born. A new heart is awakened."[38] To Katai, human degeneracy is a point at which to start afresh. The self that he sees refracted through the mirror of the ruins is a self without the trappings of society. For Baudelaire, the *flâneur* is the mirror, allowing the energies of modernization to flow through him and create him as a subject, whereas for Katai, it is the world that is his mirror, and he looks out into the devastated landscape and sees not others, the people who suffered in that landscape, but himself. This is possible only because of the distance he maintains between himself and the external world. To Katai, the outside world is empty and able to be filled with his own reflection.

Karatani Kōjin, in his discussion of the "Origins of Modern Japanese Literature," has paid particular attention to landscape in the mid- to late Meiji period. He anchors his discussion in a careful look at one of Katai's closest friends and colleagues, Kunikida Doppo. Karatani focuses on Doppo's short story "Unforgettable People" ("Wasureenu hitobito"), in which the narrator claims to be moved by his encounters with people who should be forgettable but who are not. Karatani names them "people-as-landscapes," and indeed, Doppo's narrator refers to them as "part of their surroundings, part of the moment." Nevertheless, as Karatani points out, these people-as-landscapes betray a strange paradox between the external world and the self. He claims that "Unforgettable People" reveals the "link between landscape and an introverted solitary situation": "While the narrator can feel a solidarity such that 'the boundary between myself and others' disappears in the case of people who are of no consequence to him, he is the very picture of indifference when it comes to those in his immediate surroundings. It is only within the 'inner man,' who appears to be indifferent to his external surroundings, that landscape is discovered. It is perceived by those who do not look 'outside.'"[39] Karatani suggests that, paradoxically, landscape is only being perceived by those who "do not look 'outside.'" Doppo's narrator sees the boundaries between the self and the external world disappear, but this is due not to the negation of the self, but to the expansion of the self to fill the world. The narrator easily forgets the people who should be important to him, people who have the voices to assert their own subjectivity. Instead, it is the people who have no voice, those who are emptied of meaning by his gaze, who remain in his memory. The detachment sought by writers such as Katai empties the landscape of any existence in and of itself; rather, the landscape becomes a narcissistic mirror for the self.

In the majority of *Record of the Tokyo Earthquake*, Tayama Katai offers a calm and philosophical look at an event full of emotion. At the end of "Burnt Remains," the narrator breaks down in tears standing in the ashes of the home where

38. Tayama Katai, *Tōkyō shinsaiki*, 97–98.

39. Kōjin Karatani, *Origins of Modern Japanese Literature*, trans. Brett de Bary (Durham, NC: Duke University Press, 1993), 25.

he met his mistress. The mistress is safe, but the site of their shared memories, the Mukōjima they knew, is gone forever. Kume Masao criticized this scene because the narrator's actions seemed undignified and unrealistic for a man Katai's age. Yet for Katai, it is in moments such as these that the natural ruin of the narrator is described with objective distance. Though Katai was able to show his narrator break down and cry at the loss of a way of life he had enjoyed with his mistress, this passage is less a transparent portrayal of unashamed feelings than the expected ending for a literary I-novel.

THE STORY "A SINGLE GRAIN ADRIFT IN THE SEA"

There is one long chapter in Katai's *Record of the Tokyo Earthquake* that stands apart, the exception that proves the rule. Its inclusion suggests that Katai understood the limits of detachment in dealing with the emotional urgency of disaster. Chapter 39 was first published as "A Single Grain Adrift in the Sea" ("Taikai no ichizoku") a month after the earthquake, in the popular news magazine *Sunday Mainichi*.[40] This short story was thus directed beyond the enclosed circle of the *bundan* and its readership. "A Single Grain Adrift in the Sea" is not based on any experience of Katai's, but is a fictional account of "B," who loses his father in the earthquake. When the earthquake struck, B was at work but was able to escape the collapsing building. There is a sense of urgency as he rushes home, ignoring his surroundings. He is finally able to break down in tears upon seeing his wife and child safe in the garden of their home. His joy lasts only for a moment, for he realizes that his father is absent. His father, "K," had gone into the city on an errand and had probably stopped in the movie theaters, as was his habit. After waiting in vain for a few days, B ventures out into the city. Upon his return, his fretful wife inquires after his journey. B at first remains silent, unable to speak of the horrors he observed. Finally, he begins to describe the devastation, recalling in his mind the half-burnt corpses he examined in his search for his father:[41]

> "Where did I go? Well first I went to Kudan, and there my courage gave out. It was a burnt-out wasteland as far as I could see. I had no idea where to look; I mean there was nowhere to look."
>
> "Really?"
>
> "I was amazed. I mean, it wasn't that finding the dead was the problem. No matter where you looked, there was someone burnt to death on the ground. . . ."

40. This was the first story in the October 21 edition of the *Sunday Mainichi*, 3–4.

41. This work possibly became one inspiration for a passage in Hara Tamiki's "Summer Flowers" ("Natsu no hana"), in which a character unrelated to the story (identified only by the letter N) searches among the dead of Hiroshima looking for his wife.

> "And . . ."
>
> "Well, I went to Nihonbashi, only ruins, and then I went to Asakusa. But, well, even if Dad was dead, that one death seemed like nothing compared to all this. It wasn't the time to consider a single death. There was no way of telling if he went into a theater and was crushed. . . ."
>
> His wife gave him a quizzical look.
>
> "I mean, it's all collapsed and turned to a heap of burned rubble. No trace of anything. Doesn't look like Tokyo anymore, but some other kind of place. I just don't know. . . ."
>
> "That bad?"
>
> "I just don't know what to say."
>
> So saying, B went quiet. Images swept through his mind like a movie reel. He remembered walking along the streets, stopping at every half-burnt body, looking and wondering if it could be his father.[42]

Even after days of searching like this for a "grain in the ocean," B is still reluctant to give up entirely and continues in his spare time, until the last vestiges of hope are gone. He suffers; he does not remain distant from the bodies he sees, but peers into their disfigured faces one by one, in search of his lost father. Near the end of the story, an old friend stops by and asks how B and his family weathered the quake: "B tried to say something but couldn't. Suddenly no words would come. Tears began to flow quietly over his cheeks and fell."[43] This recalls the scene of Katai weeping over the ashes of his mistress's home, but somehow these tears seem more authentic. The experience leaves B speechless, but we can feel his pain through the narration. There is no distance here; we as readers are face to face with B's horror and despair.

In this story we are also given an image of B in the crowd. He blends with the others, a single grain in the ocean of the living, searching for his father among the ocean of the dead: "Up to the fifth day, the streets were populated by earnest people searching intently with bloodshot eyes peering out from their agitated faces. B felt their silence acutely."[44] Unlike a *flâneur*, B is part of the masses, moving with them as if in a trance. The raw emotion of B in his fruitless search stands out against the studied detachment of the rest of the book. B has experienced loss, and the narrator asks for the readers' sympathy for him. In his searching and in his tears there is a sense of urgency that is contrasted with the almost leisurely stroll of the narrator/protagonist of "Burnt Remains" and the other chapters.

* * * * *

42. Tayama Katai, *Tōkyō shinsaiki*, 230–32.
43. Ibid., 234.
44. Ibid.

This break from the rest of the Tayama Katai's *Record of the Tokyo Earthquake* is striking, and it draws attention to the confines of the literary, as established by the *bundan*. "Burnt Remains" was published in a respectable journal and was considered literary, despite the criticism of Kume Masao and others. The mere fact that *bundan* critics were discussing the story suggests as much. In contrast, "A Single Grain Adrift in the Sea" was published in an affordable popular weekly. It is not mentioned in the *Year in Literature* (*Bungei nenkan*) and received no attention from critics. Similarly, scholarship on *Record of the Tokyo Earthquake* today ignores this story completely.

Authors such as Katai could not publish works like "A Single Grain Adrift in the Sea," works that addressed the perceived needs of the larger reading audience, in the customary outlets for "pure fiction." This suggests that Katai's style in "Burnt Remains" displays his awareness of the demands of the literary marketplace. "A Single Grain Adrift in the Sea," hidden in a work of detached "artistic" observation, betrays the boundaries of the *bundan*'s response to the earthquake, boundaries that I explore further in the next chapter, on other, more popular, responses to the earthquake.

CHAPTER 4

Spectacular Suffering in Earthquake Melodrama

The earthquake was an extreme event, and the suffering it caused strained the bounds of realist literature. As the literary elite's disregard for Tayama Katai's "A Single Grain Adrift in the Sea" shows, *bundan* ideas of literature were often too limited to include the horrors of the *hifukushō* (the site of the former military clothing depot in Honjo where more than 30,000 people died). Nevertheless, works recognized by the *bundan* form only one portion of the myriad texts that attempted to represent the disaster. There were *jitsuwa* (true tales), fictional stories, and feature films, all directed at mass audiences. Among these texts, melodrama was the norm. The prevalence of such narratives attests to the emotional appeal of melodrama, which struck a cord with audiences in the aftermath of the Great Kanto Earthquake. Yet, as critics such as Peter Brooks have shown, the emotion of melodrama is never ideologically neutral; it is always mobilized in the service of a moral code.

In *The Melodramatic Imagination,* Peter Brooks identifies the melodramatic mode as "a mode of conception and expression, a certain fictional system for making sense of experience."[1] This particular fictional system serves to foreground an unspoken moral code of a society, what Brooks calls "'the moral occult,' the domain of operative spiritual values which is both indicated within and masked by the surface of reality."[2] Melodrama reveals the "moral occult" through excessive emotionalism and sensationalism, as well as other characteristics he identifies as determining factors.[3] By so defining melodrama, Brooks is able to find it in places outside its standard generic boundaries, such as the high-literature writers he studies.

1. Peter Brooks, *The Melodramatic Imagination: Balzac, Henry James, Melodrama, and the Mode of Excess* (New Haven, CT: Yale University Press, 1995), xvii. I follow Brooks and Ben Singer to treat melodrama as a descriptive, rather than a pejorative, term. It was at times used pejoratively in the Taishō era.
2. Ibid., 5.
3. Brooks's actual list of characteristics is as follows: "the indulgence of strong emotionalism; moral polarization and schematization; extreme states of being, situations, actions; overt villainy, persecution of the good, and final reward of virtue; inflated and extravagant expression; dark plottings, suspense, breathtaking peripety." Ibid., 11–12.

Ben Singer, in contrast, focuses on the more narrowly defined genre of melodrama as it pertains to early twentieth-century film and stage. In his study Singer has outlined five common characteristics of melodrama as a genre: pathos, overwrought emotion, moral polarization, nonclassical narrative structure, and sensationalism.[4] Although not every melodrama has every characteristic Singer identifies, any melodrama will have several in various combinations. When we read of a wayward child coming home to his poor sick mother on her deathbed (pathos and overwrought emotion), or see a death-defying rescue of an innocent girl from the clutches of a villain (moral polarization and sensationalism), we know, to borrow a phrase from Terry Eagleton, that we are in the presence of melodrama.[5]

As Ken Ito and others have shown, melodrama has long been a part of Japanese literary production, without necessarily being named as such.[6] Nevertheless, the word "melodrama," transliterated as *merodorama*, was occasionally used as a generic category to describe plays and films during the Taishō era.[7] It is possible, however, following Brooks and Singer, to find characteristics of melodrama beyond the narrow confines of the genre. Even though *jitsuwa* (factual stories) made claims to authenticity, they were frequently melodramatic, made so in the process of retelling and collecting, and indistinguishable from fictional melodramas. Often, the only distinction was the textual and paratextual connection to actual people and events. The *jitsuwa* discussed in this chapter, entitled "At Least My Mother" ("Semete haha dake"), is not unusual in its dramatizing of the story to reinforce the virtue of the filial son.

Freed from the demands of truth, fictional earthquake melodramas were much more sensational than *jitsuwa*. Though they often borrowed plot points from the

4. Ben Singer, *Melodrama and Modernity: Early Sensational Cinema and Its Contexts* (New York: Columbia University Press, 2001), 44–49. The debt to Brooks is apparent, though Singer provides a much more explicit explanation of these characteristics and melodrama as a genre.

5. Terry Eagleton, *Literary Theory: An Introduction* (Minneapolis: University of Minnesota Press, 1996), 9. "If you approach me at a bus stop and murmur Thou still unravished bride of quietness, then I am instantly aware that I am in the presence of the literary." In the original quote, Eagleton is talking about the literary (meaning high literary), almost in the sense of the Judge Potter Stuart's famous comment on pornography: "I know it when I see it." This may ultimately be the only way we can ever strictly define melodrama, but Singer's characteristics are useful to determine its boundaries.

6. Ken K. Ito, *An Age of Melodrama: Family, Gender, and Social Hierarchy in the Turn-of-the-Century Japanese Novel* (Stanford, CA: Stanford University Press, 2008). Jonathan Zwicker explores melodrama in the Edo period. Jonathan E. Zwicker, *Practices of the Sentimental Imagination: Melodrama, the Novel, and the Social Imaginary in Nineteenth-Century Japan* (Cambridge, MA: Harvard University Asia Center, distributed by Harvard University Press, 2006).

7. In 1917 the critic Ōsugi Sakae wrote pejoratively of melodramas that "make people cry and then end with celebration." Ōsugi Sakae, "Atarashiki sekai no tame no atarashiki geijutsu," *Waseda bungaku* 143 (October 1917): 247. In 1923, the *Tokyo Asahi shinbun* described the film *Over the Hill to the Poorhouse* (dir. Harry Millarde, 1920) as a "spectacle melodrama." *Tokyo Asahi shinbun* (June 16, 1923, evening edition), 3.

news coverage of the disaster and from *jitsuwa*, they also drew heavily on tropes familiar from both Western and domestic melodramas. The result is a hybrid form that combines the claim to authenticity from the *jitsuwa* genre with the power of fiction. Both the Shōchiku studio's *Facing Death* (*Shi ni men shite*) and Nagata Mikihiko's short story "Wild Geese" ("Kari") deal with a common result of the earthquake—namely, the separation of children from their parents. Yet in these works the separation serves as the impetus to put these young women into further peril.

The texts discussed in this chapter share characteristics with the genre of melodrama as identified by Singer: pathos, overwrought emotion, moral polarization, nonclassical narrative structure, and sensationalism.[8] At the same time, they articulate a moral code in line with dominant ideology found in the imperial decrees such as the Meiji-era rescript on education and the post-quake "Rescript on Strengthening the National Spirit." By highlighting the conventional morality with authenticity, sensationalism, and emotion, they do so with a power rarely found in other works of the time.

JITSUWA AS EARTHQUAKE MELODRAMA

Jitsuwa were short, usually anonymous vignettes focused on the personal experiences of people in the disaster zone. A staple part of post-quake newspapers, magazines, and books, these stories were among the most prevalent forms of "earthquake culture."[9] Their popularity shows that people demanded more than facts and statistics about how many people had died, and where; they wanted drama. And these stories provided it. The link between drama, especially emotionally fraught melodrama, and these stories is clear in the title of Seishindō's two-volume collection of *jitsuwa* entitled *Earthquake Romances* (*Shinsai romansu*). The meaning behind the title becomes clear when contemporary definitions of the word "romance" (or *romansu*) are taken into account. *Romansu* is defined in a 1916 dictionary of foreign words as "fantastical tales of heroes and monks that emphasize the *sensational* in describing events" (emphasis added).[10] In this sense *romansu* stems not from the English word "romance" but from the French heroic tales. These are not love stories but *sensational* tales full of emotion—in other words, melodramas.

Melodrama was a key part of other *jitsuwa* collections as well, the most famous of which was Kōdansha's *The Great Taishō Earthquake and Conflagration*

8. Ben Singer, *Melodrama and Modernity*, 44–49.

9. For about a week after it resumed publication, the *Tokyo Asahi shinbun* ran a column featuring tales of sadness, improbable survival, and curiosity.

10. *Romansu* was similarly defined in a 1935 dictionary as "stories, *emotional* tales, fantastical tales." *Nihon gairaigo jiten* (Sanseidō, 1916), 241; Otsuki Fumihiko, *Daigenkai* (Fuzanbō, 1935).

(*Taishō daishinsai daikasai*). By most accounts, this comprehensive overview of the earthquake was a best seller, and as many as four hundred thousand copies were sold. The newspaper and magazine advertisements for the book give insight into what Kōdansha and its marketing team thought would pique the curiosity of the public. And the success of the book proves that they astutely perceived those interests. In addition to prominently displaying imperial approval and the number of photographs included in the book, the ad that ran in several venues stresses the inclusion of emotionally charged "true tales": "True tales of pitiful tears! Incredible tales, pitiful tales, great tales of heroism filled with tears of gratitude, strange stories, all collected here. Can there be anyone who could look on this book and not cry? Even the gods and demons would surely cry!"[11] *Jitsuwa* figure prominently in the ad, showing that they played an important part in selling the book. The ad specifically focuses on a few primary characteristics of the *jitsuwa*, claiming that these "true stories" are authentic, dramatic, and emotional.

Authenticity is built into the word *jitsuwa*; it literally means "true tales." This was part of their appeal, but *jitsuwa* offered a "true" account of the disaster that was also more intimate, and thus more emotionally engaging, than objective articles. These personal accounts allowed an imaginative connection with the event that more dispassionate reports could not offer. But it was not merely the truth of these stories, or their focus on individuals that was attractive. The ad emphasizes content both incredible and emotional; above all, however, it promises that the potent combination of truth and emotion will bring the reader to tears (along with gods and demons). As if to provide proof of this power, the ad includes an excerpt from one of these stories, introduced with a command highlighting the connection between reading and emotion: "Read! Cry!"

Though not "fiction" per se, the stories in Kōdansha's *The Great Taisho Earthquake and Conflagration* incorporate characteristics of fictional melodrama. Its table of contents describes three subgenres of *jitsuwa*, each emphasizing different elements mentioned by Singer: *sanwa* (also known as *aiwa* or *hiwa*) were sad stories full of pathos that "made gods and demons cover their faces"; *bidan* expressed the "beauty of humanity" in heroic tales that stressed moral actions under duress; and *ibun* were sensational stories that were "strange but true."[12] Each category is reflected in the ad, and each was melodramatic in its own way. The following list shows some sample titles from the book in each category:

> *Sanwa*: Suckling a dead child; An entire family killed; The pitiful death of four shopkeepers; The pitiful mad woman; Not knowing he was dead; The end of his beloved child; The sad drunk old man;

11. *Yomiuri shinbun* (October 22, 1923, morning edition), 4 (advertisement).
12. Dai Nihon Yūbenkai Kōdansha, *Taishō daishinsai daikasai*, table of contents.

Drowning out his sorrows in sake while putting his children on the funeral pyre; Holding the head of her dead husband.

Bidan: At least my mother; Saving Tokyo station amid the fires; Women are weak but a mother is strong; The assistant inspector who forgot his family to fulfill his duty; Saving an elephant from the fires; Clasping the portrait of the emperor; The servant girl who saved the valuables of her master.

Ibun: The count who borrowed money from a policeman; Falling from the top of the Asakusa twelve stories; The grace of Nyorai Buddha; Saved by a single box; A rain of beer; The people who miraculously escaped the inferno; The patients who were saved by being abandoned; The strange survival and unlikely reunion of a parent and child.[13]

These titles are replete with melodramatic excess: the pathos of dead children and crazy women, the moral fortitude of motherly strength, sensational escapes and brave rescues, joyous reunions, and the macabre.

Though all of these categories are melodramatic, the subgenre of *bidan* specifically deals with praiseworthy actions, and thus *bidan* reveal most clearly the moral code. Janet Borland has discussed a collection of *jitsuwa* produced by the Education Ministry for use in public schools, entitled simply *Education Materials Related to the Earthquake* (*Shinsai ni kan suru kyōiku shiryō*).[14] She convincingly argues that the collections were designed to teach the moral code of the Rescript on Education (specifically filial piety, harmony, benevolence, modesty, and sacrifice), using stories of ordinary people in the recent disaster. The introduction to the collection explains that the editors made an effort to collect exemplary stories along specific lines: "Actions that show a spirit of loyalty to the Emperor. Actions that show sacrificing the self to fulfill duty or responsibility. Actions that show giving one's all for society. Actions that show devotion between parent and child, siblings, or couples. Praiseworthy actions between teachers and disciples, masters and servants, or among friends."[15] Each of these moral ideals was also mentioned in the second post-quake imperial rescript on "Strengthening the National Spirit."[16]

13. Ibid., table of contents.

14. Janet Borland, "Stories of Ideal Japanese Subjects from the Great Kantō Earthquake of 1923," *Japanese Studies* 25, no. 1 (May 2005): 21–34.

15. Monbushō Futsū Gakumu Kyoku, *Shinsai ni kan suru kyōiku shiryō*, vol. 3 (Monbushō, 1923), front matter.

16. "Strengthening the National Spirit" is from my translation of the rescript title: "Kokumin seishin no sakkō no shōsho." In the official English version the title is "Imperial Edict Enjoining Sincere and Strenuous Life." The official translation of the rescript reads "Let them [Japanese nationals] be gentle and fair, be good to their parents, relatives, and neighbors, be friendly and harmonious to all, and let them observe public morality and public order, respect all responsibilities and temperance, be loyal to the sovereign and pious to parents." Fujisawa Morihiko and Bureau of Social Affairs Home Office, *Great Earthquake of 1923*; Fujisawa Morihiko and Naimushō-Shakaikyoku, *Taishō shinsaishi*, frontispiece.

Though *Education Materials Related to the Earthquake* certainly has its melodramatic moments—Borland's translation of a story about a boy losing his life in an attempt to rescue his master's baby is particularly emotional and spectacular—the overall tone tends toward the more objectively journalistic.

Tales promoting similar virtues can be found in collections produced for wider audiences, such as Kōdansha's *The Great Taisho Earthquake and Conflagration* and *Earthquake Romance*, yet in these books the melodramatic element was emphasized rather than avoided. The contrast is clear in the page and cover design. In the Kōdansha book, the characters are glossed to be understandable to a range of readers and each story is full of dialogue, giving the paragraphs an open feeling that is easily digested. Each story in the Ministry's book is a formidable unglossed block of dense text with few quotations, which are not given their own lines. Whereas the cover of *Education Materials Related to the Earthquake* merely lists the title and the Education Ministry on a white background, Kōdansha's *The Great Taisho Earthquake and Conflagration* has a striking image of the city in flames by Yokoyama Taikan (1868–1958) (see fig. 9). The stories in the latter book show a comparable sensationalism.

"At Least My Mother" ("Semete haha dake"), a *bidan* from Kōdansha's book, is characteristic of *jitsuwa* in popular media. It tells the story of a son and mother who flee the fires in Fukagawa and end up in the Sumida River. The son sacrifices himself to let his mother cling to the scrap of wood that eventually saves her. Though "At Least My Mother" would fit thematically with the Ministry of Education collection, it also displays many of the features of melodrama that Singer identifies: it depicts a sensational escape from the fires and an emotional death full of pathos. "At Least My Mother" is particularly remarkable because, unlike the more journalistic style of many *jitsuwa* and those in the ministry collection, its style borders upon the literary: it is told in a third-person narration, with an impossibly omniscient narrator and many extraneous flourishes. Thus it blurs the boundaries between nonfiction and fiction, as well as those between nonfiction and melodrama.

The opening sequence introduces the characters and gives the reader an omniscient view of the scene, privy to the private conversations of the characters: "'Well, I can already see Eitai bridge. If we can at least cross that bridge, I'm sure there will be lots of places to take refuge. No need to worry.' A thin, weak-looking man of about twenty-eight or -nine was maneuvering through the avalanche of refugees carrying an old, white-haired woman who must have been a hair shy of seventy."[17] There are three elements of this passage that emphasize its construction

17. Dai Nihon Yūbenkai Kōdansha, *Taishō daishinsai daikasai*, 120–21. The story is perhaps more readily accessible as reprinted in Gendaishi no Kai, *Dokyumento Kantō Daishinsai* (Sōfūkan, 1983), 62.

Fig. 9. The cover, by Yokoyama Taikan (1868–1958), of the Kōdansha book *The Great Taisho Earthquake and Conflagration.*

as an emotional narrative rather than objective reportage: the inclusion of quoted words, the flourishes of the metaphors ("avalanche of refugees"), and the ability of the narrator to describe the events unfolding.

The position of the narrator is among the most intriguing aspects of "At Least My Mother." In the opening scene quoted above, the narrator is able to portray the mother and son weaving through the crowd objectively, from a distance, while at the same time recounting the exact words of the son. The unrealistic narratorial position becomes much more intimate as it follows the mother and son from their spectacular leap from the bridge into the waters below. There, the narrator follows the pair as they make their way through the floating bodies, and as the son loses the strength to continue swimming and supporting his mother. At last, the narrator tells us, the son finds a floating piece of wood for his mother, but it is unable to sustain the two of them. We are privy to the thoughts of the son and his single-minded desire to save his mother: "I will certainly die, but I want at least my mother to survive."[18] It is this inner monologue of the dead son that gives the *jitsuwa* its title. Finally the narrator shows us the intimate final moments of the loyal son and dramatically underscores his sacrifice: "'Mother, I'll swim. You be sure to hold onto this wood as tightly as you can.' So saying, he gave the wood to his mother. And unable to move his arms or legs, he sank to the bottom of the river with a gurgle."[19]

It is not until the epilogue that the connection to the real is asserted. In the final paragraph the narrator tells us that the old woman in the story was from the Nakamura-ya clothing store in Fukagawa. At this point the unnamed author reveals that he or she was not privy to the events in the story, but that this was just one story he or she heard: "I just happened to hear this story, but there is no telling how many people gave up their precious lives to help others in their family or even people they did not know."[20] Though the final passage textually connects the story to a supposed actual person, the overall style is not that of a transcription of the mother's words. The author has taken the story and recast it as melodrama. The access to the words and thoughts of this particular mother and son, provided by the anonymous author, heightens the emotion and underscores the moral of filial piety.

This short retelling of the sad demise of a filial son has almost every element of the melodramatic form mentioned by Singer: the pathos of a lost son, the excessive emotion of the mother in tears as she recalls the story, the spectacle of the flight through the fires and the dramatic jump from the burning bridge, and the moral fortitude shown by this paragon of filial loyalty. This morality is the most

18. Dai Nihon Yūbenkai Kōdansha, *Taishō daishinsai daikasai*, 122.
19. Ibid., 122–23.
20. Ibid., 123.

salient aspect of melodrama for Brooks, and all other elements serve to emphasize filial piety and self-sacrifice.

A story about filial piety in the Education Ministry collection of educational materials begins much more objectively: "Haneyama Toyo, who worked at the Fukagawa Asugawa Elementary School, lived with her 70-year-old mother at number 10 Fuyuki-cho in Fukagawa. At the time of the earthquake, she had just finished the opening ceremonies at her school. Worried about her mother, she quickly took care of her workplace and hurried to her home, ten blocks away."[21] The style here eschews elaboration and emphasizes the factual, with a reference to an actual school with a legitimate address at the beginning of the *jitsuwa*. The contrast between the two is also evident in the titles: "At Least My Mother" voices the thoughts of a sacrificing son, whereas "The Female Teacher Who Fled With Her Old Mother on Her Back" ("Rōba o se ni shite nogareta jokyōshi") is dry and explanatory.

This story from *Education Materials Related to the Earthquake* attempts to adhere to an objective style, to emphasize authenticity over drama. But like "At Least My Mother," it cannot help but dramatize key moments in the narrative, moments in which the moral is most clearly articulated. After three days without food or shelter, the mother can no longer walk toward the temporary refugee camps:

> The mother sat down on the ground without moving and tearfully urged her daughter onward, saying, "Leave me here. You are young, so please save yourself." Even this filial daughter with her iron will did not have the strength to carry her mother. How could she leave her mother and flee by herself? She was at a loss. Standing there, drenched by the rain, all she could do was to pray to the gods and buddhas and resign herself to fate. Yet her filial desires finally made their way to the heavens and a car came her way. After pleading insistently, at last the driver took them to the police station, from which they were taken to the rescue camp. Finally they felt they would survive.[22]

The tearful entreaty of the self-sacrificing mother and the prayer of the rain-drenched daughter heighten the emotion of the otherwise dispassionate account of their journey. Brooks refers to such emotional climaxes of melodrama as moments that "fully articulate the terms of the drama."[23] In this particular instance the young

21. Monbushō Futsū Gakumu Kyoku, *Shinsai ni kan suru kyōiku shiryō*, 34–35. Borland briefly discusses this story in Janet Borland, "Capitalising on Catastrophe: Reinvigorating the Japanese State with Moral Values Through Education Following the 1923 Great Kanto Earthquake," *Modern Asian Studies* 40, no. 4 (October 2006): 897.
22. Monbushō Futsū Gakumu Kyoku, *Shinsai ni kan suru kyōiku shiryō*, 36.
23. Peter Brooks, *Melodramatic Imagination*, 3.

teacher faces a moral dilemma—whether or not to abandon her mother—but finally resolves to stay. Her resolve is rewarded by the arrival of help. The almost supernatural intervention of the car appearing in response to the prayer brings the tale closer to fictional melodrama. This scene relies on the melodramatic tropes of coincidence and last-minute rescue, rather than realism and stoicism. From an objective perspective it is only necessary to mention that the young teacher refused to give up on her mother, but even the educational materials produced by the government used melodrama to make their moral lessons clear.

"At Least My Mother" reveals the way true (or ostensibly true) stories were being recast as melodrama. The transformation of this story into a third-person omniscient narrative blurs the boundaries between truth and fiction. The terse objective style of journalism could tell the same story with more economy and less emotion. Yet even *Education Materials Related to the Earthquake* resorts to emotionalism at its core. Both these stories rely on a potent combination of authenticity and drama to promote virtue. But when these two are in conflict, when authenticity demands that we can never know the final thoughts of the filial son, emotion prevails. In losing the drama and the emotion, these stories would lose their moral clarity and their power; melodrama makes these *jitsuwa* powerful.

EARTHQUAKE MELODRAMAS AND *FACING DEATH*

Fiction published in high-culture journals such as *Kaizō* or *Chūō kōron* usually avoided the emotionalism and sensationalism in *jitsuwa*, but earthquake melodramas for mass audiences drew on precisely these aspects of the stories. Often the fictional narratives relied on *jitsuwa* for inspiration, though they lacked the claims of authenticity made by *jitsuwa*. Because of this, fictional earthquake stories could be crafted into more traditional melodramas with themes readily found in the genre. As Peter Brooks and, more recently, Linda Williams have noted, "innocence threatened" is a theme that often structures the moral polarization of melodrama.[24] This theme is common in print and cinema narratives directed at

24. In speaking of the play *La Fille de l'exilé*, Brooks states: "This play, and melodrama typically, not only employs virtue persecuted as a source of its dramaturgy, but also tends to become the dramaturgy of virtue misprized and eventually recognized. [Melodrama] is about virtue made visible and acknowledged, the drama of recognition." Ibid., 27. Williams has written: "If emotional and moral registers are sounded, if a work invites us to feel sympathy for the virtues of beset victims, if the narrative trajectory is ultimately concerned with a retrieval and staging of virtue through adversity and suffering, then the operative mode is melodrama." And: "Melodrama focuses on victim-heroes and on recognizing their virtue. Recognition of virtue orchestrates the moral legibility that is key to melodramatic function." Linda Williams, *Playing the Race Card: Melodramas of Black and White from Uncle Tom to O. J. Simpson* (Princeton, NJ: Princeton University Press, 2001), 15, 29.

mass audiences. The innocence threated in these examples is that of disaster victims who fall prey to the villainy of earthquake looting and opportunism.

There were at least eleven fictional films with the earthquake as a backdrop in theaters before the end of 1923, but unfortunately none is extant today.[25] One of the first was the Shōchiku studio's *Facing Death* (*Shi ni men shite*), directed by Ōkubo Tadamoto, released in Osaka only one month after the disaster. The lack of the film itself limits analysis, but it is possible to explore how others presented or reviewed the film in contemporary film magazines, which often included summaries and even full scripts of the films. In the case of *Facing Death*, an adaptation of the film written by Fukui Shirō was published in the special earthquake edition of *Katsudō kurabu* (*Movie Club*), a contemporary film journal, and a detailed summary appeared in the Shōchiku studio magazine *Kamata*.[26] Piecing these together provides an overview of the plot.

Facing Death revolved around a miner, Shōhei (Shiga Yasurō) and his daughter Ohatsu (Takao Mitsuko), who were returning to their hometown via Tokyo at the time of the earthquake. There, they stop at a cheap hotel, and a scene shows Shōhei counting out his life savings in the room. Suddenly the earthquake strikes, and father and daughter quickly flee the building. Remembering his money, Shōhei returns to the room despite the pleas of his daughter. Though she tries to wait for him, she is carried off in the fleeing crowd. Ohatsu believes her father is dead following their separation, but then hears that he is alive in a temporary hospital. She is led to a man who is unrecognizably burnt and covered in bandages. Though the man claims not to remember Ohatsu, he has her father's distinctive wallet and the nurses attribute his lack of memory to trauma. Ohatsu cares for this man and tries to nurse him back to health. There she interacts with the kind nurses and also two geisha sisters, one caring for the other who had gone mad in the chaos of the quake. One day, while collecting rations, Ohatsu meets a man also claiming to be her father, though he too is bandaged. After some effort Ohatsu is convinced he is telling the truth. Through this chance meeting, the man in the hospital is revealed as an imposter. He had taken advantage of the confusion following the earthquake to steal the father's life savings. After his confession, the imposter pleads for their forgiveness, saying that Ohatsu's kindness was his salvation. The reunited father and daughter take pity on this man and shed a tear for him before he "ascends on that journey from which there is no return."[27]

25. In his history of Japanese film, Hazumi Tsuneo has panned these films as of little interest to film history because they were nothing more than faddish works with questionable production values. Hazumi Tsuneo, *Eiga gojūnenshi* (Osaka: Sōgensha, 1951), 150. They do, however, provide insight into the moral values of the time and how those values are revealed in melodrama.

26. Fukui Shirō, "Shi ni men shite," *Katsudō kurabu* 6, no. 10 (October 1923): 40–42, and Anonymous, "Shi ni men shite: daishingai ni kakawaru aiwa," *Kamata* 16 (October 1923): 26–27.

27. Fukui Shirō, "Shi ni men shite," 42.

This summary suggests that the film included explicit references to several *jitsuwa*, which would have served to give it an air of authenticity despite the fictional story. The theme of separation and reunion of the father and daughter can be seen in *jitsuwa* such as "The Strange Survival and Unlikely Reunion of a Parent and Child" ("Fushigi ni inochi ga tasukatte oyako no saikai). The crazed geisha evokes the women crazed by the earthquake, a staple of *jitsuwa*. Some examples from Kōdansha include "The Pitiful Mad Woman" ("Aware no kyōjo") and "The Parent who Killed Her Own Child" ("Aiji wo koroshita oya").[28] Even the thief can be seen in news reports of earthquake looting and opportunism. Paratextual evidence further links the film to *jitsuwa*. The title as listed in the film journal *Katsudō kurabu* prefaces *Facing Death* with the words *shinsai aiwa*, or "earthquake tale of pathos." *Aiwa*—also referred to as *hiwa* (tragic tales) or *sanwa* (sad tales)—was a common generic category in *jitsuwa* collections.[29] The use of *aiwa* here shows an unambiguous connection between *Facing Death* and *jitsuwa* that served to heighten the authenticity of the film and thereby broaden its public appeal. The critic Tanaka Saburō recognized these tropes when he called the film "strangely plausible" in his review for the journal *Kinema junpo*.[30] The melodramatic film could have only been considered plausible following a disaster of this magnitude and the popularization of similar stories through *jitsuwa*.

The relationship between the film and the real earthquake was further emphasized in the Shōchiku fan magazines, by connecting the actual experiences of the actors in the earthquake to their performances. This real-life connection was also made in an early film melodrama of the Titanic disaster, *Saved from the Titanic* (1912). This film heavily advertised the fact that the main actress in the fictional story, Dorothy Gibson, was actually a survivor from the doomed ship.[31] In a similar move, the young child actress playing Ohatsu, Takao Mitsuko (1915–80), or Mitchan as she was affectionately referred to, was featured in the November 1923 issue of the *Shōchiku gahō* (*Shōchiku Illustrated*). In the photos, Mitchan is seen both in her role as Ohatsu, clinging to a telephone pole after the quake, and as herself, after fleeing the fires with her two cats (see fig. 10). The magazine also includes Mitchan's own earthquake survival story, supposedly told in her girlish voice. The text uses the feminine pronoun *atashi* and the feminine emphatic particle *wa*, rather than a more neutral and objective reporting style.[32] A

28. Dai Nihon Yūbenkai Kōdansha, *Taishō daishinsai daikasai*, table of contents.

29. The Kōdansha volume pairs *aiwa* with *hiwa*, and the collection *Shinsai romansu*, compiled by Arano Kōhei, includes *aiwa* as its own category. Many other collections also used the category of *aiwa*.

30. *Kinema junpo,* no. 144 (November 21, 1923): 11.

31. See, for example, the ad reproduced in Stephen Bottomore, *The Titanic and Silent Cinema* (East Sussex, England: Projection Box, 2000), 110.

32. "Atashi hontō ni kowakatta wa." Takao Mitsuko, "Koneko wo nihiki idaita mama," *Shōchiku gahō* 1, no. 11 (November 1924): 20–21.

Fig. 10. Pair of images in the *Shōchiku gahō*. The upper photo depicts Takao Mitsuko (Micchan) with her two cats after fleeing her home in Asakusa, and the bottom circle is a still from *Facing Death* showing Micchan as Ohatsu clinging to a pillar during the earthquake. *Shōchiku gahō* (November 1923).

review of the film in the same issue praises Mitchan's realistic acting and that of Shiga Yasurō, who played her father. "After the intertitle 'It's a Quake' appeared, when Mr. Shiga grabbed Mitchan and headed outside, his attitude and expression, along with Mitchan's frightened face, were so sincere they pierced my heart."[33] The reviewer later suggested that Mitchan's acting prowess derived from the fact that she had "tasted this kind of fear,"[34] thus reinforcing the authenticity behind the performance.

The characters and plot of *Facing Death* may have been inspired by *jitsuwa*, but the film itself seems to have been more closely aligned with the melodramatic tradition.[35] First, the recreation of the earthquake in the film did more than add authenticity: it added spectacle. Most stills in newspapers and magazines are of the earthquake scenes, suggesting that marketers were relying on the allure of disaster spectacle. The *Yomiuri shinbun,* for example, printed a still that depicted the recreation with the caption: "The moment the quake struck" (see fig. 11).[36] Second, *Facing Death* had the emotional excess, the pathos, and the moral polarity that Singer identifies as characteristic of the genre. Finally, although it is impossible to know the extent to which the film *Facing Death* conformed to the cinematic conventions of melodrama, the plot nevertheless traffics in several melodramatic tropes identified by other scholars. In its four reels *Facing Death* included innocence threatened, mistaken identity, emotional partings, and coincidental reunions. Linda Williams has pointed out that in melodrama the threat posed to innocence is often couched in terms of a threat to the sanctity of the home.[37] *Facing Death* is no exception. In this case, the thief invades the most intimate conception of "home": the relationship between father and daughter. This threat clarifies the moral polarity of the melodrama; the thief is the villain, and Ohatsu is the innocent heroine in peril.

Facing Death also trod the well-worn melodramatic path of the innocent country girl heading to the wicked city. According to the *Kamata* summary, the film opened with a shot of the widowed father and daughter as passengers on a horse-drawn cart traveling on a mountain path. Ohatsu's father mentions that it will be faster when they ride in an automobile. The puzzled Ohatsu has never heard of an automobile and is unaware of the technological frights of the city. When at last she sees one, she stares with a "curious suspicion," and clings to her father's knee in fright throughout her first ride.

33. Itami Saburō, "Shinsai aiwa 'Shi ni men shite' wo miru," *Shōchiku gahō* 1, no. 11 (November 1923): 18.
34. Ibid., 19.
35. "Melodrama" was a common film genre in Japan, as it was around the world.
36. In the still photograph, we can see the father carrying an unconscious Ohatsu out of a room that is in shambles.
37. Linda Williams, *Playing the Race Card*, 28.

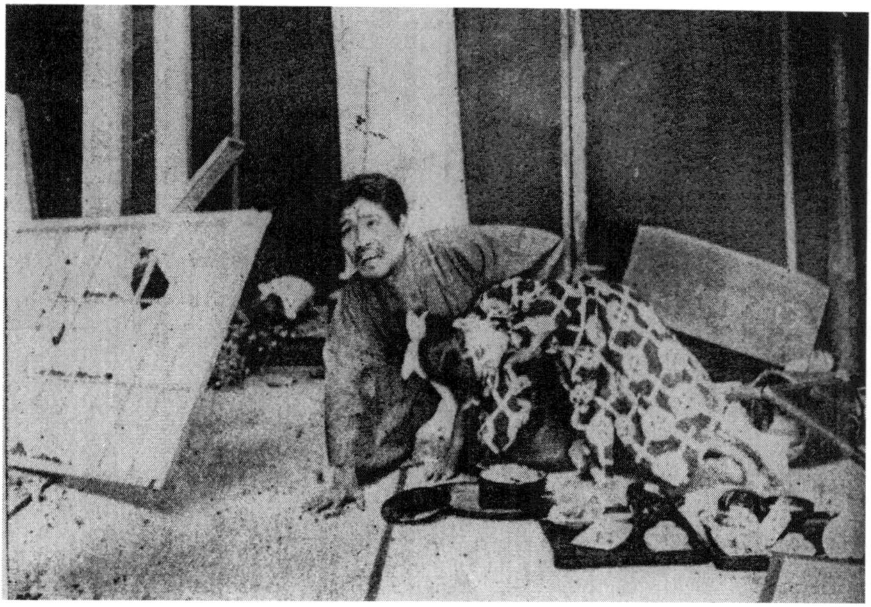

Fig. 11. Still from *Facing Death* showing Takao Mitsuko as Ohatsu and Shiga Yasurō as her father, Shōhei, in the chaos of the earthquake. This still was included in the *Yomiuri shinbun* discussion of the film. *Kamata* no. 16 (October 1923).

In her study of Meiji ideology, Carol Gluck has pointed out that migration from the countryside to the city had been treated in the national discourse as a disease dubbed *tokai netsu*, or city fever.[38] She notes that the city became seen as a site of decadence and materialism that infected the rest of the country through the (relatively easy) transportation of people and ideas. But as Gluck shows, the perceived urban maladies "represented a veritable catalogue of the attributes of a modernizing society."[39] In other words, it is impossible to separate the social ills recognized by ideologues from the progress of modernity. Ohatsu's fear demonstrates how she remains unsullied by the technological advancements of modernity that have brought with them the evils of crime and poverty.

Once in the city, Ohatsu is threatened on multiple levels—the first being the earthquake itself. The earthquake scene in *Facing Death* was reportedly frightening, and the *Shōchiku gahō* review emphasizes the acting of Mitchan, who had gone through the real thing only weeks before. But the earthquake is not shown to be the primary danger: Ohatsu safely escapes with her father. Rather, the threat is

38. Carol Gluck, *Japan's Modern Myths: Ideology in the Late Meiji Period* (Princeton, NJ: Princeton University Press, 1985), 159.
39. Ibid., 177.

posed by Ohatsu's father Shōhei abandoning her to return to the unstable boarding house (see fig. 12). It is not the earthquake but Shōhei's pursuit of money that endangers his daughter. The next threat is the overwhelming pressure of the fleeing crowds, the reason for Ohatsu's inability to wait for her father. More sinister still is the thief's invasion of the intimate father-daughter relationship by impersonating the father. The menacing force in the film is not the earthquake but the corrupting power of money (seen in both the father and the thief) and the anonymous mass of urban crowds. Both of these are contrasted with the rural innocence of Ohatsu.

The morality that motivates this story is not merely that the city is dangerous for poor young girls from the country. Rather, the various threats to Ohatsu serve to intensify the overarching moral of the tale—namely, the iniquity of earthquake opportunism and looting. The imposter represents those who took advantage of the earthquake to further their own interests, a selfish position explicitly addressed by the imperial rescripts.[40] The debased figure of the thief is contrasted with the virtue of the young girl who forgives him on his deathbed. In showing how the thief's selfish actions put Ohatsu in peril, the story has more moral power than a simple story of a thief stealing a wallet. The moral polarity is intensified through the threat to innocence, so that the film ultimately articulates the nationally promulgated virtue of sacrifice for the benefit of the whole.

These threats are resolved at the conclusion of the film. The thief dies, and Shōhei gives away his money to help the poor. But the final solution is not merely the immediate removal of the threat but a retreat to the countryside, where daughter and father can be safe. According to the *Kamata* summary, in the final scene Ohatsu asks her father where they should go, and he replies, "to our home (*furusato*) in the mountains." Shōhei and his daughter have had enough of the city. They realize that the benefits of urban living are outweighed by the costs—the masses of people, and especially those unscrupulous enough to take advantage of a major catastrophe to rob a widower and his daughter.

Melodrama exaggerates the good and evil in each character to help clarify its moral code. In this case the divide between city and country is as polarized as that between the innocent girl and the menacing villain. This divide draws on a worldview, not unique to Japan, that sees the countryside as a repository of traditional values, a respite from urban ills. The word used for "countryside" or "homeland" in the summary of *Facing Death* is *furusato*. In the Japanese case, the discourse surrounding the *furusato*, or home in the country, is linked specifically to modernization in the Meiji era. As Stephen Vlastos puts it, "the valorization of the farm village as the

40. "If, in an attempt to guarantee the interests of individuals or groups the security of the afflicted many is at all menaced—then sentiments of the people will be agitated to a limitless degree." Fujisawa Morihiko and Bureau of Social Affairs Home Office, *Great Earthquake of 1923*, frontispiece.

Fig. 12. Still from *Facing Death* showing Takao Mitsuko as Ohatsu trying to prevent her father, played by Shiga Yasurō, from returning to their room. *Shōchiku gahō* (November 1923).

heart and soil of Japan belongs to a modern discourse that developed in reaction to social cleavages and national anxieties attendant on industrialization."[41] These Meiji-era discourses that set up an idealized nostalgic homeland in the countryside *furusato* were still prevalent in 1923, and continued into the 1930s.[42]

41. Stephen Vlastos, "Agrarianism without Tradition," in *Mirror of Modernity: Invented Traditions of Modern Japan,* ed. Stephen Vlastos (Berkeley, CA: University of California Press, 1998), 80. See also Thomas Havens, *Farm and Nation in Modern Japan: Agrarian Nationalism, 1870–1940* (Princeton, NJ: Princeton University Press, 1974).
42. Mizoguchi, whose earthquake melodrama *Amid the Ruins* (*Haikyo no naka,* 1923) also ended with a happy couple returning to the countryside, made at least four films with *furusato* or *kokyō* in the title. For more on *furusato* and agricentrism discourse in this time period, see Havens, *Farm and Nation in Modern Japan;* Narita Ryūichi, "*Kokyō" to iu monogatari: toshi kūkan no rekishigaku* (Yoshikawa Kōbunkan, 1998); Jennifer Robertson, *Native and Newcomer: Making and Remaking a Japanese city* (Berkeley, CA: University of California Press, 1991); and Christine Yano, *Tears of Longing: Nostalgia and the Nation in Japanese Popular Song* (Cambridge, MA: Harvard University Press, 2002). Stephen Dodd analyzes the theme in high literature of the time. See Dodd, *Writing Home: Representations of the Native Place in Modern Japanese Literature* (Cambridge, MA: Harvard University Press, 2004).

The moral polarity in *Facing Death* is, ultimately, class-neutral. That is, the imposter and the poor father and daughter are all members of the same disadvantaged class. From the opening, we know that the father had been working in a coal mine and was just returning to his hometown with his earnings. Though we are given little background on the imposter, his presence at the same boarding house implies a similar class position. In *Facing Death*, the "moral occult" is operative only in the sense that Ohatsu is an innocent girl threatened by a thief. In the earthquake melodramas of Nagata Mikihiko, the melodrama and the morality behind it often hinge on class difference.

NAGATA MIKIHIKO'S EARTHQUAKE MELODRAMAS

Just over three months after the earthquake Nagata Mikihiko (1887–1964) published a collection of earthquake-related material. Mikihiko is most famous for his love stories set in Hokkaido and the Gion district of Kyoto, part of a genre called *jōwa*, or "emotional tales." *Jōwa bungaku* was a particular brand of melodramatic literature emerging from late-Meiji aestheticism that peaked around 1916. *Jōwa* were seldom seen in the primary *bundan* literary outlets at the time of the quake, but continued to be a recognized genre in more popular magazines. This exclusion was due in no small part to criticism of sentimentality in literature, a key example being Akagi Kōhei's scathing 1916 critique of popular literature.[43] His essay, entitled "Toward the Eradication of Self-Indulgent Literature" ("Yūtō bungaku no bokumetsu"), criticized Mikihiko's works in particular as "fake art," the product of "childish sentimentalism" and "inferior romanticism." Akagi bluntly recommended that Mikihiko "quietly retreat to the world of popular literature writers and keep focusing on making money."[44] Though he continued to publish profusely, Mikihiko remained a marginal figure in the *bundan*.

Mikihiko's earthquake book, *The Earth Shakes* (*Daichi wa furū*, 1923) contains twenty shorter works, each depicting an aspect of the earthquake. Some are personal accounts of his experiences in the quake, and the rest are stories either told to him or completely fictional.[45] The line between fact and fiction is at times

43. Akagi Kōhei, "Yūtō bungaku no bokumetsu," *Yomiuri shinbun* (August 6–8, 1916); reprinted in *Kindai bungaku hyōron taikei*, vol. 4 (Kadokawa Shoten, 1971), 260–66.

44. Ibid., reprint, 265.

45. Several chapters about Mikihiko's own experiences—"Standing in the Ruins" ("Haikyo ni tachite"), "After the Disaster" ("Saika no ato"), and "Night Watch" ("Yakei")—were first published in journals alongside other personal essays describing the experiences of well-known figures. They were published in the October 1923 editions of *Josei* (*Woman*), *Bunsho kurabu* (*Literary club*), and *Fujin sekai* (*Woman's world*), respectively. His stories "The Tale of an Old Policeman" ("Rokeiji no hanashi"), "Observations on the Great Quake" ("Daishin kanbō"), and "Outdoor Play" ("Yagaigeki") appeared in the *Jiji shinpō* newspaper on October 1, 2, and November 1, respectively. They were later incorporated into various chapters in the book.

hard to distinguish, because even the *jitsuwa* that Mikihiko includes are embellished. The story "Wild Geese," from the middle of *The Earth Shakes*, is one of the most explicitly fictional works in the collection. It is told by a third-person omniscient narrator and focalized through the protagonist Hamako. Unlike several of the other stories, there is no reference to the narration or how the narrator heard the tale. In "Wild Geese" Mikihiko uses the common melodramatic trope of innocence threatened to draw out the pathos in social instability following the earthquake.

Before the earthquake, Hamako and her younger brother Kyūzō lived with their widowed father, a used clothing dealer in Kanda. They were at one time comfortably wealthy, but the recession has meant that they are just making ends meet. And then the earthquake strikes. Their store collapses in the initial shock, crushing their father's leg and destroying everything they own. Though he is rescued from the flames by young volunteers, their father is put in a temporary hospital, leaving Hamako and her brother to fend for themselves. Luckily, while taking refuge from the rain one day, Hamako chances upon a woman who used to be their servant when the business was more prosperous. This woman, Okatsu, is starting a *gyūdon* (beef over rice) shop in a stall built on the ruins of Kanda, and she agrees to employ Hamako and Kyūzō.

We learn this information about Hamako's background in an analepsis from the middle of the main narrative: that of a drunken man who sexually harasses Hamako. The man has been paying close attention to Hamako throughout the evening, asking her to pour his drinks, as do girls in other kinds of establishments. Though Hamako has been assailed verbally on other occasions in her new job, the narrator states, this particularly traumatic attack turns physical. When Okatsu and Hamako are finally closing up and Hamako asks the man to leave, he offers a proposal: "'Hey, cutie (*neesan*)! Once you close up here, how 'bout you and I find somewheres nice, have a bath, and I'll lay you down on a nice linen futon? Ha ha ha ha ha!' Hamako tries to flee, but he grabs hold of her. 'Hey, no need to get all ruffled up, I say. I bet you don't get much from running this *gyūdon* shop all day? Why not relax that body of yours? I've got a job that makes a pretty penny. Why not listen to me? Your innocent airs could be a real moneymaker. Ha ha ha ha.'"[46] Hamako screams and, with the help of Okatsu, escapes the man's grasp. The man leaves, but Hamako is left sobbing in the corner. Okatsu comforts Hamako and promises not to serve beer in the future. Soon afterward, Hamako's brother Kyūzō returns from middle school, and Hamako is forced to hide her tears. As they walk back to Okatsu's home after this traumatic day at work, Kyūzō hears wild geese migrating for the coming winter and points them out to Hamako. He remarks that

46. Nagata Mikihiko, *Daichi wa furū* (Shun'yōdō, 1923), 178–79.

though others were able to flee the earthquake like the geese, they were forced to remain in the city: "Today I was talking with Dad about how those of us born in Tokyo have a really hard time when things like this happen. I mean, even Dad often made fun of people from the country, calling them 'hick,' but Kondō and Taniguchi from the shop are probably back at home in the country relaxing. Dad was a bit jealous of them, saying how he wished we had a home in the country to go back to. Even those geese have a home (*kokyō*) to return to in the fall."[47] It is here that the story concludes, with two unfortunate children, whose only parent has been left an invalid by the disaster, reflecting on their lost home and their lack of a *furusato* in the country. "Wild Geese" similarly posits the *furusato* as a place of refuge, a contrast not only to the devastation but also from urban corruption. Yet, unlike *Facing Death*, the *furusato* is not set up in a clear moral binary, but rather exists to deepen the pathos of the story. In this case, the siblings' loss of their home is compounded by their fall in social status.

Hamako, like Ohatsu in *Facing Death*, is made vulnerable by her separation from her father and the impossibility of returning to her previous sheltered life. But her separation from home is also inflected with class difference. Though they had fallen on hard times even before the earthquake, Hamako is from a merchant family and thus is part of the "old middle class" in Tokyo. The narrative further mentions that Hamako graduated from a girl's school, underscoring her social status. Although education through elementary school was compulsory at the time, going to a secondary women's school was limited to those who had the means to pay for it. Hamako condescends to serve *gyūdon* amid the ruins due to necessity. This is made explicit when Okatsu first talks to Hamako about working in the stall: "Why don't you forget about your previous status and work with me selling *gyūdon*, at least to tide you over?"[48] The earthquake disaster has put Hamako in a position she is unaccustomed to, namely, that of serving those who were once socially beneath her.

This contrast is made clear in a passage describing Hamako's usual interactions with other members of her clientele, immediately after mentioning her education: "Hamako was generally capable of rising to whatever situation she was put in and so, *though she had graduated from a women's school*, she was not embarrassed by working in a place such as this. However, the one thing she could not get used to was when laborers would come to the store, get drunk on beer, and tease her with all sorts of distasteful talk. Whenever they would say such things, she would squeal and retreat to the back of the store. Amused by her reaction, the sweaty men would tease her with even more lewd remarks" (emphasis added).[49] Hamako is not embarrassed by working at the stall, though the passage suggests

47. Ibid., 182.
48. Ibid., 176.
49. Ibid., 177.

that most graduates of a women's school would never stoop so low. She recognizes that she is fortunate to be able to have a place to stay and a way of earning much-needed money. Nevertheless, the treatment she receives at the customers' hands is too hard to bear, especially for a young woman of her upbringing.

The class-based dimension of the story is apparent from the specific mention of Hamako's education, but it is also a key part of Hamako's interaction with Okatsu. Okatsu was once Hamako's servant but now is the proprietor of the *gyūdon* shop, and thus Hamako's employer. Though Hamako ignores her status to work at the *gyūdon* shop without embarrassment, the social distance between Hamako and Okatsu remains in the language they use toward each other in the shop. At the end of the story Hamako suggests that the alcohol they sell causes the problem: "Hey, nursemaid, maybe let's stop selling beer tomorrow?" Okatsu replies using deferential language. "Yes, we should do that. We only get 7 sen profit for each one we sell, anyway."[50] Hamako refers to Okatsu by her former position as her maid, rather than as her employer, and speaks down to her. The difference does not come through as forcefully in translation, but in the original Japanese Okatsu uses deferential speech patterns. In contrast, even the polite form of the copula is lacking in Hamako's speech.

Nagata Mikihiko uses speech patterns and other class cues in "Wild Geese" to accentuate a kind of social upheaval that he imagines having been caused by the earthquake: a former servant offering to help and employ a young woman who was once her mistress. This theme of social reversal, impossible in less chaotic circumstances, was a popular one following the quake, though difficult to document in reality. Among the *jitsuwa* collected in the Kōdansha volume were stories like "The Count Who Borrowed Money from a Policeman" ("Junsa kara kane wo karita hakushaku"), "The Bank President Who Stuck His Hand out from beneath the Floor for Rice Balls" ("Yukashita kara te wo dashite nigirimeshi wo morau ginkō tōdori"), and "The General in Deference to a Worker" ("Rōdōsha ni saikeitai suru shōgun"). It was a theme that appeared in film as well; for example, the Nikkatsu studio production *The Earth Shakes* (*Daichi wa yuragu*, 1923, discussed in Chapter 6) depicted a wealthy family forced to rely on their cook for survival. Mikihiko appears to call attention to the strange possibilities for role reversal elicited by the earthquake, as did these *jitsuwa* and films, but he does so also to emphasize the villainy of Hamako's attacker.

Class is an important part of the villain's identity as well. He is said to look like an *ukeoishi*, or a middleman who deals with day laborers.[51] This description

50. Ibid., 180.

51. The majority of the articles in the *Asahi shinbun* mentioning *ukeoishi* in 1922–23 dealt with some criminal activity. Kikuzō II visual, Ritsumeikan University, January 20, 2011. <http://database.asahi.com/library2/main/start.php>.

means that he is associated with the world of the lowest stratum of laborers, and yet he profits without working himself. The villain is marked as evil because he threatens Hamako's purity, but being an *ukeoishi* suggests that he also preys upon the unfortunate for his own benefit. He displays a great deal of money to Hamako, and his proposition to her implies that it is a moneymaking venture. The implication is that he is a pimp and that she would work for him. The connection is explicitly made between a middleman who procures day laborers for employers and one who provides prostitutes. This character embodies disaster opportunism and exploitation at its worst: preying on earthquake orphans to make them prostitutes.[52]

The *ukeoishi*'s villainy is brought into stronger relief because the innocent young woman he is propositioning is from another social sphere. The *ukeoishi* is specifically described as coarse (*gehin*), a term supported by his rough language. When propositioning Hamako, he talks down to her by saying that he will "lay her down on a nice linen futon," using language that debases her ("*nekashite yaru ze*"). The contrast with Okatsu's language toward Hamako is stark. If Okatsu's attitude toward Hamako is deemed proper, then the *ukeoishi*'s is an affront to the moral standards of the old middle class that Hamako represents. It is Okatsu who is ultimately able to act as a bridge between the two worlds and rescue Hamako. This is possible because the *ukeoishi* exists in Okatsu's world. She has been forced to deal with people like him in the past and has developed the skills to do so. It is only the naïve Hamako who lacks the strength and knowledge to respond appropriately.

The morality in this story is specifically directed against earthquake opportunism, and especially that involving the buying and selling of the labor of others for profit. People taking advantage of the earthquake for selfish reasons is a theme that Mikihiko visits in other stories in the collection. One story shows his horror at discovering an old woman hoarding food provided by relief workers. Another depicts a woman and a man (also described as an *ukeoishi*) who hide severed fingers, with rings still on them, in their own bandages.[53] In these other stories, however, there is no visible threatened party. To make the moral clear, to stress the evil of earthquake opportunism, Mikihiko needed not only a villain, but an innocent victim. He needed melodrama.

* * * * *

52. This is one thread in another earthquake-related melodrama, the 1924 film *Chimata no ko* (*Children of the Street*). A crime boss forces a female earthquake orphan to work for him. Though not explicit, prostitution is certainly a possible interpretation of her imprisonment. Eventually she is rescued and ends up in a loving adopted family.

53. They are "Nightwatch" ("Yakei") and "Evil Demon" ("Akuki"), respectively. Nagata Mikihiko, *Daichi wa furū*.

There is a move in these two fictional earthquake melodramas that separates the action and the plot from the pathos caused by the earthquake. They use the fact that children were left abandoned by the earthquake, but do so to tell a different story of victimization. There is a natural pathos surrounding children orphaned by the quake, but without a villain there is little moral outrage behind the emotion. In contrast to these fictional stories, most *jitsuwa*, though melodramatic, do not have villains. Rather, they rely on stories of sacrifice to engage emotions, clarifying the ethical message not by the contrast to wickedness but by highlighting righteousness. The drama of "At Least My Mother," for example, is explicitly linked to the earthquake and to the emotion-ridden sacrifices that come with disaster. In this case the melodramatic elements of the story helped articulate the dogma of filial piety emphasized in the "Imperial Rescript on Education." By focusing on death, sacrifice, and pathos, "At Least My Mother" speaks more to the intensity of the actual disaster than do *Facing Death* and "Wild Geese," which focus on the aftermath. Certainly there were children separated from parents temporarily, and it was unfortunate, but the melodramas truest to the suffering caused by the disaster were those that dealt with people losing everything, those without the possibility of reuniting parents and children. The truly tragic earthquake melodramas were *jitsuwa*.

Chapter 5

Quiet Suffering in Masamune Hakuchō's "The Suffering of Another"

Masamune Hakuchō's "The Suffering of Another" ("Tanin no saigai," 1924) was published only four months after the earthquake, in the New Year's edition of *Chūō kōron*, a general-interest journal that was one of the primary outlets for the high-culture literature of the *bundan*.[1] Though there were several works of fiction written by members of the *bundan* about the earthquake, most, such as Tayama Katai's *Record of the Tokyo Earthquake* (see Chapter 2), revolved around the experiences of the authors. The same New Year issue of *Chūō kōron*, for example, also included Tokuda Shūsei's I-novel "Amid the Uncertainty," which described his concern about his family in Tokyo from his location at his sister's home in rural Kanazawa.[2]

Hakuchō's work stands out among *bundan* writing on the earthquake because it deals explicitly with "the suffering of the other." In this sense it shares more with the earthquake melodramas of Nagata Mikihiko and others than with the work of Hakuchō's *bundan* peers. It is a fictional story of a woman who has experienced the earthquake and the fires. At the same time, its treatment of class establishes "The Suffering of Another" as a high-culture alternative to the sensational melodramatic stories that were popular at the time.

Class difference was the source of dramatic tension in several post-quake melodramas, with Nagata Mikihiko's "Wild Geese" as a prime example (see Chapter 4). In "The Suffering of Another" Hakuchō turns his gaze not to the experiences of the old middle class of shopkeepers depicted in Mikihiko's "Wild Geese," but to the new urban middle class of office-workers populating the western half of Tokyo. This attention to a different segment of the population sets Hakuchō's story apart from most of the earthquake melodramas, but the real difference is found in his mobilization of "taste," in Pierre Bourdieu's sense of the word. Hakuchō denigrates what he sees as the distasteful interest in earthquake suffering found in "low-class" representations of the earthquake by critiquing a

1. Masamune Hakuchō, "Tanin no saigai," *Chūō kōron* 39, no. 1 (January 1924): 1–25.

2. Tokuda Shūsei, "Fuan no naka ni," *Chūō kōron* 39, no. 1 (January 1924): 248–73; reprinted in *Shūsei zenshū*, vol. 6 (Kyoto: Rinsen Shoten, 1991), 171–205.

broad swath of earthquake-related popular culture: sensational depictions of death and destruction in postcards and nonfiction films, and the disaster tourism phenomenon of *yakeato kenbutsu* ("viewing the ruins"). Hakuchō's refusal to dwell on the spectacle of the disaster in his story and his explicit dramatization of the difference between his story and other types of post-quake culture serve as a critique of popular voyeurism, particularly in his juxtaposition of disaster tourism (*yakeato kenbutsu*) with a personal story of loss.

The protagonist of "The Suffering of Another," Kitako, injures her leg when her house in Kanda collapses. She imagines that she would have been killed by the fires had her husband, Senkichi, not returned to carry her to safety. Though she loses no one dear to her, everything she and her husband possessed is gone. Thankfully, she has family in Kōfu, a rural town in Yamanashi prefecture, and she returns there to recuperate. In contrast to the characters in Nagata Mikihiko's melodramas, Kitako's parents can take her in without hardship and can help her get back on her feet, both physically and economically.

The story opens as Kitako begins to walk again, and sets out to visit her friend Masako across town. Unlike Kitako, Masako had remained in her childhood town and is unmarried. After speaking with Masako at length, Kitako learns from Masako's mother that the earthquake personally affected Masako as well—she had begun marriage negotiations with a man from Tokyo who was killed in the disaster. Masako dismisses the matter as unimportant, and refuses to discuss it further, but Kitako senses that Masako is hiding a deeper pain. On the train back to Tokyo, Kitako learns the details of Masako's story from Oei, Masako's palsy-afflicted aunt. I will return later to the story, and the mystery behind Masako's loss, but first wish to locate these characters, particularly Kitako, in the matrix of class and earthquake experience introduced earlier (see Introduction).

Hakuchō specifically situates the primary characters in his story as members of the "new" middle class. The term has been used by David Ambaras and other historians who have identified this group as those Meiji-era newcomers to the city who worked in "white-collar" management and bureaucratic occupations.[3] In terms of income, some may not have differed greatly from the "old" middle class of shopkeepers, but their occupations and the requisite cultural and educational capital set them apart.[4] Specifically, Kitako is shown to be a young, privileged woman from the provinces who moved to Tokyo with her husband. The home they lived in was in Kanda, a transitional city ward between the *shitamachi* and

3. David Ambaras, "Social Knowledge, Cultural Capital, and the New Middle Class in Japan," 1; and Minami Hiroshi, *Taishō bunka* (Keisō Shobō, 1965), 44.

4. For information on income differences (and the lack thereof) between the "new" and the "old" middle classes, see Hiromichi Ishizuka, "The Slum Dwellings and the Urban Renewal Scheme in Tokyo, 1868–1923," 187. I take my discussion of cultural and educational capital from Pierre Bourdieu, "Forms of Capital."

the *yamanote*. This makes for an extreme earthquake experience while allowing Kitako to be interpreted as a part of the new middle class. She is not shown to be employed, but is married to a man with a stable office job, one that remains after the earthquake.

When Kitako returns to Tokyo after recuperating at her childhood home, her husband has found a house to rent in the suburbs. As Jordan Sand has shown, suburbia was a distinctly middle-class goal, cultivated by developers who "played to class desires by hinting that suburbanites would be guaranteed the exclusive company of others like themselves."[5] Masako is shown to be in a very similar position. Kitako and Masako have grown up in the same town, gone to the same schools, and their families seem to exist within the same socio-economic circle in Kōfu.

Kitako's position as a comfortably middle-class housewife is reinforced in a conversation she has with Masako. After Masako expresses her belief that women should be able to support themselves, Kitako replies:

> "It's no good for women to support themselves. I can't stand those Tokyo working women."
>
> "What don't you like about them?" Masako responded with probing eyes, but Kitako couldn't come up with a satisfactory reply. She then remembered that when they had met a few days before, Masako intimated that she was secretly reading women's magazines to get a sense of the working woman's life.
>
> Masako continued emphatically, "Didn't you tell me on a previous visit, that a woman should have some skill that would allow her to be independent?"
>
> "It's not that I've given up on that idea. It's just that I can't seem to learn anything myself."
>
> "That's not true. Even I have come to believe that I can do most things if I put my mind to it. I have spent three or four years here doing nothing but housework. When I think about not learning anything useful over these years, my regret almost brings me to tears. Haven't you ever regretted anything like that?"
>
> "Of course. I'm not perfect and have made my share of mistakes."
>
> With that, their conversation fell into silence.[6]

Whereas Kitako has found comfort and stability in her marriage, Masako seeks independence in employment after the death of her fiancé. This she does not for economic reasons, but for freedom from the constraints of her provincial family life in Kōfu. For Masako, these aspirations are explicitly linked to her consumption of women's magazines, which keep her abreast of the latest fashions and trends.

5. Jordan Sand, *House and Home in Modern Japan*, 137.

6. Masamune Hakuchō, "Tanin no saigai," in *Hennentai Taishō bungaku zenshū*, vol. 13 (2003): 57–58.

Employment, economic freedom, and marriage prospects situate Kitako and Masako and their families as members of the new middle class both in Tokyo and the provincial cities. In other words, they are people in a class position not unlike that of Masamune Hakuchō himself and the readers of *Chūō kōron*. Hakuchō was born into a wealthy established family in rural Okayama. He moved to Tokyo in 1897, and eventually became a literary critic for the *Yomiuri shinbun*, a major newspaper. Through his activities as a critic and his associations from school, he met and became friends with several established and upcoming authors, notably Tayama Katai. Though he began his career as a critic, Hakuchō soon started writing fiction in the Naturalist vein and came to be considered one of the four giants of Naturalism, along with Tayama Katai, Shimazaki Tōson, and Tokuda Shūsei.[7] In all respects Masamune Hakuchō was a "high-culture" writer and critic, and an established member of the *bundan* almost equal in stature to Katai himself. The high-culture aspirations of "The Suffering of Another" are apparent not only in the class positions of the protagonists, but also in the explicit condemnation of popular culture and tastes. Hakuchō takes pains to point out what his story is *not*, to establish "The Suffering of Another" as anti-melodrama.

"The Suffering of Another" as Anti-Melodrama

The topic of popular culture was one not often addressed by Hakuchō in his criticism, which was almost exclusively focused on the works of *bundan* writers. In a discussion of popular literature (*tsūzoku bungaku*) published in 1925, Hakuchō reveals his thoughts on the popular period pieces, or, in his words, "warmed-over and rehashed Edo tales." He summarizes his general opinion of them in this way: "[Popular stories] may have something striking, but they do not touch the human heart. Thus, though they may dazzle and be fine for one reading, if you read them again, they begin to stink."[8] In his essay, Hakuchō takes the samurai tales of the 1920s as a jumping off point to discuss popular culture in general, including cinema. He sees all popular culture as playing to the same superficial desires of the masses—and hence as "striking," but ultimately hollow at the core.

Although Hakuchō does not use the term "melodrama" in his critique, he specifically addresses such tales' reliance on the emotional, the sensational, and the clear difference between good and evil, wherein "the bad guy is destroyed and the good guy prospers."[9] In essence, Hakuchō is conflating the popular and the

7. Hakuchō also contributed to the dominance of Naturalism through his criticism. See Yamamoto Kenkichi, "Masamune Hakuchō," in *Nihon kindai bungaku daijiten*, vol. 3 (1977): 232.

8. Masamune Hakuchō, "Tsūzoku bungaku sono hoka," in *Masamune Hakuchō zenshū*, vol. 7 (1965): 75; originally published in *Shinchō* 42, no. 4 (April 1925).

9. Ibid., 76. This statement critiques the Edo-era popular tales written along the theme of *kanzen chōaku* ("rewarding good and punishing evil").

melodramatic, and criticizing them both. Hakuchō positions "The Suffering of Another" in opposition to his conception of the popular in several crucial ways. First, it eschews melodrama. It lacks a villain, and avoids overwrought emotion, moral polarity, and sensationalism. Second, it explicitly points to the absence of these qualities in several key passages. And finally, it openly critiques the other more popular forms of earthquake culture.

The story's divergence from melodrama is most apparent in Hakuchō's refusal to offer a spectacular view of emotional women suffering in the disaster. None of the characters in "The Suffering of Another" indulges in obvious expressions of emotion. Kitako is a stoic, independent woman who ventures out on her own, despite her injury. Masako downplays her pain at the loss of her prospective husband, despite others' assertions that she must be upset. "The Suffering of Another" highlights the absence of female emotional spectacle by hinting at the more dramatic stories that could be told about these characters, without reveling in the sensational details.

As a survivor who lost her home, Kitako's story could have been the stuff of melodrama. We learn that her husband helped her flee the flaming city, seemingly an appropriate topic for exploration in a sensational mode. Yet the description of Kitako fleeing the fires is told succinctly, without details such as jumps from bridges or a dramatic separation from her husband amid the fires. Rather, in introducing Kitako the narrator merely tells us that: "The loss of her home and possessions, the events that left her injured, the difficult flight as a refugee remained only as a memory of the past and no longer caused her pain. The compassion of her parents had all but made up for the material and psychological damage she incurred in the earthquake."[10] Hakuchō hints at the drama behind Kitako's escape by mentioning her injuries and by alluding to "psychological damage," but scrupulously avoids sensational details. These untold details suggest that Hakuchō's story is about something different, that this story is about the quiet moments that follow a sensational disaster, rather than the disaster itself.

Hakuchō's critique of popular culture within the story becomes explicit when it directly mentions earthquake postcards, one of the most prevalent forms of earthquake sensationalism. In an early scene, the narrator describes Kitako's impressions on seeing postcards depicting earthquake suffering being sold on the streets of the provincial city of Kōfu:"She gazed with interest at the stores to the right and to the left and she stopped in front of the temporary stalls. Among these stalls there were those selling earthquake postcards. The movie theaters also advertised films of the earthquake."[11] This passage illustrates the ubiquity

10. Masamune Hakuchō, "Tanin no saigai," 53. All page numbers are from the reprinted version in *Hennentai Taishō bungaku zenshū*, vol. 13.
11. Ibid., 55.

of earthquake culture beyond the devastated city and into the provinces. And, as the passage continues, Hakuchō criticizes them for catering to the voyeuristic desires of those distant from the catastrophe: "As a survivor herself, Kitako found it distasteful that the earthquake suffering was being turned into a commodity. Nevertheless, she took it as a sign that those in this town were just country folk (*inaka-ppei*) behind the times. Besides, they hadn't experienced the earthquake."[12] In this passage Hakuchō distinguishes Kitako from the people in Kōfu in two ways. First, he asserts her identity as a survivor who experienced the earthquake. Through Kitako's internal musings, Hakuchō suggests that the commodification of disaster is distasteful to people who experienced it.[13] The last line emphasizes this difference. However, Kitako's thoughts also differentiate her from the people of Kōfu based on her association with the metropole. She is a city girl. The word used for "country folk," *inaka-ppei,* is a derogatory term closer to "hick." This implies that the people of Kōfu are less refined, less educated, less culturally aware. By attributing the trade in postcards to the fact that the people in Kōfu are *inaka-ppei*, Kitako places herself above them.

Though in the story the term *inaka-ppei* criticizes provincials in Kōfu, these postcards and films were in fact at least as popular in Tokyo as they were outside it. Thus this comment seems directed not so much at the residents of Kōfu as at people throughout Japan who indulged in the spectacle of the earthquake. In so doing, Hakuchō defines a category of people interested in the voyeuristic spectacle, in contrast to Kitako and others like her. Sociologist Pierre Bourdieu has shown that by classifying some cultural objects as "good" and others as "bad," members of one class invoke the idea of "taste" to differentiate themselves from others. As he puts it, "Taste classifies and it classifies the classifier."[14] Hakuchō classifies popular earthquake culture as "distasteful" and thus links consumption of spectacular earthquake commodities to a lower category of people, setting Kitako (and other middle-class Tokyoites) apart from those who are less educated and less sensitive.

It is precisely this distinction in taste that defines the boundaries between popular literature and high literature. In "The Suffering of Another," Hakuchō emphasizes the difference between his writing and other types of earthquake spectacle, the difference between high and low culture. In his 1925 article on popular

12. Ibid.

13. The artist Takehisa Yumeji also expressed disgust with the phenomenon of earthquake postcards, though he, too, trafficked in images of the disaster. He described the postcards as "cruel" in his sketches and musings on the quake serialized in the *Miyako shinbun*. Takehisa Yumeji et al., *Yumeji to Karyō, Kōka no kantō daishinsai rupo* (Kuresu Shuppan, 2003), 42. Part of this passage has been translated by Gennifer Weisenfeld in her *Imaging Disaster*, 131.

14. Pierre Bourdieu, *Distinction: A Social Critique of the Judgement of Taste* (Cambridge, MA: Harvard University Press, 1984), 6.

literature, Hakuchō seems resigned to the fact that the masses crave melodrama. Unlike Kikuchi Kan, however, Hakuchō sees himself growing ever distant from the tastes of the masses: "It seems that I am increasingly unsatisfied by popular art. I suppose a connoisseur of art must necessarily depart from the popular."[15] Hakuchō's "The Suffering of Another," with its focus on the quiet suffering of everyday people, attempts to distance both the author and his work from the masses and their tastes.

Hakuchō's attitudes toward mass entertainment are clear in his protagonist Kitako's dismissal of the popular earthquake postcards and films. But the most effective critique comes through the way Kitako is herself drawn toward the site of someone else's suffering, in the same way that masses of people were drawn to the devastated city. In "The Suffering of Another" this practice of *yakeato kenbutsu* (viewing the ruins, or disaster tourism) plays a central role. On the one hand, this type of "disaster tourism" is shown to resemble the postcards and films in the way it brings people who have no connection to the disaster to view the suffering of others. On the other hand, the story goes beyond merely criticizing the practice from afar, for it highlights the tension between the attraction of "other people's suffering" and moral revulsion at that attraction.

DISASTER TOURISM (*YAKEATO KENBUTSU*)

The postcards, the films, and the stories depicting the disaster engendered a desire among the people to see the sights for themselves.[16] In his autobiography, the film director Kurosawa Akira wrote of his brother escorting the young Kurosawa through the ruins to see the sights and the bodies.[17] They were far from alone. Soon after it resumed printing, the *Yomiuri shinbun* reported on the masses of "tourists." According to the September 13 article, the influx of people was causing major problems with the reconstruction effort. Furthermore, the article claimed, many of those who entered Tokyo ostensibly to help merely used that as an excuse to see the ruins.[18] Though some certainly came to offer assistance or to check on relatives, the astonishing figure of almost two million people entering Tokyo in the fifteen days following the quake suggests something more.[19]

15. Masamune Hakuchō, "Tsūzoku bungaku," 76.
16. This phenomenon is not unusual, as visitors to the site of the World Trade Center in New York can attest. Chris Rojek has written about visitors to the sites of other disasters, such as the Lockerbie Pan Am disaster and other sites of death, which he calls "Black Spots." Chris Rojek, *Ways of Escape: Modern Transformation in Leisure and Travel* (Lanham, MD: Rowman & Littlefield, 1994), 137–38.
17. Kurosawa Akira, *Something Like an Autobiography* (New York: Vintage, 1983), 47–56. Kurosawa wrote that the sights he saw influenced his raw depiction of violence in his films.
18. *Yomiuri shinbun* (September 13, 1923), 2.
19. Fujisawa Morihiko and Bureau of Social Affairs Home Office, *Great Earthquake of 1923*, 66.

Among those viewing the ruins were contemporary writers who described what they saw for readers, perhaps encouraging others to see for themselves. Tayama Katai's *Record of the Tokyo Earthquake* is a prominent example of this kind of writing, but younger members of the *bundan* such as Kawabata Yasunari, Akutagawa Ryūnosuke, and Kikuchi Kan, as well as writers such as Nagata Mikihiko all recorded their thoughts and impressions of the destruction. One writer, Takegawa Shigetaro, reported visiting the remains of the Yoshiwara pleasure quarters on three separate occasions in three months, twice as a guide for visiting acquaintances.[20] In "The Suffering of Another" Masamune Hakuchō seems to condemn the popular desire to "view the ruins," but at the same time acknowledges the attraction.

What was the attraction? Why did people visit the ruins in such numbers? Tourist sights are marked by their difference from the ordinary, and as John Urry claims in *The Tourist Gaze*, that difference is reinforced by the way people look at these sights, the "tourist gaze" of his title. This gaze is socially constructed through activities that direct attention to one place over another: "Places are chosen to be gazed upon because there is an anticipation [especially through daydreaming and fantasy] of intense pleasures, either on a different scale or involving different senses from those customarily encountered. Such anticipation is constructed and sustained through a variety of non-tourist practices, such as film, TV, literature, magazines, records and videos, which construct and reinforce the gaze."[21] In the case of the 1923 earthquake, the anticipation Urry refers to was created by the dissemination of popular stories and images of the destruction, the "spectacle of suffering." The postcards, films, *jitsuwa*, and other examples of popular earthquake culture fostered a desire to see the devastated sites in person. Yet, unlike other touristic practices, in *yakeato kenbutsu* the difference from the everyday is marked by death and loss, a phenomenon sociologists Malcolm Foley and John Lennon call "dark tourism."[22] Like Auschwitz and other sites associated with death, the earthquake disaster zone became a location marked as different through the suffering that had occurred there. Sites that focus on the dead seem to encourage a connection (through sympathetic identification) with the people who died.

The crux of "The Suffering of Another" is centered on *yakeato kenbutsu*, and the phenomenon is repeatedly discussed as the story progresses to its climactic scene amid the ruins themselves. During Kitako's initial visit with her friend Masako, they discuss their expectations, dreams, and fantasies of viewing the ruins.

20. Takegawa Shigetarō, "Yoshiwara," *Bungei shunjū* 2, no. 1 (January 1924): 39–40.

21. John Urry, *The Tourist Gaze: Leisure and Travel in Contemporary Societies* (London; Newbury Park: Sage Publications, 1990), 6.

22. See J. John Lennon and Malcolm Foley, *Dark Tourism* (London; New York: Continuum, 2000).

Masako qualifies her desire to visit the ruins by saying that she does not want to go to any of the famous places like the *hifukushō* or Asakusa. She is interested in going where no one else will go, a place she has seen in her dreams. Kitako replies by saying that the ruins are different from the photos: "Where do you want to go and see? The real *yakeato* are even worse than you can imagine from the photographs. They're filthy and repulsive. No matter how grand the house, they are all alike when they are burnt-out ruins." Masako, however, claims to be different from the standard tourist: "You're probably right, but it's exactly the dirty and decrepit parts that I want to see so badly. You say that it's different than I imagine, but I don't see nice dreams of the ruins. I see birds picking at corpses, the pungent fires burning, the eggs of the devil seething up from the ashes in swarms, the souls of the blackened dead moaning from beneath the burnt earth. If I go and it isn't quite like that, I'll probably find it a bore."[23] The masses may want to visit the popular places—the *hifukushō* and the devastated entertainment district of Asakusa—but Masako is interested in the fantastic and the imaginary, a place that exists in her dreams, not in the images available through illustration and photography. Within the story, several months have passed since the earthquake by the time this conversation takes place. The fires are gone and the corpses cremated. The dark vision Masako sees is not available to those want to experience the disaster vicariously. Yet the fantasy she describes to Kitako can be interpreted as a desire for an impossible experience of suffering, similar to that undergone by those who were actually there. The specifics behind her desire become apparent further on in the story.

After a substantial period of recovery following her visit with Masako, Kitako's leg has improved enough for her to return to Tokyo. She views the return with trepidation, but also excitement at seeing her husband and her new home. Kitako's brother accompanies her on the journey, to help her and to see the ruins. After they have settled in Kitako's new house in the suburbs, Kitako goes with her brother on a *yakeato kenbutsu* excursion. She agrees to do so not because of the impersonal sites her brother is interested in, but because she wants to see where her old house was: "I need to go [to the ruins], to look carefully and remember, remember this moment in my life."[24] Hakuchō takes care to emphasize that Kitako wants to visit a place that she connects with personally, to remember her own experiences and be moved by sorrow for her loss and gratitude for her good fortune.

Kitako and her brother begin with the barracks village on the grounds of Yasukuni Shrine and then proceed down toward the completely flattened area of Kanda, where Kitako had lived previously. Her brother's initial response is revealing:

23. Masamune Hakuchō, "Tanin no saigai," 59–60.
24. Ibid., 67.

> "These ruins are a mess!" Her brother commented, looking around. The ruins he had imagined after seeing the films were nowhere to be seen. It was merely dusty, smelly, dirty, and somewhat of a disappointment. "Is this it? Isn't there something worse?"
>
> Kitako responded with surprise, "Isn't this enough? You don't know what it was like here before the fires. That's why you're not affected. On that corner was a big Western clothing store. Senkichi got his suits there, and now look at it." Kitako recalled her husband's lost suits as she solemnly gazed back at the ruins of the store.[25]

Through the point of view of Kitako's brother, the author states that the reality of the ruins does not live up to the anticipation created by movies and other popular representations of the earthquake. This disappoints Kitako's brother because he is looking for an authentic experience, but one that also lives up to the media hype. The brother's response identifies him within the story as one of the "country folk" whose motives are voyeuristic. This is explicitly contrasted with Kitako's response. Her sadness derives from the way the ruins of the Western clothing store works as a metonym for her loss. Kitako's response to the ruins is coded as "proper" within the narrative because she has a personal connection with the devastation.

This trip to the ruins leads to the climax of the story. As Kitako and her brother are heading toward the *hifukushō*, Kitako changes her mind. Rather than seeing "a pile of bones of people she didn't know at the *hifukushō*," Kitako wants to see where Masako's prospective husband had been crushed to death—Nishiki-chō in Kanda. Using Masako's aunt's story as a guide, Kitako leads her brother toward the area. They pause to look at the ruins of a hospital, and Kitako's brother draws her attention to a figure heading toward them—Masako: "Kitako wanted to avoid Masako, but she couldn't very well go off to the side without feeling even more ashamed, so she went up to greet her. Masako's face turned color, and she seemed to be at a loss for words." They exchange pleasantries for a while, and then it is Kitako who is at a loss for words: "Masako continued with a deliberately calm expression. 'I came with my mother, but she's at the Yoshimuras and I went out to see the ruins (*yakeato kenbutsu*) by myself.' At that point they both glanced over and discovered the sign of the XX Office at the same time. . . . It was only a pile of burnt bricks with no hint of future rebuilding."[26]

Kitako is motivated to see the place where Masako's prospective husband died because of an embarrassing curiosity. Just as *jitsuwa*, postcards, and films encouraged disaster tourism, so Masako's aunt's story encouraged Kitako to seek out this place. In this way the aunt marks this particular pile of burnt bricks with

25. Ibid., 68.
26. Ibid., 68–69.

suffering—not that of the man who died, but Masako's suffering. In contrast to the difference between Kitako and her brother looking at the ruins of the clothing store, in this case it is Masako who has a personal connection to the landscape and Kitako who does not.

Again Masako breaks the silence, saying, "It's like this no matter where you look. No one's to blame." She takes leave of Kitako, who struggles to find parting words. The narrator explains: "She had come to this site out of curiosity and regretted hurting Masako's feelings. Kitako lost all interest in seeing the *hifukushō* ruins . . . and decided to hurry home."[27] By meeting Masako in the ruins, Kitako's motives are exposed and she becomes no different from the other "tourists." Following her shame at being discovered, Kitako has no more desire for *yakeato kenbutsu*.

This moment of coincidental confrontation reveals the moral code of the story. Kitako's palpable discomfort at being caught indulging in the voyeurism she condemned earlier brings out both the allure and the moral ambiguity in disaster tourism. By acknowledging Kitako's interest in the site where Masako's fiancé met his demise, "The Suffering of Another" validates her desire as natural, though in need of suppression. Kitako's embarrassment gives insight into the title of the story. We may share in the suffering of other people, but it must be on a personal level, and shared through personal interactions rather than in the simple viewing of ruins out of curiosity. "The Suffering of Another" seems to deride the popular sightseeing of places where unknown people died. It suggests that because the masses have no personal connection to the suffering, such visitors are merely voyeurs. This is not necessarily the case. Though there were certainly those who were interested in the devastation because of a morbid curiosity, others were seeking a connection to the larger catastrophe that affected the national community.

* * * * *

Who is the "other" in the title "The Suffering of Another"? Is it Masako—whose loss of her fiancé draws Kitako's interest? Or is the "other" perhaps all those whose disaster experience exceeded Kitako's own, those whose bones were heaped in the *hifukushō*? The "other" in the title leads us to ask: What is the proper way to represent the suffering of the other? Does the impossibility of truly knowing that suffering preclude its representation? The story does not answer these questions, but it does suggest a respect for the unknowable suffering of others.

There is another victim of the earthquake in "The Suffering of Another"—a boy who escaped from the Yokohama inferno. Though he returned to his home

27. Ibid., 69.

in the country after the quake, he was sent to work as a store boy near Kitako's parents. He did not have the luxury to recuperate with family. He cries in pain, shattering the idyllic mountain scene of Kitako's convalescence. The boy recovers after being taken back to his home, and Kitako's mother wonders whether his cries were not just an act. Kitako replies, "You can't cry out like that with just a feigned illness. I heard many similar screams at the time of the quake. It is as if they are stuck, echoing in my ears, even now. People make those kinds of sounds when they are in pain."[28] "The Suffering of Another" suggests that there is no way to truly access the pain of others. This comes through most strongly in the boy's painful shrieking. His suffering is not explained, but only cries out into the night, asking for understanding but defying interpretation.

28. Ibid., 54.

Chapter 6

Survivor Anxiety in Nagata Mikihiko's "Wild Dance of the Flames"

Ten days after the Great Kanto Earthquake of 1923, Nagata Mikihiko set out to view the ruins of a destroyed Tokyo. In his book *The Earth Shakes* (*Daichi wa furū*), he describes preparing for his journey in a peculiar manner: "To walk into the devastated area, I couldn't dress as I normally do. I wore a shirt that I'd worn for several days, short pants, a blackened straw hat, and an old hand-towel around my neck. As I walked along with my thick staff dragging along the ground, I could only be considered a laborer. If I hadn't dressed like that, I'd have felt so badly (*ki no doku*) for the city people who had been affected by the disaster that I wouldn't have been able to go out at all."[1] In this passage Mikihiko shows his awareness that the clothes and appearance of a worker will allow him to blend in with the "city people," the earthquake survivors in the devastated *shitamachi*, or downtown area of Tokyo. This masquerade is an attempt to make him appear to be an authentic sufferer—a person who lived through the disaster to the same extent as those among whom he travels. Although the reason for such a costume is not fully articulated, its use hints at the fact that, though the impetus for the catastrophe was natural, certain social classes centered in the *shitamachi* bore the brunt of the destruction. Mikihiko's inner monologue shows not only an awareness of the disparity in the distribution of the damage, but the anxiety felt by a writer who experienced little of the devastation himself.

This description of Mikihiko preparing for his excursion reinforces the idea that authenticity is performative. In his collection *The Earth Shakes*, Michiko creates a chain of authenticity out of literary techniques and tools that link his writings to his personal experiences. He accomplishes this through his introduction, narrative voice, and style. But he also must clothe his work in the moral and aesthetic authority of the witness. To do so requires the voices of others. In one particular story from his collection, "Wild Dance of the Flames" ("Honoo no ranbu"), he recounts meeting a man who lived through the *hifukushō* inferno, the site where more than 30,000 people died. To recount this man's story, authenticity

1. Nagata Mikihiko, *Daichi wa furū* (Shun'yōdō, 1923), 58.

required Mikihiko to identify the man as a member of a particular class. This is not the case in the official imperial rescripts and sensational tales of suffering such as *jitsuwa* (true stories). There, class and other distinctions are often elided in favor of a universalizing conception of the disaster as affecting the country as a whole, though some citizens were more unlucky than others. This is the expected response from a nation working to erase distinctions of class in favor of what Benedict Anderson calls "a deep horizontal comradeship."[2] In contrast, Mikihiko's account of his costumed journey in *The Earth Shakes* consciously portrays class difference. In so doing it lays bare his anxiety about the difference between suffering in the *shitamachi* and weathering the disaster in the *yamanote*, showing that the "national" disaster was fraught with tension and revealing the myth behind the universalizing discourse of the state ideologues.

CLASSLESS AUTHENTICITY IN *JITSUWA*

Nagata Mikihiko's *The Earth Shakes* was part of the wave of earthquake-related books discussed in Chapter 1, the first of which, Kōdansha's *The Great Taisho Earthquake and Conflagration* (*Taishō daishinsai daikasai*), set the standard for books that followed. The large proportion of melodramatic *jitsuwa* in the Kōdansha volume was a major selling point. Many of the books that followed it were entirely devoted to *jitsuwa*; notable examples include Arano Kōhei's *Earthquake Romances* and the government-sponsored *Educational Materials Regarding the Earthquake*.[3] Yet despite the fact that most of the people featured in these stories came from the poorer regions of the city, none of these *jitsuwa* deal with the underlying socio-economic realities that had resulted in the vast disparity in the damage. In general, they subtly shift blame for the disaster away from socio-economic factors by stressing the tragedy's natural causes.

One *jitsuwa* in the Kōdansha collection elides class in a way that contrasts nicely with Nagata Mikihiko's story "Wild Dance of the Flames." "In the Muddy Water" ("Doromizu no naka"), one of the many anonymous *jitsuwa* found in the Kōdansha book, is about a man named Ochiai Matsujirō who, like the protagonist in Mikihiko's story, survived the fires at the *hifukushō*. He had taken refuge there with his brother and thousands of others as the fires approached his nearby home. After the flames descended on the refugees, he and his brother survived by covering themselves with the muddy water referred to in the title of the story. Like many *jitsuwa*, "In the Muddy Water" relies on some literary devices, such as different narrative stances and points of view, to intensify the emotion and to

2. Benedict Anderson, *Imagined Communities: Reflections on the Origin and Spread of Nationalism* (London: Verso, 1991), 7.

3. Arano Kōhei, *Shinsai romansu*; Monbushō Futsū Gakumu Kyoku, *Kyōiku shiryō*. Both are discussed in Chapter 4.

encourage sympathy.[4] The description of Mr. Ochiai amid the flames, relying on the shallow pool of water to keep him and his brother alive, is especially dramatic:

> Surrounding him on all sides were sounds like wood blazing in flames, which reverberated in his ears like the rumblings of the earth, and he could not open his eyes. He was pouring water, pouring mud on himself and praying to the gods and buddhas unceasingly, knowing that if he were to stop for one minute he would be dead. Forgetting that he was hungry, forgetting that he was tired, forgetting that he was scared, he was mechanically pouring the muddy water over himself without any thought beyond survival. He could tell his brother was tired and at times appeared to resign himself to death as the sparks fell down upon them. "Watch out! If you stop you'll die." "I can't go on, brother. . . ." "Hang on! What'll happen if you give up now? Pour!"[5]

These vivid descriptions and dramatic quotes enhance the impact of the brothers' extraordinary survival. Yet the emotional force in the story also arises from its connection to the real, emphasized from the opening lines: "A man named Ochiai Matsujirō (40) lived in Honjo, Kamezawa-chō 2–5."[6] The story concludes with a factual epilogue that gives similarly detailed location information: after walking over the innumerable dead, the postscript claims, the brothers escaped to relatives in Ichikawa, in Chiba prefecture. The combination of objective journalism emphasizing authenticity and dramatic description creates a powerful emotional impact.

The specific Honjo address in the opening lines of this *jitsuwa* not only gives the story an aura of authenticity but obliquely suggests the Ochiai's socio-economic class. Nevertheless, "In the Muddy Water" refrains from any concrete mention of social position or occupation. In this way, the story allows for an identification with the protagonist that is uncomplicated by class or other difference. The brothers' experience is wretchedly unique, but the story provides no explanation as to why they suffered so much while the vast majority of those who are reading their story did not. Any factor that might have made the Ochiai brothers more vulnerable to the disaster than these readers is completely ignored.

NAGATA MIKIHIKO'S AUTHENTIC EARTHQUAKE COLLECTION

Nagata Mikihiko's earthquake collection included several *jitsuwa* that were not much different from those found in other collections. At the same time, *The Earth*

4. Chapter 4 discusses some of the ways literary techniques are used in *jitsuwa*. The use of the word *jibun* ("self") in this story blurs the distinctions between first- and third-person narration in a way often found in the I-novel (*shishōsetsu*). See Edward Fowler, *Rhetoric of Confession*, 5–6.
5. Dai Nihon Yūbenkai Kōdansha, *Taishō daishinsai daikasai*, 176–77.
6. Ibid., 176.

Shakes was unique in that it contained fictional stories along with the *jitsuwa* and Mikihiko's personal account of the disaster. This variety would have suggested to contemporary readers that Mikihiko's collection offered a more comprehensive depiction of the disaster than could be found elsewhere. Like the other popular earthquake texts, most of the stories in *The Earth Shakes* do little to undermine prevailing ideas about the universality of the disaster and the class dynamics of the aftermath. The story "Wild Dance of the Flames," however, contains a framing narration that describes an encounter between the narrator (presumably Mikihiko himself) and a man who, like the Ochiai brothers, lived through the *hifukushō* inferno. In this framing narration, Mikihiko reveals that the disparity between his earthquake experience and that of those who suffered the most mirrors the distance between them in terms of socio-economic class.

The Earth Shakes was published just over three months after the earthquake. The hardcover volume was reasonably priced at 1.8 yen, meaning that Mikihiko's usual middle-class audience would have been able to afford it.[7] It contains twenty short works, all depicting the earthquake. They are undifferentiated in the table of contents, but there are nevertheless three categories of stories: (1) accounts based on the author's experiences, (2) stories told to the author (including *jitsuwa*), and (3) fiction. Each type is discernible only by certain stylistic elements and other clues: focalization, narration, and point of view. Chapters relating the experiences of the author use limited focalization and explicitly connect the narrator and the author. For example, characters refer to the narrator as "Nagata." When describing secondhand stories, the narrator is careful to show how he heard about the events through a framing narration. For the third category, fiction, the defining factor is the point of view. Several make use of a third-person narrator unassociated with the author. The third-person narration in the story "Wild Geese" is focalized through the young female protagonist Hamako. This is an unrealistic narrating position for the real Nagata Mikihiko without deploying the imaginary prowess of an author. Yet even in fictional stories like "Wild Geese," Mikihiko applies a realistic style to his representation of events.

In the introduction to *The Earth Shakes*, Mikihiko claims that the value of his work derives from its faithful recording of the disaster. Though internal markers contribute to its aura of authenticity—focalization, framing narrations, and explicit connections to newspaper stories—in his introduction Mikihiko asserts an unmediated connection to reality for the entire book:

> I need not explain that the works contained within this book are not pure artistic works (*jun'itsu naru geijutsuhin*) attained after

7. Nagamine Shigetoshi shows that a salaryman family would spend between 6–8 yen a month on books, newspapers, and magazines. See Nagamine, *Modan toshi no dokusho kūkan*, 225.

> countless revisions. After being approached by Mr. Wada [the head of Shun'yōdō, Mikihiko's publisher], I wrote furiously, beginning on the seventh day after the earthquake, and finished a mere three weeks later. I do not think that the value of a work stems from experience, but I took my brush in hand and faced the unparalleled disaster. I researched this book by personally examining the actual locations. Thus I believe that I have, at least in some way, faithfully captured the situation of the time. I sat, industriously sending my brush running across the page, as I was threatened by the recurring aftershocks, as I shuddered at the rumors of attacks by unruly gangs, at times relying on the flickering light of a small candle, at times writing with a sword for night watch at hand, at times writing while slurping gruel of unpolished rice in a tent filled with the cries of the wounded. Thus, to me, it is all the seed of memory.[8]

In his assertion that literary value does not stem from experience, Mikihiko rejects the valorization of the life of the author triumphed by I-novel writers. Nevertheless, he also draws from that discourse to declare that the lack of artistry, the temporal immediacy, and his own bodily experience make his work more authentic. *The Earth Shakes* was written immediately after the earthquake and *while* he was experiencing the aftershocks, hearing the rumors of unruly gangs, standing guard, and eating rice gruel.

Thus, this introduction claims, the work is artless precisely because there was no time to write it artistically. By drawing the connection to hardships that occurred as Mikihiko was writing, the introduction to *The Earth Shakes* evokes the genre of the "disaster diary." James Young's examination of Holocaust testimonial writing notes that "because the diarists wrote from within the whirlwind, the degree of authority in their accounts is perceived by readers to be stronger than texts shaped by hindsight."[9] By asserting that he was writing "within the whirlwind" of aftershocks, Mikihiko is claiming the authority to record the disaster as a whole.

The introduction serves the dual purpose of highlighting Mikihiko's proximity to the disaster for those who did not experience it, and at the same time offering a "seed of memory" to other *yamanote* residents. Yet Mikihiko remains limited in his earthquake experience. The hardships mentioned in the introduction were those endured specifically by the middle-class residents of the *yamanote*. This is accentuated by the lack of reference to the fires, the primary concern for residents of the *shitamachi*. The introduction is therefore directed toward two kinds of readers: (1) those in Tokyo who experienced the quake as Mikihito did, and who can

8. Nagata Mikihiko, *Daichi wa furū*, 4. "Unruly gangs" is a likely reference to rumors of Korean gangs, since word for *futei* ("unruly") was often paired with Koreans.
9. James Young, "Interpreting Literary Testimony: A Preface to Reading Holocaust Diaries and Memoirs," *New Literary History* 218 (1987): 414.

thus recognize the list of hardships as resembling their own; and (2) those who did not live through the earthquake and for whom this passage establishes the author as someone who did. Neither of these categories encompasses those who suffered most. For their experience, Mikihiko relied on his research—conducted by traveling to specific sites to "faithfully capture the situation of the time." One result of that research was the story "Wild Dance of the Flames."

"WILD DANCE OF THE FLAMES"

Though the introduction to *The Earth Shakes* focuses on his *yamanote* earthquake experiences, Mikihiko strives for an authentic and affective portrayal of the entire disaster in his collection. Other chapters relate the author's experience, but to authentically convey the broader experiences of the earthquake, Mikihiko saw the need to give voice to the people who felt the heat of the fires or lost someone to the flames. These were experiences to which he had no immediate access. "Wild Dance of the Flames" attempts to remedy this oversight. A similar move can be found in Sadamura Seihyō's post-earthquake writings. Sadamura first wrote a book detailing his experiences in the quake and his flight to the safety of Chiba. Realizing that the focus on his own experiences alone made for a limited view of the disaster, he published a second book devoted to *jitsuwa* accounts. In the introduction to that book he wrote, "I felt something lacking in my first book and decided to compile this collection of other people's stories."[10] Like Sadamura's *jitsuwa* book, "Wild Dance of the Flames" adds to Mikihiko's own experiences those of others whose suffering he could only imagine. For this story Mikihiko turned to the tragedy that, in its extremity, came to stand metonymically for the disaster as a whole: the inferno at the *hifukushō*.

"Wild Dance of the Flames" attempts to go beyond the experiences of the author while simultaneously providing an authentic representation of intense suffering. Though the *hifukushō* experience was extreme, Mikihiko endeavors present it through firsthand experience. This he does by calling attention to the narrating situation and linking it to himself. According to the story's introduction, Mikihiko heard the account directly from a man who survived the *hifukushō*, and the encounter between Mikihiko and the man reveals the class distance between the two, a distance that is mirrored in their different experiences of the earthquake. Though the tale itself is filled with markers of the man's social class, the conclusion of the story attempts to make him one sufferer among "tens of thousands." That is, the man becomes a statistic, the victim of a natural disaster rather than of rapid urbanization and socio-economic inequality. Nevertheless, the clues to class

10. Sadamura Seihyō, *Sōnan hyakuwa*, 3–4.

difference are never erased completely, and the narrator's palpable anxiety reveals his awareness of the unspoken imbalanced distribution of damage.

Previous chapters of *The Earth Shakes* describe the narrator's journey into the ruins of the city from his home in the *yamanote* region of Tokyo. "Wild Dance of the Flames" begins with the narrator emerging from the grounds of the *hifukushō*. He had gone there out of curiosity, as did many other disaster tourists, but he was also interested in gathering material for his writing. Just outside the *hifukushō*, the narrator observes a man sitting directly on the gravel by the road and offering to repair bicycles. The narrator notices the burns on the man's skin and the bandages on his chest. These physical marks betray the presence of a story to be told, and the narrator successfully coaxes it from the injured man.

The repairman had taken refuge with his family in the *hifukushō*, but was separated from them before the fires engulfed the crowd. He recounts the flames descending on the area, the crowd surging in panic, and his losing consciousness. He awakes to find himself buried under dead bodies and badly burned. Though he returns to look for his family among the tens of thousands of dead, his search is futile.

Despite its claims to authenticity, the story is too carefully constructed to have been faithfully transcribed by the author exactly as it was recounted, and there is no guarantee that Mikihiko even met the man in question. However, the main question is not whether or not the story is "true" but how it is rhetorically constructed to give it an aura of authenticity. For the narrator to relate the horrors of the *hifukushō* and maintain the authority of truth he has asserted throughout the book, he must show how he received that knowledge. Mikihiko's framing narrative accomplishes this by using a first-person narration in which he describes meeting the bicycle repairman. To give further immediacy to the story, the narrator lets the repairman who experienced the conflagration firsthand speak for himself as well.

Thus the repairman's story is differentiated from the framing narration because it is given in his own "voice." That is, the embedded narration is set apart from the rest of the text by quotation marks and by the use of language that mimics actual speech patterns. This linguistic mimicry is differentiated from the more common use of *genbun'itchi* (vernacular prose) that characterizes the framing narrative.[11] For the dialogue of the repairman, Mikihiko attempts to convey

11. *Genbun'itchi* is the style of vernacular prose adopted by Meiji intellectuals to have the written word more closely mirror speech. The result, however, was nevertheless distinct from the spoken language. For more on the development of *genbun'itchi*, see Nanette Twine, *Language and the Modern State: The Reform of Written Japanese* (London; New York: Routledge, 1991). The story of the repairman includes interjections such as *iya* ("not really"), verbs and verb endings such as *masu* and *desu*, and dialect such as the use of *asuko* rather than *asoko* ("o'er there" rather than "over there").

speech by using interjections, dialect, verbs and verb endings that are inconsistent with literary *genbun'itchi* as it was practiced in the Taishō era. This ostensibly transcribed spoken language suggests that the author is merely the transparent medium through which this sufferer tells his ghastly tale.

Mikihiko uses voice, language, point of view, and other formal attempts to maintain narrative consistency and establish authenticity. Each of these rhetorical moves adds a link in the chain of authenticity that Mikihiko creates to connect the repairman to his readers. But there is another appeal to truth within this story, namely, the appeal to the emotional and moral authority of the witness.[12] Mikihiko's repairman speaks after having experienced the "whirlwind" in the *hifukushō* inferno. This gives him a privileged position among survivors. Anyone who encountered the earthquake was a survivor, but there was a considerable difference in how each survived. Some living outside the damaged region endured prolonged uncertainty about whether loved ones survived; some closer to the epicenter were shaken but suffered no damage that a day of cleaning would not solve. Others lost homes but suffered no physical injury. Many others were injured by the falling beams, burned by the fires that engulfed their houses, and lost loved ones to the flames.

Those who most acutely felt the disaster, however, were the "victim-survivors." Ross Chambers uses this term in his work on testimonial writing to describe those whose "education in trauma, unlike that of other survivors, has involved extremely close proximity, a proximity not only physical, but also moral and psychological, with those who did not survive the trauma."[13] This proximity gives the stories of victim-survivors additional authority and poignancy because they have felt death approaching and lived to speak for those who were killed beside them.

In the case of "Wild Dance of the Flames," this proximity to death is highlighted by the burns on the repairman's body and his liminal position as a survivor who returned from the dead after living through a literal hell. The description of the man at the opening of the story is particularly striking:

> I looked at him, and around his knees were old bike tires, a small pump, and a very few tools. Beside him in the burnt remains by the roadside was a small white cotton flag, in poor handwriting, declaring "Bike repairs." . . . As I walked past, I glanced in his direction and his

12. Lubomìr Doležel has written, "The basis of the Ich-narrator's [first-person narrator's] authentication authority is his privileged knowledge. Two kinds of devices are essential for establishing and maintaining this quality of the narrator: a) devices limiting the scope of the narrator's knowledge [narrow focalization]; b) devices identifying the source of his knowledge." Doležel, "Truth and Authenticity in Narrative," *Poetics Today* 1, no. 3 (Spring 1980): 18.
13. Ross Chambers, *Untimely Interventions: AIDS Writing, Testimonial, and the Rhetoric of Haunting* (Ann Arbor, MI: University of Michigan Press, 2004), xxiv.

> pitiful face entered my sight. Beneath the towel covering his head I could see his painful scalp, burned crimson, and the burns, still raw, remained black along his cheek and down to his jaw. As I looked closer, I noticed he had a dirty bandage wrapped around his chest, covering what appeared to be more burns.[14]

This arresting image arouses the pity and curiosity of the narrator and indicates a story hidden behind the burns. The burns mark this particular survivor as having encountered death face-to-face, inscribing his status as a sufferer on his body. The burns thus serve as an indexical sign of suffering—that is, they point to the cause of the burns, the fact that this man suffered through the fires. The indexical nature of the burns also suggests how they function as a metaphor for writing. Not unlike the way the burns point to the suffering and the story behind them, the words on the page are physical traces of that same story, creating a chain of authenticity that links the reader to the sufferer through the mediation of the author and his text.[15] At the same time, this chain of authenticity is a rhetorical construct, and relies on artifice to establish the connection between reader and sufferer.

The burns in "Wild Dance of the Flames" that mark the repairman as a victim-survivor also show him to be in a liminal state between the dead and the living: he has the marks of the fire that killed his family and 30,000 people around him. After admitting that he survived the inferno, the man tells the narrator, "When I think about it, I can't help imagining that I died then and my life now is but a dream. It may sound strange, but sometimes, when I get lost in thought, I have to pinch myself to check whether or not I am really alive."[16] Similarly, when the repairman first regains consciousness under the bodies of the dead in the *hifukushō*, he initially believes himself to be dead. His liminal position is repeatedly emphasized, and as such contributes to the complicated foundation of authority and authenticity created by this chapter of *The Earth Shakes*. Being on the boundary of life and death gives the repairman's story more weight than those of survivors like Mikihiko, who suffered relatively minor inconveniences.

"Wild Dance of the Flames" builds on the claims of authenticity in the introduction to the book by describing the narrating situation and limiting the point of view to a narrator who resembles Mikihiko. But the unique ability of a victim-survivor to speak of the destruction further emphasizes a truth that lies beyond Mikihiko's own experiences. The repairman's liminal connection with

14. Nagata Mikihiko, *Daichi wa furū*, 146–47.

15. Burns are also used in an earlier chapter in *The Earth Shakes* for a similar purpose. An aristocrat tells the narrator: "Nagata, this one was in her home in Yokohama when the quake struck and barely survived. Listen to her story. Look her right arm. Those are the traces of the fires" (Nagata Mikihiko, *Daichi wa furū*, 93–94). The aristocrat calls specific attention to the girl as a source of a story and links the story directly to the burns on her skin.

16. Ibid., 149.

the dead as well as the emotional weight of real suffering combine with other rhetorical gestures to give this story a mantle of authenticity. This authority is accomplished by personalizing the disaster, by creating a traceable chain that extends from the dead to the liminal repairman's singular experience of extreme suffering through the narrator and the author to the written page.

To authentically convey the man's story, Mikihiko identifies him with a certain social class from the very first depiction of him in the opening lines of the story. Yes, the man has burns that mark him as a sufferer, but according to the narrator he also has few resources. His bandages are dirty and his handwriting is poor, all of which implies a lack of money and education. Furthermore, his mere presence in the city at a time when many had fled to the countryside shows that he has nowhere to turn. Because the majority of those who gathered in the *hifukushō* lived in the lower-class districts of Honjo, realism demanded that Mikihiko describe the repairman as lower class. Nevertheless, Mikihiko displaces the class identity of the repairman at the conclusion of "Wild Dance of the Flames." There, the narrator muses on the repairman's situation and that of others like him:

> He had lost everything, and so he had no choice but to squat here by the side of the road repairing bikes as he had before, earning enough for his daily meal. . . . *What happens to men like this? There must be tens of thousands of them, sunk as they are in their misfortunes. I was struck at my own helplessness in the face of it all.* There are a few among those tens of thousands who interpreted their survival as the protection of the gods and set about as if reborn, working with renewed vigor. They are fine. But what can save the spirits of those sunk in the depths of a despair that even denies life?
>
> I couldn't just leave the man like that, so I took a measly yen from my own depleted wallet and gave it to him as I left.
>
> The sun was setting behind the muddy pools of the Sumida River and the shadows of monks performing services for the suffering spirits blended with the thin smoke from the incense as it became one point in the desolate scene.[17] (emphasis added)

In the eyes of the narrator, the repairman is not working "with renewed vigor" toward reconstruction of the nation but has sunk into the despair of the victim-survivor. More importantly, he becomes one of "tens of thousands," merely one of those men who suffers from the effects of a natural disaster and thus loses his specific identity. This universalizing of the repairman's suffering is the most problematic aspect of the story. In his discussion of post-quake magazines, Narita Ryūichi points out the way such magazines painted a universalizing picture of the disaster using the individual stories of suffering found in *jitsuwa*, but subsuming

17. Ibid., 166–67.

them into the whole. As he puts it, "The experiences of these victims become single lines in the image of the disaster. Doing so takes their singular experience [of the disaster] and treats it not as particular or distinct, but as a stereotypical frame of reference subordinate to a larger image of the earthquake."[18]

Throughout the story, the bicycle repairman is associated with two collectives—his socio-economic class and the collective of sufferers. The former could be a source of class confrontation, but the latter displaces conflict onto the more universal and politically neutral category of earthquake victim. The narrator ignores differences in vulnerability linked to class and shifts the focus to the "tens of thousands" of other unspecified and classless sufferers. In so doing, he removes the blame from socio-economic inequality. This displacement is further emphasized by the narrator's assertion of his own helplessness. By claiming to be helpless, and thereby disavowing any sort of power, the narrator distances himself from any responsibility for the suffering of the "tens of thousands."

There is a contradiction in the text between the universalizing conclusion and the detailed specificity that makes up the bulk of the story, and it is this contradiction that reveals the class anxiety present in the story. Authenticity demands that the repairman be depicted as part of a certain class, yet that specificity directs attention to the uncomfortable division between the relatively unscarred middle class and those who lived through, or died in, the worst of the disaster. "Wild Dance of the Flames" may attempt to ultimately submerge the issues of class into the less problematic category of sufferer, but a close reading of the text actually highlights class difference.

Though apparent in the initial description of the repairman, the class difference between the narrator and the man remains unspoken. Nevertheless, linguistic clues show that it is very much a part of the way they relate to each other. After initially walking past the scene, the narrator returns to ask the man for a match as a means of initiating conversation, though he is careful to note to his readers that he already had one. He uses a casual tone, marked by words that signal either that he is conscious of his superior social status or, more likely, that he wants to appear more familiar. The narrator's words could be roughly translated as:

> "Hey you, s'cuse me, but you got a light?"
> "*Nee, kimi. Shitsurei daga, kimi wa macchi wo motteiyashinaikane.*"

The man replies in a very deferential language, illustrating that despite the casual approach of the narrator he recognizes the difference between them. His reply is considerably more polite:

18. Narita Ryūichi, "Kantō daishinsai no metahisutori no tame ni: hōdō, aiwa, bidan," 72.

> "Why yes, sir. Are you going to smoke?"
> "*Anata, tabako wo o-nomi-ni narun desu ka.*"[19]

Linguistic markers of polite speech continue throughout the retelling of the tale, despite the fact that pages go by without a word from the narrator. By maintaining this deferential language, Mikihiko creates a social gap between the repairman and the narrator.

This distance is exacerbated by the difference in earthquake experience, and the magnitude of the repairman's suffering further separates him from the narrator. His story starts out with experiences not unlike those of Mikihiko. The man felt the initial shocks while on an errand for his bicycle repair business. He returned to find his shop damaged but not beyond repair, and his wife and two children uninjured. They proceeded to make themselves comfortable, taking refuge in a nearby space until a young relative came to warn them of the approaching fires.

This is where the story begins to diverge from the experiences of Mikihiko, who was able to remain in his garden through the aftershocks. The repairman's family quickly gathers important possessions and flees to the *hifukushō*, where he struggles to find a place in the shade for his children. The man then describes the relative calm and peace among the refugees, sitting down and laughing, drinking beer and eating *onigiri* (rice balls), ignorant of the shadow of impending death. Having left without many supplies, the repairman then returns to his home for a few items. He returns to the *hifukushō* as the flames are closing in. He mentions the valiant policemen trying to force people to drop their flammable belongings before entering the *hifukushō*—a reference to the *bidan*-type *jitsuwa* that lauded the noble efforts of officials. The crowd has grown, and he struggles to find his wife and family. His wife is relieved when he makes his way back, and they relax as their children play with friends from school. "Don't go far," warns their father, without knowing he has spoken his last words to them. It is at that moment that he sees the flames, so close that he can hear their crackle. This intense scene, the continuation of the *hifukushō* scene excerpted earlier, warrants being quoted at length:

> The people below the fires fled toward us like a wave. They clambered one upon the other, like mountains of people, rising up and collapsing. I could hear the cries and screams of women as the commotion drew closer. I began to fear for my children and called their names I as scrambled about. A burning hot wind arose that seared my lungs. At that moment, a nearby mountain of luggage burst into flame. I was enveloped in smoke and heat and almost instinctively took shelter behind someone close. I heard a fearful sound from the sky and whirlwinds

19. Nagata Mikihiko, *Daichi wa furū*, 147.

> arose on this side and that, tearing things up into the air and twirling them about. A bright red sheet of corrugated metal flew about like it was a sheet of paper. A flaming wardrobe was taken up, and the people standing there were lifted up in unison, flailing their arms and feet as if they were walking amid the smoke. I even saw a fully loaded cart fly through the air. As the corrugated metal came down, people in its path were cut on their faces and shoulders. I wanted to do anything I could to look for my children, but my path became a wall of fire as I was enveloped in a whirlwind. I couldn't breathe as I felt myself being lifted up. The last thing I remember is people on fire twirling around me as if they were swimming insanely in the air.
>
> When I awoke it was after nightfall. I was lying in a shallow pool of water, with my left hand and face exposed. I couldn't move and it was as if there were weights piled on my back. My eyes were hazy so I couldn't see a thing. . . . I could faintly hear voices calling out from somewhere, "Hey! Hey! Anyone alive—get up, get up!" . . . I cried out with all my strength. Then right near me was a voice saying "Hold on! Hold on in there!" I could feel the weight on me get lighter and I felt someone's arms pulling me up. Finally I could see and looked around me. I had been buried under about five burned bodies, but, aside from burns on my hand and scalp, I was unharmed. Above all else I was tormented with an unbearable thirst, so I put my lips to that pool of water, made muddy by human fat and burnt blood, and drank. As I looked about me, all I could see were mountains of bodies.[20]

The ghastly description of the man drinking from water "made muddy by human fat and burnt blood" emphasizes the extremity of his experience. This graphic tone continues through the conclusion of the man's story, as he describes searching in vain for his wife and children among the innumerable bodies. The ultimate horror of these experiences is reflected in the man's inability to finish his story, which trails off in his blank gaze toward the smoke still rising from the *hifukushō* cremations.

The story told by the man is designed to elicit a sympathetic response in the narrator (and the reader), and thus an emotional connection as a result of the chain of authenticity that the story has established. However, his extreme experiences, which Mikihiko recounts in the man's own voice, reassert the unbridgeable distance of class and suffering. The narrator recognizes this difference, and, despite his initial attempts to bridge the gap through language, he is uncomfortable with his status as a relatively well-to-do and unscathed survivor. To solicit the story from the man, the narrator had consciously lied about his own earthquake experience to represent himself as a fellow sufferer. (We know it is a lie because the narrator tells us so.) The narrator claims that he was burned out of his home in

20. Ibid., 162–63.

Kanda, a destroyed district on the border between the *yamanote* and *shitamachi*. The narrator justifies this lie because he "couldn't just casually say [he] was from the *yamanote*."[21] As a member of the privileged class, and one who escaped extreme suffering, the narrator is shown to be cognizant of the insurmountable gap between himself and the repairman.

The narrator's admission of uneasiness with his own relatively comfortable state mirrors the scene earlier in the book describing his donning the garb of a laborer for his excursion to the *hifukushō*. His reasons for dressing up are instructive: "If I hadn't dressed like that [in costume], I'd have felt so badly (*ki no doku*) for the city people who had been affected by the disaster that I wouldn't have been able to go out at all."[22] His costume reveals his discomfort and his desire not to provoke the lower classes with even a normal middle-class wardrobe. The narrator speaks as though he changes clothes out of concern for those who suffered there, but the description of the action betrays an uneasiness with his status as a member of the middle class and as a resident of the *yamanote*. The posturing of the narrator, juxtaposed with the intense experiences of the bicycle repairman, makes the narrator's minor hardships in previous chapters seem inconsequential. The man's story of suffering thus overshadows the narrator and his attempt to shift the focus to the many sufferers at the conclusion of the story. Ironically, it is Mikihiko's insistence on the identity of the repairman as not only a sufferer but a member of the lower classes that makes untenable the narrator's simple displacement of the man's experiences onto the whole.

At the conclusion of the story Nagata Mikihiko works to make this man represent the numerous sufferers of the earthquake, and thus to strip him of his individuality. This move toward the universal mirrors that of the imperial rescripts. However, the individuality and poignancy of the man's story problematizes the universal national subject posited by the rescripts. As Benedict Anderson has argued, the nation requires a shared imagination; yet class and earthquake experience show how difficult that shared imagination can be. The rescripts, and even most *jitsuwa*, attempted to make the quake a national disaster that could be shared by the entire population, but the sufferer in "Wild Dance of the Flames" has a connection with disaster that makes a shared imagination impossible. The man's story and the narrator's discomfort show that the unspoken difference in vulnerability cannot be erased completely.

The discomfort of trying to bridge the gap between survivor and victim-survivor, *yamanote* and *shitamachi*, comfortable middle class and poor working class, is readily apparent in this text. Although "In the Muddy Water," the *jitsuwa* of the Ochiai brothers in Kōdansha's *The Great Taisho Earthquake and Conflagration*,

21. Ibid., 148.
22. Ibid., 58.

portrays a similar tale of surviving the *hifukushō*, in that story the markers of class are erased and the relationships between the victim-survivor, the reporter, and the audience are undefined. Like most *jitsuwa*, "In the Muddy Water" traces the causes of suffering not to society but to nature.[23] Such *jitsuwa* depict the suffering of the lower classes, but without the anxiety shown in "Wild Dance of the Flames." Despite its problematic universalizing shift from single sufferer to the whole, "Wild Dance of the Flames" not only gives voice to the victim-survivors, but also lays bare the class anxiety felt by the author, and presumably by his audience.

* * * * *

Stories such as "Wild Dance of the Flames" reveal an attempt to address the problems presented by the earthquake. Nagata Mikihiko sought an authentic representation of earthquake experience, and he saw the need to include viewpoints and experiences other than his own. This places Mikihiko among the very few writers who actually grappled with class anxiety in the aftermath of the earthquake. However, in exploring issues of class and victimhood, Mikihiko also perceived the threat of these narratives to the universality of the earthquake experience. That is, he perceived their threat to the homogenous imagined national community, as idealized by the state. Though the narrator of "Wild Dance of the Flames" tries to displace that threat by universalizing the sufferer and offering the repairman a bit of money as he goes on his way, in the end these gestures do not hide the class difference palpable in the narrative. It was perhaps Mikihiko's moral and literary ethics that made this story what it is. No matter the cause, "Wild Dance of the Flames" offers crucial insights into how those on one side of the city viewed the experiences of those on the other.

23. Franco Moretti has explored this idea in his study of Italian melodramas. See Moretti, "Kindergarten," translated by David Forgacs in *Signs Taken for Wonders: Essays in the Sociology of Literary Forms* (London; New York: Verso, 1988), 181.

Chapter 7

Divine Retribution and Its Critics

Soon after the March 11, 2011 earthquake and tsunami hit northeastern Japan, Ishihara Shintarō, then governor of Tokyo, said: "Japanese people have become selfish. Politics are overly enamored with populism. We must use the tsunami to wash away selfishness, the grime that has accumulated on the hearts of the Japanese over these last few years. I think this is divine punishment (*tenbatsu*), but I feel sorry for the disaster victims."[1] With this statement, Ishihara invoked a long history of statements linking the movements of Heaven and Earth to human actions. At the same time, Ishihara's use of the term "divine punishment" descends directly from a modern discourse that arose after the 1923 Great Kanto Earthquake. In this particular usage, the disaster becomes a punishment for national degeneracy.

Human beings have long interpreted natural phenomena as "signs from Heaven." Throughout much of China's history, people thought that disasters presaged a shift in the Mandate of Heaven. This idea was perhaps best articulated by the Han-era Confucian philosopher Dong Zhongshu: "If the ruler expresses his four emotions in accord with moral principles, then the world will be well governed, but if not, the age will be chaotic."[2] For Dong, any instability in the realm, natural or not, reflected a moral instability in the emperor. There are countless examples of natural phenomena interpreted in such a way as to affect politics. Wolfram Eberhard

1.. "Ishihara Chiji 'Tsunami wa tenbatsu, gayoku wo arai otosu hitsuyō,'" *Yomiuri shinbun* March 15, 2011 <<http://www.yomiuri.co.jp/politics/news/20110314-OYT1T00740.htm>> (accessed August 1, 2013). For English, see *Kyodo News*, "Ishihara apologizes for 'divine punishment' remark," *Japan Times* March 15, 2011 <http://search.japantimes.co.jp/cgi-bin/nn20110315x7.html> (accessed January 17, 2012).

2. Dong Zhongshu lived second century BCE. Patricia Buckley Ebrey, ed., *Chinese Civilization: A Sourcebook* (New York: Free Press, 1993), 59. For more on Chinese interpretations of natural phenomena, see Wolfram Eberhard, "The Political Function of Astronomy and Astronomers in Han China," in *Chinese Thought and Institutions*, ed. John K. Fairbank (Chicago: University of Chicago Press, 1957); Donald J. Munro, *The Concept of Man in Early China* (Stanford, CA: Stanford University Press, 1969); and Joseph Needham, "Seismology," in idem, *Science and Civilisation in China*, vol. 3 (1954): 624–35. At the same time, there is another more "rational" trend in Chinese thought, discussed by Charles Hammond in his article, "The Interpretation of Thunder," *The Journal of Asian Studies* 53 (1994–05–01): 487–503.

relates an occasion when one Han-era faction was saved from prison and brought back into power because of an earthquake, only to lose power again after another.[3]

In another cultural tradition, the Hebrew Bible tells of Sodom and Gomorrah, which were destroyed by fire due to God's judgment. To cite a more recent example, many interpreted the Lisbon earthquake of 1755 as God's wrath meted out to sinners. In one sermon Lisbon was faulted as "greedy, devoted to material wealth, immoral, licentious, and irreverent."[4] In this case, religious leaders felt the population should return to God to avoid further destruction.

Though both Western and Chinese traditions ascribe disasters to supernatural forces responding to human actions, these two ideas of heavenly punishment are different. On the one hand, in the Confucian idea of the Mandate of Heaven, disaster shows corruption of the government. On the other, in the Judeo-Christian tradition, heavenly punishment stems from the sins of the people.

In the heavenly punishment discourse following the Great Kanto Earthquake, no blame fell to the government or the emperor (at least none that made it past the censors). Rather, in popular discourse appearing in newspapers and magazines, blame was placed squarely on the Japanese people. It was as if the Judeo-Christian idea of a sinning populace was combined with conservative Japanese Confucian morality. The result is a discourse on heavenly punishment that looks remarkably similar to the clergy's condemnation of eighteenth-century Lisbon. Ten days after the Great Kanto Earthquake, industrialist Shibusawa Eiichi, one of the foremost apologists for heavenly punishment, was quoted as saying that Tokyo's moral laxity made it ripe for a punishment from heaven, or *tenken*.[5] The idea was soon sanctioned in official government pronouncements that sought to mobilize the people toward rebuilding by distributing the responsibility among them.

The idea of divine punishment following the 1923 disaster was not limited to discussions among elites, but reached into the realm of popular culture. Many films and books treated the idea in some way or another, most often in the guise of an attack on materialism, excesses of which were commonly blamed for the disaster in essays on the subject. Contemporary authors also played a crucial role in *tenken* discourse. Some authors lent their voices to the choir calling for repentance. Other authors were themselves considered to be both causes and symptoms of the trend toward depravity. And there were still other writers who critiqued the very idea of divine punishment as both illogical and inhumane, much as Voltaire

3. The faction in question was that of Liu Xiang. See Wolfram Eberhard, "The Political Function of Astronomy and Astronomers in Han China," 53. Similar stories can be found in accounts of Ming- and Qing-era politics.

4. Thomas D. Kendrick, *The Lisbon Earthquake* (Philadelphia: Lippincott, 1957), 123.

5. This excerpt originally ran in the *Hokkai Times* on September 11, 1923. It is quoted in Hori Shin, "Kantō daishinsai to tenkenron: Shibusawa Eiichi wo chūshin ni," in *Rekishi to bungaku: Kantō daishinsai* (Kyōritsu Joshi Daigaku Sōgō Bunka Kenkyūjo Kanda Bunshitsu, 2004), 133–34.

did after the 1755 Lisbon quake.[6] This chapter follows the idea of divine punishment as it appeared across various iterations, in government discourse and popular culture and the vigorous critique of the idea from authors.

Divine Punishment Discourse

Public discourse in Taishō Japan was largely grounded in a post-Enlightenment rational worldview, and most did not believe that "the heavens" were actually responsible for the 1923 earthquake. Nevertheless, the disaster was seen as an ideal opportunity to critique the status quo from a variety of rational and supernatural directions. The basic idea behind the divine punishment or *tenken* discourse—seen in countless articles by government officials, priests, businessmen, reporters, writers, and artists—is that the earthquake punished Japan from straying from a path of Confucian morality and served as a warning for the people to correct their ways. The reasons cited for the punishment are as diverse as the people expounding it, yet they seem to congeal around two related and often conflated faults: lax morality and materialism.

Historian Charles Schencking has collected examples of this line of thinking from a wide array of prominent figures: General Ugaki Kazushige, philosopher Fukusaku Yasubumi, Home Ministry bureaucrat Suematsu Kaiichirō, and Keio University economics professor Horie Kiichi.[7] The name most often associated with the divine punishment or *tenken* philosophy after the earthquake, however,

6. In a poem written not long after the disaster Voltaire wrote:

> To those expiring murmurs of distress,
> To that appalling spectacle of woe,
> Will ye reply: "You do but illustrate
> The iron laws that chain the will of God"?
> Say ye, o'er that yet quivering mass of flesh:
> "God is avenged: the wage of sin is death"?
> What crime, what sin, had those young hearts conceived
> That lie, bleeding and torn, on mother's breast?
> Did fallen Lisbon deeper drink of vice
> Than London, Paris, or sunlit Madrid?

For the complete poem see: Voltaire, "Poem on the Lisbon Disaster: Or an Examination of the Axiom, 'All is Well,'" in idem, *Toleration and Other Essays by Voltaire* (1912).

7. The best overview of the *tenken* discourse in English is J. Charles Schencking's article "The Great Kanto Earthquake and the Culture of Catastrophe and Reconstruction in 1920s Japan," *The Journal of Japanese Studies* 34, no. 2 (2008): 295–331, found in a revised form in his book *The Great Kanto Earthquake and the Chimera of National Reconstruction in Japan.* Gregory Clancey and Orihara Minami also discuss *tenken* in their article "The Nature of Emergency: The Great Kanto Earthquake and the Crisis of Reason in Late Imperial Japan," *Science in Context* 25, no. 1 (2012): 103–26, especially 111–16. In Japanese, Hiroi Osamu offers a survey in his book, *Saigai to Nihonjin.* Others who supported the *tenken* idea include the architect Itō Chūta, the poet Kitahara Hakushū, and Masuda Giichi, editor-in-chief of the business magazine *Jitsugyō no Nihon.*

was that of industrialist Shibusawa Eiichi. In his discussions of heavenly punishment across several essays, Shibusawa, a member of the government's reconstruction committee, expressed his concern about the spiritual as well as the physical reconstruction of Japan.

Shibusawa first introduced the idea in an article published in the *Hokkai Times* a mere ten days after the earthquake. In it, Shibusawa is quoted as saying: "Though this was a natural disaster (*tensai*), one could also say it was a divine punishment (*tenken*). The tendency in Tokyo lately has been like a demon of chaos, normalcy has fallen by the wayside, morals have deteriorated from laxity, the five filial relationships of Confucius can no longer be seen, and immorality is rampant. Conditions were truly ripe to meet with divine punishment."[8] Shibusawa does not expound on the precise reasons the heavens decided to unleash the destruction, even in his later essays. Rather, he claims that the reason for this heavenly action is a prevailing moral laxity and rejection of Confucian virtues. Though nuances changed slightly in the other iterations of his theory, the central ideas remain constant—namely, that the disaster was in response to degeneracy among the people and that a return to moral fortitude would be necessary for rebuilding.

Shibusawa's brand of divine punishment discourse soon found its way into the second imperial rescript on "Strengthening the National Spirit," which drew upon similar rhetoric.[9] The initial imperial rescript, issued the week after the quake, emphasized the natural cause of the disaster, but by the time the second rescript was announced in November, more than two months later, heavenly punishment had become the dominant conservative theme and Shibusawa had become a prominent member of the reconstruction committee: "In recent years much progress has been made in science and human wisdom. At the same time, frivolous and extravagant habits have set in, and even rash and extreme tendencies are not unknown. If these habits and tendencies are not checked now, the future of the country, we fear, is dark, the disaster which befell the Japanese nation being very severe."[10]

The rescript particularly shows the influence of Shibusawa, who called for a moral rebuilding in conjunction with the physical one. Though the "frivolous and extravagant habits" are not mentioned by name, a link between national decadence and the disaster is implied by the assertion that the future of the country

8. Quoted in Hori Shin, "Kantō daishinsai to tenkenron," 133–34. A similar sentiment ran in the September 13, 1923 edition of *Yorozu chōhō*, quoted in ibid., 134. In that version Shibusawa uses the love suicide of Arishima Takeo and his lover Hatano Akiko earlier that year as evidence of widespread moral degeneracy. Another, less specific version from the September 11, 1923 evening edition of *Yorozu chōhō* is collected in Kŭm Pyŏng-dong, *Chōsenjin gyakusatsu ni kansuru chishikijin no hannō*, 85.

9. This is my translation of the rescript title, "Kokumin seishin no sakkō no shōsho."

10. Fujisawa Morihiko and Bureau of Social Affairs Home Office, *Great Earthquake of 1923*, frontispiece.

rests on reversing the moral decay. As Shibusawa put it, "We must not be satisfied with rebuilding the physical infrastructure, but rather there is a great need to consider our spiritual state (*seishin*)."[11] By incorporating *tenken* into this rescript, heavenly punishment became the national discourse on the earthquake, and it endeavored to put the nation on a unified path toward state-sanctioned morality.

While Shibusawa and the rescript were vague about the actual causes of the divine punishment, other critics spelled out their problems with the state of Japanese morality with great clarity. Ironically, one of the more vitriolic attacks on popular depravity came from *Shinseinen*, the magazine that would itself become a byword for decadence later in the 1920s. In its first post-quake issue, the magazine published an article by army colonel Tadokoro Shigeyasu, a regular columnist for the magazine, praising the role of the earthquake in opening Japan's eyes to its own moral degeneracy. Tadokoro distributes the blame evenly throughout society:

> There is a spirit of falsehood, vanity, deception, laziness, meanness, unrighteousness, and immorality. Politicians sell the nation for their own profit. Scholars, priests, and educators do nothing but self-promotion, thinking nothing of how it affects the country. Capitalists overindulge in debauchery while laborers are reckless, and both forget the honor in their divine role. The intellectual world is in confusion and has forgotten its sense of direction. If there is anyone who praises Confucian morality, they are derided as behind the times. If there is anyone who happens to speak of honor, they are derided as being narrow-minded. There are even some modern people whose immorality knows no depths. They seduce wives and assault virgins, knowing no shame, but rather announce their depravity with pride, prattling that romantic love is the pinnacle of life.[12]

Barring the emperor and the military—presumably bastions of virtue for this soldier—hardly any aspect of Taishō Japan was spared in Tadokoro's tirade. In fact it is likely that Tadokoro's criticism of the government, not merely politicians, was equally scathing, as large sections of the essay were censored.

Though Tadokoro was particularly broad in his critique, several ideas emerge that are common among many who discussed the issue: first and foremost is the reference to Confucian morality that Tadokoro shares with Shibusawa; second is the focus on selfishness and vanity that he sees plaguing politicians, intellectuals, capitalists, and laborers alike; and third is the specific mention of sexual immorality in a veiled reference to authors who were advertising their antics in I-novels. The cure for all of these social ills for Tadokoro—as well as for Shibusawa and

11. Originally from Shibusawa's essay "Ryoritsu shigatai futatsu no jōken," published in the October 1923 issue of *Gendai*, quoted in Hori Shin, "Kantō daishinsai to tenkenron," 136.
12. Tadokoro Shigeyasu, "Tenken no moto ni hirefu shite," *Shin-seinen* 4, no. 12 (October 1923): 4.

the imperial rescript—is a return to "traditional" morality that is imagined to predate modernity. In his conclusion Tadokoro states: "We might think that it is cruel to call this punishment from heaven, but if we look carefully at ourselves, we must be grateful that this was the reward for our sins. . . . Thanks to the great compassion of this heavenly punishment, we have, at least for the moment, returned to the diligent characteristics of the people of old."[13]

Christian thinker Uchimura Kanzō, one of the few literal interpreters of the disaster as divine punishment, similarly saw the earthquake as compassionate punishment. As early as September 5, he wrote in his diary that he felt "as if an angel had brought down his sword against the entire city in judgment. But I believe this was a benevolent judgment."[14] Uchimura developed the idea in an essay for *Shufu no tomo* that directly referenced Shibusawa. After a quote from Isaiah, Uchimura adapted the chapter and verse to Tokyo: "Ah, sinful nation, a people laden with iniquity, a seed of evildoers, look at the Diet and the city council. Look at the theaters and the department stores and the frivolous men and women who frequent them. Look at the literati and intellectuals they worship, and the magazines and newspapers that encourage them. If this is Japan, then I would be embarrassed to have been born here. Japan before the earthquake, especially Tokyo, was the kind of place in which the righteous could not endure."[15] Continuing his moralistic crusade in his monthly Bible study column, Uchimura compared Tokyo to Sodom and Gomorrah: "Pre-quake Tokyo may not have been as depraved as Sodom, but it is undeniable that it was heading that way."[16] Though "frivolity" was a catchphrase he used as well, for Uchimura the sins of the people of Tokyo were mostly those of sexual immorality—the focus of his discussion on Sodom and Gomorrah—and he saw authors as particularly to blame for Tokyo's debauchery.

As Tadokoro and Uchimura's insinuations suggest, authors were often implicated in the heavenly punishment discourse, both as symptomatic of decadence and as tempters who lured others into sin. Uchimura directs much of the anger in his essays against "literati and intellectuals," whom he blames for spreading immorality. Authors had long been viewed disapprovingly by those charged with fortifying state morality, but there had been a recent scandal that kept them at the forefront of any

13. Ibid., 10.

14. Quoted in Hori Shin, "Kantō daishinsai to tenkenron," 153, note 11. The idea of a benevolent punishment seems out of place with Chinese thought on the matter and is probably a Christian import. Other, non-Christian thinkers also called the punishment benevolent. Colonel Tadokoro is one example.

15. Uchimura Kanzō, "Tensai to tenbatsu oyobi tenkei," in *Uchimura Kanzō zenshū*, vol. 28 (1983): 18; originally in the October 1923 issue of *Shufu no tomo* (vol. 7 no. 10). Uchimura references Isaiah 1:4–6.

16. Uchimura Kanzō, "Sodomu to Gomora no fukumetsu," in *Uchimura Kanzō zenshū*, vol. 28 (1983): 54; originally in the November 10, 1923 issue of *Seisho no kenkyū* (no. 280).

discussion on immorality.[17] This was the love-suicide of Arishima Takeo.

In July 1923, less than two months before the earthquake, Arishima Takeo's body was discovered in his mountain villa, alongside that of his lover, the married *Fujin kōron* editor Hatano Akiko. Their affair had been a messy and public one, and their deaths only compounded conservative disapproval of their actions. After the earthquake, critics singled out Arishima's suicide as a particular symptom of degeneracy linked to *tenken*. The "Arishima Incident" was mentioned specifically by Shibusawa Eiichi in the *Yorozu chōhō* as proof of Japan's decadence, and this scandal is likely the context for Colonel Tadokoro's condemnation of people who "seduce wives" and "announce their depravity with pride."[18]

Uchimura's harsh focus on authors, however, stemmed from a much more personal betrayal. Arishima had been a disciple of Uchimura in his younger years, but Arishima's public rejection of his faith in Christianity had brought about an equally public falling out between them. After Arishima's affair and subsequent love-suicide with Hatano Akiko, Uchimura was vocal in his condemnation of Arishima and all who supported him. Both Uchimura and Tadokoro specifically mention "romantic love," or *ren'ai*, as false morality. For them, authors such as Arishima, who championed romantic love in their works, thus became proof of Japan's decadence.

We can see Uchimura beating at Arishima's ghost in his comparison of Tokyo to Sodom. After citing a scriptural passage about the sins of selfishness and slandering the sacred, Uchimura wrote: "Those people called literati (*bunshi*) are particularly bold in breaking conventions. They are selfish and put their own ideas above everything else. Should anyone oppose such men, they are derided as outdated and oppressive. They do not particularly fear slandering the sacred, in other words, God. And many of them are apostates."[19] Though the reference to selfishness and breaking conventions might arguably apply to several authors active at the time (especially those writing I-novels), the reference to apostates specifically links the invective to Arishima.

While lax morality and sexual impropriety were targets for some proponents of *tenken* discourse, most commentators mentioned their corollary, materialism, in some form or another.[20] The complaint that Japan had become overly materialistic

17. See, for example, Jay Rubin's discussion of Meiji-era literary censorship in his *Injurious to Public Morals: Writers and the Meiji State* (Seattle: University of Washington Press, 1984).

18. Tadokoro Shigeyasu, "Tenken no moto ni hirefu shite," 4. Shibusawa's reference to the Arishima Incident was in the September 13, 1923 issue, quoted in Hori Shin, "Kantō daishinsai to tenkenron," 134. He wrote, "Our morals have become so degenerate that we sing the praises of the Arishima Incident. This disaster was by no means a chance occurrence."

19. Uchimura Kanzō, "Sodomu to Gomora no fukumetsu," 54. Uchimura gives no citation, and I have been unable to track down the scriptural passage that precedes this quote.

20. Schencking cites Fukasaku Yasubumi, who included "sexual slackness" in his list of traits that brought on the disaster. Schencking, "The Great Kanto Earthquake and the Culture of Catastrophe," 304. Most of the critics Schencking cites, even Fukasaku, focus their attacks on Japan's rampant materialism.

was cited by almost all critics expounding on divine punishment. In several versions of his *tenken* theory, Shibusawa decries the "audacious luxury" of the current "*nouveau riche* age"; Colonel Tadokoro singles out vanity among his list of moral failings; and the rescript mentions "frivolous and extravagant habits."[21] Materialism was the primary focus of all the critics whom Charles Schencking cites as emblematic of this discourse.

The few authors who discussed the disaster as a divine reckoning also concentrated on materialism. In his essay published in the October 1923 edition of *Kaizō*, I-novelist Chikamatsu Shūkō wrote, "No one would contest the fact that we Japanese, drunk on our own repeated successes and good fortune, have recently fallen into useless luxurious self indulgence. . . . Abundance leads to immorality. Just as lack leads to unhappiness, so too does wealth."[22] This is particularly surprising coming from an author whose literary career had been built on showcasing his own sexual desire for both a wife who left him and an Ōsaka prostitute.[23] Yet the immorality Shūkō mentions is not the sexual immorality that Uchimura and Tadokoro refer to, but an immorality based on excess materialism, "useless, luxurious, self indulgence."

Expressing a similar sentiment and using similar imagery, the author Uchida Roan (1868–1929) wrote in *Taiyō* that, rather than divine punishment, the disaster was "divine assistance that will help save us from the hangover of the *nouveau riche*."[24] Nagai Kafū (1879–1959) also addressed the perceived greed in his diary more than a month after the disaster: "When one looks back on the general arrogance, the limitless greed, one cannot but think of the disaster as divine punishment."[25] Even the left-leaning writer Akita Ujaku took the earthquake as an opportunity to critique the excesses of capitalism. In a poem entitled "Capital of Death" ("Shi no miyako"), Ujaku wrote:

> War victories continued.
> Wealth gained.
> The drive for conquest sated.
> They gave no thought to the lives of people
> or the joys of human harmony.

21. These terms appear in Shibusawa's writing as quoted in Hori Shin, "Kantō daishinsai to tenkenron," 134, 137. See also Tadokoro Shigeyasu, "Tenken no moto ni hirefu shite," 4, and Fujisawa Morihiko and Bureau of Social Affairs Home Office, *Great Earthquake of 1923*, frontispiece.
22. Chikamatsu Shūkō, "Tensai ni arazu tenken to omoe," *Kaizō* 5, no. 10 (October 1923): 217.
23. For more on Chikamatsu Shūkō, see Edward Fowler, *Rhetoric of Confession*, especially chapter 7. In a 1916 essay, Akagi Kōhei linked Shūkō with several other writers whom he saw as immoral, little better than those who produced pornographic books. Akagi Kōhei, "Yūtō bungaku," 263.
24. Uchida Rōan, "Daihakai to fukkō," *Taiyō* 29, no. 12 (October 1923): 73.
25. Edward Seidensticker, *Kafū the Scribbler: The Life and Writings of Nagai Kafū, 1879–1959* (Ann Arbor: University of Michigan, Center for Japanese Studies, 1990), 108; first published by Stanford University Press in 1965.

> They only wanted to gain more for themselves.
> They built a morality of oppression and greed
> upon a foundation of free-market philosophy.[26]

In this excerpt, Ujaku shares some of the rhetoric of the conservative critics such as Shibusawa. Both discuss "wealth" and "greed" and a lack of attention to "human harmony." Nevertheless, rather than a call for renewed attention to the Confucian morality of the emperor, Ujaku called for an end to imperial expansion and capitalist greed. That the socialist Akita Ujaku and the conservative wealthy businessman Shibusawa could share a common target in the audacious display of wealth by the *nouveau riche* shows the extent of the anti-luxury discourse in post-quake Japan. This broad critique found expression in the popular films of the day as well.

Anti-Materialism in Popular Melodrama

The film industry was a relative newcomer to popular culture, and the medium of film was struggling for acceptance both as an art form and as something worthwhile in the eyes of the state. Hence it is not surprising that the film industry allied itself with conservative discourse. Of the eleven fictional films made about the quake in 1923, about half depicted the earthquake as an awakening for those who had been "infected" with materialism in the heady years leading up to the disaster. Some, such as the Shōchiku studio's *Facing Death* (*Shi ni men shite*), directed by Ōkubo Tadamoto, did so subtly (see Chapter 4). Though the unfortunate characters in this film could hardly be considered overly materialistic, the hardships borne by the daughter were caused by the father's concern for his money. The happy ending includes the father giving up his money to help those less fortunate than himself. In Mizoguchi Kenji's earthquake film *Amid the Ruins* (*Haikyo no naka*), also not extant, the message was more specifically targeted at the affluent. *Amid the Ruins* was about a woman who had grown dissatisfied by her overly materialistic existence with her wealthy husband. While looking for her husband after the earthquake, she finds an old beau who shows her what a simpler life could have been.[27] Other films specifically targeted the wealthy in attacks that are closely aligned with the heavenly punishment discourse.

The film *Two Minutes to Noon* (or *11:58*, the time of the initial Kanto earthquake, also no longer extant) drew specifically upon critiques of luxury

26. Akita Ujaku, "Shi no miyako," *Bunshō kurabu* 8, no. 10 (October 1923): 37. For a brief discussion of authors' contributions to divine punishment discourse, including Akita Ujaku, see Takematsu Yoshiaki, "Metsubō suru teito."

27. Anonymous, "Haikyo no naka," *Katsudō zasshi* 10, no. 8 (August 1924): 138. See also Dudley Andrew and Paul Andrew, *Kenji Mizoguchi: A Guide to References and Resources* (Boston: G. K. Hall, 1981), 47.

following the quake. *Two Minutes to Noon* depicted an affluent housewife shaken out of her worldly lifestyle. In a scene noted by reviewers, she appears at a relief meeting in her finery, only to be embarrassed by the contrast with everyone else, who had dressed simply, either out of respect or necessity.[28] This scene especially reinforced the anti-luxury discourse of Keio economics professor Horie Kiichi, reformer Abe Isō, and Chikamatsu Shūkō, among others. As Charles Schencking has pointed out, Abe even praised Japan Women's University for banning "wasteful Western-style clothing" after the disaster.[29] Chikamatsu Shūkō, like Abe, also called for the complete banishment of "useless luxury goods and vain decorations," singling out diamonds and silk kimonos.[30]

Though all these films reflected the trend against materialism and luxury in heavenly punishment discourse, two films explicitly invoked the *tenken* idea. The first, *The Direction of the Flames* (*Honoo no yukue*), from the Shōchiku studios, included a prophet character who appears before the disaster calling for the world to change its ways or face the punishment of Heaven. The second, a Nikkatsu film directed by Suzuki Kensaku, entitled *The Earth Shakes* (*Daichi wa yuragu*), reworked a Hollywood movie to depict an upper-class family who refuse to heed the warning provided by the disaster.

The Direction of the Flames was based on a novel serialized in the *Osaka Asahi shinbun* about a couple whose future together is jeopardized by the greed of a father. Everything is resolved after the earthquake, when they realize that some things are more important than money. Though the general theme of the story is an oft-repeated trademark of romantic films, the film explicitly invokes heavenly punishment discourse in the figure of a prophet who calls for repentance before the disaster. It is difficult to determine how large a role the prophet played without access to the film itself. Nevertheless, in the *Kinema Junpō* review of the film, the prophet (played by Okada Sōtarō) is third on the list of cast members. Furthermore, the serialized novel hints at how he may have appeared in the film.

The novel begins with the prosperous Dōzawa family commenting on a prophet talking to a crowd outside their home. His sermon, though set before the earthquake, resembles the post-quake heavenly punishment discourse: "Beware, and keep your pride in check. Do you think your duty to the gods is merely to wear beautiful kimono, eat rich foods, and live in gaudy palaces? Something dreadful will come of it. When the world is touched by Heaven's anger, it will be turned upside down." This phrase would have clearly signaled the recent earthquake to the readers of the novel. The patriarch of the family, Dōzawa Keigorō,

28. Reviews of the film *Two Minutes to Noon* are found in Anonymous, "Jūichiji gojūhappun," *Kinema junpō* 147 (January 1, 1924): 20, and Anonymous, "Jūichiji gojūhappun," *Katsdō zasshi* 10, no. 2 (February 1924): 95.

29. J. Charles Schencking, "The Great Kanto Earthquake and the Culture of Catastrophe," 312.

30. Chikamatsu Shūkō, "Tensai ni arazu tenken to omoe," 219.

agrees: "He speaks the truth. . . . Those who grow too prideful will incur Heaven's wrath—no, Heaven's punishment."[31] In the world of *The Direction of the Flames*, even the wealthy, it would seem, recognized the excesses of late Taishō-era Japan.

Although it is difficult to ascertain how the *tenken,* or heavenly punishment, idea appeared in the film version of *The Direction of the Flames*, evidence suggests Nikkatsu's *The Earth Shakes*, released in October 1923, was particularly influenced by heavenly punishment discourse. Though the Nikkatsu Mukojima studio (located just northeast of Honjo ward) was damaged and most subsequent production shifted to Kyoto, this film was shot amid the ruins of Tokyo.[32] An on-location photo emphasizing this fact ran in the November1923 issue of the *Nikkatsu gahō* (*Nikkatsu Illustrated*). It featured Suzuki Kensaku directing two of his actresses, with burned-out trees, rubble, and a few curious onlookers in the background (see fig. 13). This connection to the real helped underscore the film's moral message.

The Earth Shakes takes its premise from the 1919 Cecil B. DeMille melodrama *Male and Female*.[33] In *Male and Female*, a rich family must survive on a deserted island with help from their butler; in the Nikkatsu remake, the situation is changed to post-quake Tokyo. As its title implies, the DeMille film takes its drama from the interaction between the sexes, especially the love between the butler and the daughter of the wealthy family. Based on paratextual evidence, the love-interest aspect in *The Earth Shakes* was muted and the film instead focused primarily on the social reversal brought about by the earthquake and the concomitant opportunities for education and reform in response to a disaster of that magnitude. Ultimately, it was about the perils of extravagance and the pleasures of the simple life.

Like *Male and Female*, *The Earth Shakes* opens with images of the aristocratic family, the Kurauchis, emphasizing their wealth and idleness. According to the summary printed in the *Nikkatsu gahō* magazine, the patriarch, played by Yamamoto Kiichi, "has a keen sense of class-consciousness."[34] His three daughters "change their outfits both morning and night," as just one example of the lives of profligacy they lead.[35] This detail about the clothing not only

31. Tachibana Sueo, *Honoo no yukue* (Osaka: Seibunkan Shoten, 1923), 6–7.
32. The film *The Earth Shakes* (*Daichi wa yuragu*) debuted in October 1923, but was being advertised as late as May 1924 in an Asakusa theater.
33. The connection between the films *The Earth Shakes* and *Male and Female* was pointed out in Peter High, "Japanese Film and the Great Kanto Earthquake of 1923," *Kokusai kankei gakubu kiyō* 31 (1985): 80. DeMille's film was in turn an adaptation of J. M. Barrie's play *The Admirable Mr. Crichton*, which may have been inspired by a German play by Ludwig Fulda called *Robinsons Eiland.* See Arthur Walkley, *Drama and Life* (New York: Bretano's, 1908), 198.
34. Anonymous, "Daichi wa yuragu," *Nikkatsu gahō* 1, no. 5 (November 1923): 40.
35. Ibid., 41.

Fig. 13. Location photo from the filming of *The Earth Shakes*. *Nikkatsu gahō* (November 1923).

points to their wastefulness but calls attention to the importance of clothing in discourses criticizing the wealthy, a fact also seen in *Two Minutes to Noon*. As further evidence of their extravagance, the Kurauchi family has many servants in their household.[36] The film focuses on one of these servants, the cook, Yūzō, who is simply happy with his lot in life despite working from dawn to dusk. In strong contrast to the family, Yūzō is described in the summary as "pious toward nature and full of common courtesy."

The audience's interpretation of the film as a *tenken* allegory is not left to chance. The name Kurauchi itself implies both wealth and insularity—the *kura* character means "storehouse" or "treasury," and the *uchi* means "within." In other words, they are living in a storehouse full of wealth without a concern for the outside world. The summary in the Nikkatsu fan magazine describes the Kurauchis as not only extravagant but "absorbed in the dream of prosperity, *just as if representing Japan*" (emphasis added).[37] By equating the Kurauchis with Japan, the anonymous author of the summary makes the allegory explicit: This is a story about what Japan was like before the earthquake, and what Japan must do to survive the subsequent tribulation.

As if to make the link to *tenken* discourse even more explicit, when the earthquake strikes, the summary simply says, "One day, heavenly punishment (*tenken*) arrives." The Kurauchi family, coddled by their wealth, must rely on their kind

36. Four are credited.
37. Ibid., 40.

cook. Yūzō helps them deal with their new situation by gathering food and making a shelter. Despite the change in circumstance, the patriarch of the family remains firm in his ideas of class and propriety. A contemporary reviewer praised the actor Yamamoto Kiichi for his depiction of Kurauchi Kanzō as a man who "retained his strong class-consciousness even in a disaster."[38] A still included in the November 1923 issue of *Nikkatsu gahō* supports the reviewer's assessment. In it, the actor Yamamoto sits eating a rice ball while being waited upon by a servant, keeping up Kurauchi Kanzō's image of propriety despite being incongruously surrounded by rubble. Though Yamamoto was praised for his acting skills, the character of Kurauchi Kanzō was certainly not seen as an ideal, and the incongruity seems to have been played for humor (see fig. 14).

In contrast to the humorous persistence of her father, the youngest daughter Ranko, played by Mizuki Kyōko, adapts to her surroundings and finds joy in the menial labor necessary for survival. This she does under the kind tutelage of the cook, Yūzō (see fig. 15). Once Ranko begins to repent of her materialism and starts to work, she is rewarded by a new sense of accomplishment. As the summary tells us, "Compared to the boredom of idling away her time, she clearly felt the exhilaration that came welling up from sweat and toil." The rest of the family does not fare so well. As a whole, they follow the father and refuse to let go of their aristocratic ways. Finally, in the words of the summary, they leave the ruins, "without realizing that they were the rotting corpses of a society clinging to its own emptiness on a ghostly carriage of death."[39] The bold metaphor condemns the Kurauchi family, along with the other decadent citizens of Japan.

The message is clear—the nation needs people unsullied by urban materialism, such as Yūzō, or repentant urbanites, such as Ranko, who are willing to work toward recovery. Should Japan desire to avoid a ride on a "ghostly carriage of death," it must follow the trajectory of Ranko by recognizing the error of its ways and returning to the exhilaration that arises from "sweat and toil." *The Earth Shakes* and other post-quake films that criticize urban materialism saw the disaster as a corrective force that led back to morality and simplicity. In this, they shared much with critics such as Shibusawa and Uchimura.

Critiquing the *Tenken* Idea

Though many voices expounded on various aspects of the *tenken* idea, there were also many who criticized it. The editor and humorist Miyake Gaikotsu called the very idea "barbaric."[40] One of the most direct critiques came from Kikuchi Kan,

38. Anonymous review, "Daichi wa yuragu," *Katsudō zasshi* 10, no. 8 (August 1924): 139.

39. Anonymous, "Daichi wa yuragu (*Nikkatsu gahō*)," 42.

40. Miyake Gaikotsu, "Tenpenchii wo dōtokuteki ni kaisuru wa yaban shisō nari," *Shinsai gahō* 3 (November 1923): 41. Hori Shin has a list of critiques of Shibusawa in his notes. See Hori Shin, "Kantō daishinsai to tenkenron," 155, note 31.

Fig. 14. Still from *The Earth Shakes* depicting Yamamoto Kaichi as Kurauchi Kanzō being waited upon by a servant amid the ruins. *Nikkatsu gahō* (November 1923).

in a short essay for the October 1923 issue of the magazine *Kaizō*, worth quoting in full:

> I saw the huge destructive power of nature. I learned that nature cares nothing for humanity. I learned that it is nonsense to believe in an entity who protects or rebukes us. If the earthquake is a heavenly punishment, as Shibusawa Eiichi suggests, then several people who should have been killed are still living. In fact, if he sat and thought about the fact that he survived, Shibusawa could not think this to be a heavenly punishment. Before nature there are no good people or bad people, just chaos. We have no choice but to remain in awe at the powerlessness of humanity. Not to recognize the violent power of nature is merely humanity's poor excuse for its weakness.[41]

Here Kikuchi scoffs at the idea that nature could be influenced by the actions of humanity. To ascribe meaning to the whims of nature ignores its indiscriminate violence. Kikuchi's final sentence suggests that to see this violent disaster as a response to human actions ascribes to humanity more power than it has.

41. Kikuchi Kan, "Saigo zakkan," *Kaizō* 5, no. 10 (October 1923): 228. In the original, the German word *ohnmacht* is the gloss attached to the characters for "powerlessness" in Japanese, *muryoku*.

Fig. 15. Still from *The Earth Shakes* depicting Mizuki Kyōko as Ranko and Kuzuki Kōichi as Yūzō. *Katsudō zasshi* (January 1924).

Akutagawa's response in the same issue of *Kaizō* similarly highlights nature's indifference to humanity and the unfair distribution of damage, and thus the impossibility of imagining the disaster as punishment:

> Viscount Shibusawa has said that we should think of this earthquake as a heavenly punishment. There is surely no one who remains unscathed

> by this disaster. . . . Looking upon the deaths of his own wife and child, and then to others whose houses remain undamaged, who would not be surprised at the injustice of the heavenly punishment? It is better to forgo belief in heavenly punishment altogether than to believe in a partial heavenly punishment. We should recognize nature's cruel indifference to us humans.
>
> Nature is cruelly indifferent toward humanity. The earthquake did not differentiate between proletarian and bourgeoisie, the good and the bad. It is just as Turgenev wrote in his poems: in the eyes of nature, humans are no different from insects.[42]

Both authors critique Shibusawa by appealing to a scientific view of nature as a force divorced from human will or actions. Curiously, Akutagawa appeals not to famous scientists and philosophers of the Enlightenment but to Turgenev, a writer. His is a rational argument laced with lyricism.

A post-Enlightenment, science-based worldview was the standard in Taishō-era Japan. Though science and superstition can coexist, Shibusawa's argument did not depend on an actual scientific or supernatural connection between the degeneracy of Japan and the earthquake. Rather, he used divine punishment as a means to modify the moral trajectory of the nation. As Hori Shin points out, Shibusawa changed his ideas on *tenken* in subtle ways in response to criticism.[43] Shibusawa continued to argue for interpreting the earthquake as "heavenly punishment," but did so with a few caveats that were absent from his first essays. First of all, in his November 1923 essay "The Reconstruction of the Capital and My Hopes," he included himself among those who were targeted by the wrath of Heaven. He was, as he wrote, "too careless," which resulted in his losing valuable books in his storehouse.[44] This inadequate *mea culpa* seems particularly addressed to critics, such as Kikuchi, who thought that Shibusawa would not have been spared had this really been a "heavenly punishment."[45]

The more salient critique, common in the writing of Kikuchi, Akutagawa, and other critics, was that the punishment was unequal—and, more specifically, that it was unethical to speak of divine punishment without being on the receiving end of that punishment. Miyake Gaikotsu implied as much in the opening essay

42. Akutagawa Ryūnosuke, "Daishin ni saiseru kansō," *Kaizō* 5, no. 10 (October 1923): 194; reprinted in *Akutagawa Ryūnosuke zenshū*, vol. 10 (Iwanami Shoten, 1995), 152–54.
43. Hori Shin, "Kantō daishinsai to tenkenron," 140–44.
44. As quoted in ibid., 141; the original essay was published in *Fujinkai* 28, no. 5 (November 1923).
45. Shibusawa also places a disclaimer—the phrase "a kind of"—before his use of the term *tenken*. In other words, he emphasizes his use of the term *tenken* as an interpretive move rather than a categorical one equating divine punishment with an unscientific idea of religious punishment. There is evidence of a similar idea in Chinese discussions of heavenly punishment and the Mandate of Heaven; see Wolfram Eberhard, "The Political Function of Astronomy and Astronomers in Han China," and Charles E. Hammond, "The Interpretation of Thunder."

of his post-quake magazine series, *Shinsai gahō*: "There were certainly many bad and many good people among those who lost homes and possessions, those separated from fathers or children, those who lost husbands or wives. Those who survived are not all good, and those who suffered from the effects of the disaster are not all evil. To label the disaster as heavenly punishment or divine providence is a harmful and barbaric way of thinking that ignores science, the inequalities of nature, and the intermixture of good and evil."[46] Miyake points out that the problem with the heavenly punishment interpretation is not only that it ignores science and the realities of the disaster but that it lumps the myriad effects of the disaster into a single unifying trope, and does so from a remote vantage point. As he states elsewhere in the essay, anyone who suffered from the disaster and believes it to be heavenly punishment "should be numbered among the fools."

Ogawa Mimei's critique of divine punishment discourse is more indirect. Rather than critiquing it on rational grounds, Mimei provides an unflattering look at a *tenken* proponent in his short story "Immeasurable Things" ("Hakarazaru koto," 1923). In this story the narrator, K, walks around the city after the earthquake and encounters a man speaking to a crowd on the subject of Japan's decadence, not unlike the prophet in Shōchiku's *The Direction of the Flames*:

> For many days afterward, everyone lost their sense of order and the normal modes of life were in chaos. With this in mind, K could not look at the man in front of him without fear. From the man's bloodshot eyes, K had the impression that if anyone were to contradict him, they might be killed on the spot. So he just stood there listening.
>
> "People have become too arrogant. They've laughed in the face of nature once too often. They no longer respect the heavens. This is a punishment, a heavenly punishment. A lesson for everyone. Don't you know that Odawara and Atami were hit harder?"
>
> "Yeah, I heard it was pretty bad down there," agreed a man next to K. . . .
>
> "When I had no money and was coming to Tokyo, I was hungry and without options. I came to Odawara and walked to Kōzu. It was the end of March, so all those people who had gone south to Atami for the winter were crowded into the trains. When I saw young girls with some sort of feather or silk boa wrapped warmly around their necks, with their powdered faces, lipstick, and rouge, mixed in with the crowds, standing shoulder to shoulder with boys, I was repulsed stronger than I have ever been. I will never forget that feeling of disgust. But now, what sweet revenge! Those women, those ladies, now have become paupers with nothing to wear. What becomes of people like that?"
>
> The tall man with bloodshot eyes arched his back and yelled, "I bet they have no choice but to become prostitutes amid the smoldering

46. Miyake Gaikotsu, "Tenpenchii wo dōtokuteki ni kaisuru wa yaban shisō nari," 41.

> corpses and burnt-out ruins." He continued his hysterical laughter.
> "Humanity was just too proud."[47]

With this excessive vitriol, Mimei caricatures the agitator as a raving madman. The imagery of modern girls turned prostitutes amid corpses recalls the characterization of the Kurauchi family in *The Earth Shakes* as "the rotting corpses of a society clinging to its own emptiness on a ghostly carriage of death."[48] The streetcorner demagogue's rhetoric exceeds even Colonel Tadokoro's ravings, yet it is not so far removed from mainstream heavenly punishment discourse as to be unrecognizable. The excesses of the speech serve as a critique, but the characterization of the demagogue is the most damning.

The repeated emphasis on the demagogue's "bloodshot eyes" gives him an aura of insanity, and the way the protagonist fears for the life of anyone who might contradict the speaker links the demagogue to the excesses of the *jikeidan*, or "self-protection groups," that emerged in the chaos after the quake. This connection is reinforced later in the story, when we encounter the man with bloodshot eyes again, this time as the leader of a *jikeidan*. After a failed attempt to catch a man, possibly a Korean, who fled from a checkpoint, the man with the bloodshot eyes brandishes his sword ominously and remarks, "No matter what, I'd like to cut at least one head off."[49] Mimei combines in one character a man who both grouped the wealthy together as targets of divine rage and directed his own wrath against an ethnic group in a bloodthirsty rampage. By so doing, Mimei highlights the dehumanization inherent in both divine punishment discourse and the post-quake Korean massacre, and thus attacks bigotry in all its forms.

These critics show the faults in the divine punishment discourse. They point out the abstractions necessary to categorize all Japanese together as "materialistic." They show that, by universalizing the disaster as a message to the entire nation, divine punishment discourse took the focus away from those who really suffered in the disaster. The heavenly punishment discourse required an erasure of individual suffering, because the individual pain described in *jitsuwa*, or even in Nagata Mikihiko's "Wild Dance of the Flames" (see Chapter 6), exposed the lie that any such suffering could be caused by "sin." As Voltaire wrote in his poem after the Lisbon earthquake, "What crime, what sin, had those young hearts conceived/ That lie, bleeding and torn, on mother's breast?"[50] It is exceedingly difficult to lay blame on individuals, especially when the suffering they endured is so extreme.

47. Ogawa Mimei, "Hakarazaru koto," *Kaizō* 5, no. 11 (November 1923): 9–10.
48. Anonymous, "Daichi wa yuragu (*Nikkatsu gahō*)," 42.
49. Ogawa Mimei, "Hakarazaru koto," 18.
50. Voltaire, "Poem on the Lisbon Disaster."

* * * * *

Ultimately, Mimei's juxtaposition of divine punishment and the Korean Massacre is revelatory. In both instances, individuals were subsumed in false master narratives linked to the nation. Meiji-era ideologues had worked to create the idea of the nation, and the earthquake threatened to tear it apart. Divine punishment suggested that the nation had lost its moral focus and that the earthquake was necessary to redirect the people toward morality and a shared purpose. Such an idea implied that the imagined overabundance of wealthy, vain, and decadent people populating Tokyo needed to be humbled in the earthquake—completely ignoring the fact that it was the poor and the humble who suffered most. The justification of the Korean Massacre suggested that all Koreans must be punished for imagined crimes committed by a few, that foreign threats must be expunged from the nation so that it could remain whole. The chapters that follow explore the consequences of this latter narrative, and how authors responded to it.

CHAPTER 8

Authors and the Korean Panic

Author Ema Shū, who had safely weathered the disaster in his *yamanote* home, first heard the rumors about Koreans on the day after the earthquake. An elderly lieutenant general in his neighborhood came up to him and said in a low voice, "They are saying that Koreans are taking advantage of the confusion to go around setting fires."[1] When Ema at first expressed doubt, the lieutenant-general replied that Korean violence was a possibility: "After all, for *those* people, the ones who hate the Japanese nation in normal circumstances, this is the perfect opportunity, isn't it?"[2] This exchange shows not only how the rumors spread from person to person, but also the way preexisting ideas about Koreans worked to convince people that the rumors could be true. In addition to setting fires, rumors accused Koreans of poisoning wells or massing to attack neighborhoods, spreading widespread fear across the disaster zone. The rumors, and the crazed reaction to them, became known at the time as the "Korean Panic" (*Chōsenjin sawagi*).[3]

Individual accounts of the panic most often mention hearing the rumors from others, as was the case with Ema, but the rumors were also spread by more dependable sources. Some reported seeing official posts on telephone poles and police bulletin boards.[4] Soon after the September 1 earthquake, newspapers,

1. The word "Koreans" is censored in the original, but the most likely candidate was inserted by the editors of the reprinted edition cited here. Ema Shū, *Hitsuji no ikaru toki* (Kage Shobō, 1989), 81.
2. Ibid., 81–82.
3. I am indebted to Andre Haag for this translation of "Korean Panic" for the phrase *Chōsenjin sawagi*.
4. Ikuta Hanayo (the wife of poet Ikuta Shungetsu) reported seeing several newspaper extra editions posted in her neighborhood soon after the earthquake, relaying rumors that inactive volcanoes were becoming active and that Koreans were gathering for an attack, among other things. Ikuta Hanayo, "Hinan no niya," *Bunshō kurabu* 8, no. 10 (October 1923): 58. The origin of the rumors is debated, between those who believe the rumors were consciously started by the government and those who believe they emerged spontaneously from the masses. In one of the first scholarly examinations of the massacre, Saitō Hideo asserted that the government was responsible for the rumors; Saitō Hideo, "Kantō daishinsai to chōsenjin sawagi: sanjūgo shūnen ni yosete," *Rekishi hyōron* 99 (November 1958): 25–39. Later scholars followed this line of thinking with circumstantial evidence as support. Kang Tŏk-sang in particular argues that the rumors were consciously started. See Kang Tŏk-sang and Kŭm Pyŏng-dong, *Kantō daishinsai to Chōsenjin*; and Kang

desperate for whatever information they could acquire, spread the rumors in the authoritative voice of the headline. In several extra editions that ran on September 3, 1923, the *Tokyo Nichinichi shinbun* wrote of Korean attacks with headlines reading: "Outlaw (*futei*) Koreans Setting Fires across the Disaster Zone," "Koreans on the Rampage across the City—200 Gathering with Drawn Swords," and "10 Japanese Men and Women Killed."[5] The rumors spread quickly from the devastated metropolis to the far reaches of the archipelago and the empire. On September 4, the *Kahoku shinpo* based in Sendai ran the headline "Arson, Robbery, Rape, Looting: The Astonishing Violence of Outlaw Koreans."[6] In response to the alarming details they heard and read, neighborhoods formed *jikeidan*, or self-protection groups. Some *jikeidan* took aggressive measures to seek out and capture or kill Koreans rather than merely to defend in case of an attack. In other cases military and police took the lead in the massacre. Ultimately, thousands of Koreans living in the disaster zone were killed.

As the military man who whispered to Ema suggested, people believed these rumors in part because of the threatening portrayal of Koreans in the media prior to the disaster. In an essay written not long after the earthquake, Nakanishi Inosuke (1887–1958) criticized the media for making Koreans into "dark, scary shadows." It was this stereotypical image of the Korean as villain that informed the story "Red Moon," Nagata Mikihiko's fictionalized story of a Korean attack—a rare example of an author treating the rumors as fact. Most authors, such as Tayama Katai, dismissed the rumors in their writing. Katai's text would be unremarkable in this respect if not for an alternate portrayal in an editor's diary showing

---

Tōk-sang, *Kantō daishinsai*. In contrast, Matsuo Takayoshi argues that the rumors arose naturally amid the populace; see Matsuo Takayoshi, "Kantō daishinsai ka no Chōsenjin gyakusatsu 1," and "Kantō daishinsai ka no Chōsenjin gyakusatsu 2," *Shisō* 476 (1964): 110–20. Their 1973 debate, published in *Rekishi hyōron*, outlines the basics of each argument; see Kang Tōk-sang, "Kantō daishinsai ka 'Chōsenjin bōdō ryūgen' ni tsuite," *Rekishi hyōron* 281 (October 1973): 21–30. According to the *Nihon kingendaishi kenkyū jiten*, Saitō and Matsuo later suggested that it was some combination of the two; see Toriumi Yasushi et al., *Nihon kin-gendaishi kenkyū jiten* (Tōkyōdō Shuppan, 1999), 315.

5. Reproduced in Yamada Shōji, *Chosenjin gyakusatsu hōdō shiryō*, 139–40. The word *futei*, or "outlaw," was often associated with "Korean" at the time, and was particularly linked with conspiracy theories following the 1919 independence movement. See Yamada Shōji, "Kantō daishinsai to Chōsenjin gyakusatsu," *Sanzenri* 36 (November 1983): 41; Ken C. Kawashima, *The Proletarian Gamble: Korean Workers in Interwar Japan* (Durham, NC: Duke University Press, 2009), 154; Andre Haag, "Nakanishi Inosuke to Taishōki Nihon no 'futei senjin' e no manazashi," *Gengobunka kenkyū* 22, no. 3 (January 2011): 81–98; and Barbara Brooks, "Peopling the Japanese Empire: The Koreans in Manchuria and the Rhetoric of Inclusion," in *Japan's Competing Modernities*, ed. Sharon Minichiello (Honolulu: University of Hawai'i Press, 1998), 30.

6. Reproduced in Kang Tōk-sang, and Kūm Pyōng-dong, *Kantō daishinsai to Chōsenjin*, 160. There were also newspapers reporting as early as September 8 on the danger of rumors. See, for example, several stories in the *Hōchi Shinbun* and the *Nichinichi Shinbun* on September 8. Yamada Shōji, *Chosenjin gyakusatsu hōdō shiryō*, 10–11, 145–46.

considerable revision in Katai's record. Some authors went further and criticized the rumors and the mob mentality behind the panic, despite heavy censorship. Akutagawa, for example, offered up an ironic critique of the national subject in his account of the rumors. Similarly, Tokuda Shūsei's allegorical exploration of the panic used humor to criticize the rumor mongering and intellectual posturing that had helped fuel the panic.

Yet while Mikihiko, Katai, Akutagawa, and Shūsei portrayed the panic in black and white (one way or another), Ema Shū openly acknowledged his belief in the rumors but criticized the subsequent massacre. His refusal to oversimplify the forces shaping perception is a refreshingly honest and nuanced exploration of the panic. Taken as a whole, these texts show the range of responses to the Korean Panic, how tenaciously the "shadowy" figure of the Korean in the media took hold among the populace, and how that image led to violence.

REBELLIOUS KOREANS IN THE MEDIA AND THE FEAR OF THE COLONIZED

Koreans living in Tokyo and across Japan were subject to widespread bigotry, caused in part by repeated negative portrayals of Koreans in the media. On the one hand, there were reports of anti-Japanese sentiment due to Japan's colonization of Korea, exemplified by the coverage of Itō Hirobumi's assassination by An Jung-geun, a Korean nationalist, in 1909. On the other hand, Koreans were inordinately identified in the press as perpetrators of crimes such as robbery and rape, or as the instigators of brawls.[7] These two trends merge after the 1919 Korean independence movement. The movement was portrayed as a "riot" (*sōjō*) in the Japanese press at the time, and reports of outlaw Koreans (*futei senjin*) and Korean conspiracies were even more common in the newspapers afterward.[8] *Futei senjin*—pairing *senjin,* a pejorative word for "Korean," with the adjective *futei*, meaning "outlaw" or "rebellious"—was a key term in the press that effectively associated being Korean with criminality and rebellion. This association in turn led to greater scrutiny by police, and thus to more negative coverage. As Ken Kawashima explains, "*Futei senjin* . . . became a policing sign that operated less through the identification of Korean lawbreakers, and more through a general

7. An unscientific survey of headlines in a database covering Koreans in Japanese newspapers shows that approximately 40 percent were negative. A few examples from soon after the official annexation of Korea in 1910 include "Suspicious Korean" from the *Kobe shinbun* on August 31, 1910, and "Korean Rampage" from the *Yorozu chōhō* on March 21, 1911. Mizuno Naoki and Horiuchi Minoru, "Senzen Nihon zaijū Chōsenjin kankei shinbun kiji kensaku (Database of prewar newspaper articles related to Koreans in Japan)," http://www.zinbun.kyoto-u.ac.jp/~mizna/shinbun/shinbun.html (accessed May 3, 2011).
8. This statement is based on searches in the *Yomiuri shinbun* database, *Kikuzō II Visual* database (*Asahi shinbun*), and the database of Koreans in the newspapers set up by Kyoto University Professor Mizuno Naoki, ibid.

misidentification of all Koreans as potential or probable criminals."[9] Just a few months before the earthquake, the *Kobe yūshin nippō* ran the headline: "*Futei senjin* Sneaking into the Homeland."[10] Headlines like this groomed the Japanese to believe the rumors of a Korean uprising when they heard them immediately after the disastrous earthquake.

The connection between the portrayal of Koreans in the media and the rumors after the earthquake was articulated three months later by proletarian author Nakanishi Inosuke. In his article "Speaking for the Koreans" ("Chōsenjin no tame ni benzu"), Nakanishi laments the lack of information on Korea and its culture in the newspapers and the difficulty in learning about this addition to the empire. He continues: "Koreans have been unthinkingly sacrificed on the altar of journalism, and as such they have been engraved in the minds of the Japanese as dark, scary shadows (*kuroki kyōfu no gen'ei*). . . . Did not these recent rumors of Korean violence naturally emerge from the Japanese subconscious? Was this not because of unfounded fears of these dark, shadowy figures?"[11] Nakanishi blames sensationalistic journalism for creating an ominous image of Koreans instead of depicting them as real people with a history and customs of their own. In turn, he claims that these representations led directly and spontaneously to the rumors, and thus, by extension, to the massacre.

Nakanishi's sentiment is echoed by the journalist Hasegawa Nyozekan (1875–1969) in an essay on the rumors for the October 1923 issue of the women's magazine *Fujin no tomo*. After explaining that rumors had to be believable to spread, Nyozekan argued that if people had not been worried about Koreans rebelling before the earthquake, the rumors would not have spread so easily. He concluded by writing that the way to combat rumors was to encourage truth before disasters happen: "If people actually knew beforehand what kinds of people Koreans were, or what kinds of people socialists were, these kinds of rumors would never have taken hold."[12] Education and knowledge were, in Nyozekan's mind, the best way to combat the violence stemming from ignorance.

The frequent mention of criminal and rebellious *futei senjin* made Koreans into scary figures. But there was another reason behind the fear—namely, what Jinhee Lee, in her study of the Korean Massacre, has called "the imagined

9. Ken C. Kawashima, *The Proletarian Gamble*, 154.

10. From a search for "*futei senjin*" in Mizuno Naoki and Horiuchi Minoru, "Senzen Nihon zaijū Chōsenjin kankei shinbun kiji kensaku" (Database of prewar newspaper articles related to Koreans in Japan).

12. Nakanishi Inosuke, "Chōsenjin no tame ni benzu," *Fujin kōron* 8, no. 12 (December 1923): 55.

12. Reprinted as Hasegawa Nyozekan, "Ryūgen higo wa dōshite okoru ka," in *Chōsenjin gyakusatsu ni kansuru chishikijin no hannō*, vol. 1 (Ryokuin Shobō, 1996), 144. A similar sentiment is also in Yanagisawa Takashi's essay "The Violent Actions of the *Jikeidan*" ("Jikeidan no zangyaku kōi") in the following issue of *Fujin kōron*. See the reprint in Kūm Pyŏng-dong, *Chōsenjin gyakusatsu ni kansuru chishikijin no hannō*, 211.

inversion of power," in which colonial violence was projected onto subjugated Koreans.[13] As Lee explains, many Japanese felt a "self-conscious anxiety that the subjugated people in the metropole might seek revenge."[14] In other words, recognition of Japanese guilt led to fear of reprisal, a fear punctuated by occasional instances of actual insurgence. This fear remained despite the clear military superiority of Japan, and the swift and brutal oppression that met any signs of rebellion. It was a fear that came from understanding that Koreans had reason to hate Japan. This fear and the negative coverage of Koreans in the press created a mutually reinforcing combination, a perfect petri dish in which the rumors could be expected to multiply.

The Sinister Mirage of "Dark, Shadowy" Koreans

The shadowy figures of marauding, rebellious Koreans that Nakanishi mentions make a regular appearance in authors' accounts of the earthquake. In some cases, rumors are merely mentioned with little to no commentary; in others, rumors are believed only by the ignorant and unenlightened. One exception was Nagata Mikihiko, who embellished a scandalous story about Koreans raping and murdering a woman in his 1923 earthquake collection *The Earth Shakes* (*Daichi wa furū*, also discussed in Chapters 4 and 6). In the story "Red Moon" ("Akai tsuki"), two liberated working girls, Nobuko and Kinuko, flee the fires into the suburbs of Tokyo, where Kinuko's family lives. Nobuko is timid and scared, but Kinuko, confident and strong, encourages her. These two women are painted in broad strokes, but their manner of speaking, dress, and occupation signifies that they are the modern girls who so captivated the popular press at the time.

After walking miles into the sparsely populated suburbs, Nobuko can walk no longer. Saying she will be back in twenty minutes, Kinuko leaves to ask directions. As hours pass, Nobuko gets worried, and seeing other refugees nearby, heads for some people milling around a clump of houses nearby. She walks up to a group of women to inquire if anyone has seen Kinuko. A woman in her fifties replies, "Well, there was someone done up all fancy and Western, like you. If it's her you're talking about, then it doesn't look good. She passed this way a little while ago, but just up there, she was taken off somewhere by some [*futei senjin*]. Everyone in the village is in a state because of it."[15]

Nobuko searches for more information from members of the *jikeidan* (self-protection group), but ultimately can do nothing but sit on the grass and cry.

13. Jinhee Lee, "Instability of Empire," 34.

14. Ibid., 49.

15. Nagata Mikihiko, *Daichi wa furū*, 216. The word in brackets was censored, but the four characters missing could only be *futei senjin*. Future instances of censorship will also be so marked when the missing word(s) are intelligible by context.

It is not until one in the morning that she hears what has become of her friend. Some police officers have found Kinuko in a shed near a work site, along with two other women: "The [*futei senjin*] did unspeakable things to them. Their hands were tied together with thick wire, and their bodies were covered with bruises. It looked like they had been bludgeoned. The two others were revived through the nurturing care of the police officers, but Kinuko lay on the floor, dead from a brutal wound to her stomach."[16] The narrator is careful to note that the criminals who killed her were never found. After a few days Nobuko returns to her home in northern Japan, but according to the narrator she seemed strange, altered forever by her near encounter with rampaging Koreans.

"Red Moon" participates in a broader discourse of comeuppance for women too strong and independent for their own good—a common trope in pulp stories. It is a perfect mixture of two sensational topics of Taishō-era tabloid journalism: liberated modern girls and villainous Koreans. The story is also likely to be a complete fabrication. In contrast to other pieces in his collection *The Earth Shakes*, there are no indications that Mikihiko spoke with anyone involved. Furthermore, the story contains fictional elements and the narrator is privy to information and dialogue impossible for the author to know plausibly. Nevertheless, Mikihiko is intent on declaring its authenticity. As an epilogue to the story, he includes a parenthetical statement: "This story actually happened in the Kanagawa area. In fact, it was a tragedy more fearsome than that which I include here. It is not certain that the culprits were [*futei senjin*], but the government forbids telling the true story, so this is something I have modified considerably at the editing stage."[17]

The basis for the story could have been one of several newspaper articles or personal rumors. Similar accounts appeared after the ban on reporting on the massacre and Koreans was lifted on October 20, 1923. For example, in the evening edition that night, the *Hōchi shinbun* reported on lifting the ban and provided a list of "true" crimes caused by rampaging Koreans. Though the newspaper took pains to note that "outlaw Koreans" were a small minority, it nevertheless included the gang rape and murder of a teenaged girl in the Nankatsu area.[18] It is likely that this newspaper story, like so many others, was based on rumor and hearsay. Neither the perpetrators nor the victim were found.

With "Red Moon," Nagata Mikihiko attempts to maintain a chain of authenticity linking his sensational melodrama to newspaper reports and thus to actual events, something he does throughout his earthquake collection. In this case, his

16. Ibid., 221.

17. Ibid., 222.

18. The *Hōchi shinbun* cited the Justice Department for the information, but it is hard to verify these claims. Yamada Shōji, *Chōsenjin gyakusatsu hōdō shiryō*, 47. A similar list can be found in other newspapers on the same day, for example, the *Nichinichi shinbun*.

sources are shrouded in mystery. This concession to censorship makes it difficult to verify the authenticity of Mikihiko's story, but hinders criticism that that story is unsubstantiated. With his detailed description of the two modern girls and their struggle to reach the suburbs, Mikihiko turns a groundless headline into a more sensationalized story that appropriates the authenticity of the news media. In so doing, he uncritically vilifies Koreans in Japan and further perpetrates the myth of Korean criminality.

Revisionism, Censorship, and the Korean Panic

In contrast to Mikihiko's indiscriminate use of the image of scary Korean criminals, many authors claimed that they disbelieved the rumors in their accounts of the disaster. In Shiga Naoya's diary-like account, published in *Shinkō* early in 1924, he wrote: "Karuizawa. Dusk. They were serving ice cream to the passengers at the station. Heard that Koreans were running around Tokyo with bombs, but didn't believe it."[19] Like Shiga, most authors were writing well after the confusion had died down, and it is possible that there were revisions in these personal accounts to paint the author in a more favorable light. Tayama Katai is a particularly egregious example of duplicity in this respect. In Katai's *Record of the Tokyo Earthquake,* he shows scorn for those who believed in the rumors on several occasions. One of the most telling comes from an exchange with his wife after he returns from visiting the ruins:

> She sidled up next to me and in a low voice said, "There are all sorts of rumors going around. Like that there are a hundred of *those* people in Hori no uchi and that they are coming this way."
>
> "What foolishness!" I exclaimed.[20]

Katai's reply shows his disdain for those who believed the rumors, yet as Kūm Pyōng-dong points out, Kisaki Masaru (1894–1979), an editor at *Chūō kōron,* gives a different view of Katai in his diary. According to Kisaki's diary entry for September 11, 1923, Kisaki went to visit Katai about ten days after the earthquake and was relieved to see that he had weathered it so well. While Kisaki was there, Katai regaled him with an anecdote of encountering a Korean soon after the earthquake. Katai told him that one night a Korean was chased by a *jikeidan* into Katai's yard and hid under the veranda, "so I dragged him out and

19. Shiga Naoya, "Shinsai mimai," originally published in the February 1924 issue of *Shinkō*; reprinted in Kūm Pyōng-dong, *Chōsenjin gyakusatsu ni kansuru chishikijin no hannō*, 188–92. Shiga also reports seeing soldiers chasing a Korean.

20. Tayama Katai, *Tōkyō shinsaiki*, 49–50.

gave him a beating."[21] According to Kisaki, Katai seemed pleased that he could do such a thing at his age, but Kisaki was "unimpressed by the foolhardy bravery of an old man."[22] Katai clearly displaced his belief of the rumors onto his wife, whom he calls foolish. Revealing himself to be a believer in the rumors, let alone a participant in the Korean persecution, required more honesty than did his frank depiction of his darkest sexual desires in his I-novels. Other authors may have made similar revisions in their accounts, but none was caught out quite so blatantly in doing so.

The substitution of "those people" for "Koreans" in Katai's account shows that censorship remained an issue in April 1924, when his book was published. Censorship was especially a factor in the early months after the earthquake, when even the most benign mention of the rumors had to contend with the possibility of government intervention. Anything related to the massacre, or even to the rumors of Korean crimes, was expressly forbidden in the first month and a half after the earthquake by the peace preservation edicts associated with martial law. This meant that any book, magazine, or newspaper deemed "dangerous" to civil order would be confiscated, with the publisher bearing the costs. Nevertheless, because Taishō-era Japanese censorship allowed the publication of controversial texts as long as certain words were replaced by blanks (often in the form of OOOO or XXXX), it is possible to read texts where the word "Korean" is excised, yet implied by the context and the number of missing characters.[23] In general, it was the publishers and authors who chose to self-censor in order to avoid confiscation of the entire run of their magazines, worried that even a slight reference would result in significant economic losses. Newspapers had less risk because they published daily. A single issue did not have much impact on the overall profit, and by the time the officials decided to confiscate a given issue, a large portion of the run would have been sold.

The ban was officially lifted on October 20, 1923, but the Korean Panic and the massacre remained a sensitive topic long afterward.[24] After permission was granted to publish information on the massacre, newspapers were more willing to print information about Koreans, but magazines had to be more careful because of the higher losses they would sustain from being banned. Despite making efforts to self-censor, some magazines still faced government bans when the material was deemed questionable. The April 1924 issue of *Engeki shinchō,* in which Akita

21. Quoted in Kūm Pyōng-dong, *Chōsenjin gyakusatsu ni kansuru chishikijin no hannō*, vol. 2 (Ryokuin Shobō, 1996), 410. Kisaki Masaru's diary was first published after the war, decades after Tayama Katai's death.

22. Quoted in ibid. Katai was 51 at the time.

23. For a discussion of Japanese censorship in the interwar era, see Richard H. Mitchell, *Censorship in Imperial Japan* (Princeton, NJ: Princeton University Press, 1983). For the Meiji era, see also Jay Rubin, *Injurious to Public Morals*.

24. The self-censorship in magazines and books continued at least into the late 1920s.

Ujaku's play *Dance of the Skeletons* (*Gaikotsu no buchō*) first appeared, was confiscated due to the play's controversial depiction of the Korean Massacre.[25] It was later published in a significantly redacted form.[26]

Censorship was particularly severe in the October 1923 issues of magazines, which appeared when the ban was still in effect. As a result, many authors published their memoirs with the word "Korean" replaced by OOO or XXX. Alternatively, if the word "Korean" was included, the details would be censored. Hosoda Tamiki (1892–1972) wrote about seeing a Korean youth (with the word "Korean"—*senjin*—intact) being accosted first by a member of a veterans' group and then by a policeman. The work is censored, but it does not take much imagination to fill in the gaps. "[The policeman] took the youth and forcibly XXXXXXX. I was surprised at the extraordinary strength in the human fist. To be XX like that, I wonder why XXXX. Or perhaps he was XX. From the way he looked, this youth was in no way part of a so-called outlaw gang (*futei no to*)."[27] The implication is clearly that the youth was severely beaten.

In some cases the missing words can be reconstituted by examining the original manuscripts. Thankfully, several of the original manuscripts from the first post-quake issues of *Kaizō* and *Josei kaizō*, held at the Kawaguchi Magokoro literary museum, act as a kind of Rosetta Stone to interpret the censored lines of other texts from the time.[28] For example, in the case of the artist Takehisa Yumeji, editors removed a line that merely mentioned the rumors without using the word "Korean" at all. In the original handwritten manuscript the line read: "There was a report that a group of about 100 on a rampage had come as far as Ebisu station."[29] Kume Masao's diary-like account of his experiences, in contrast, was full of detail. In the print edition, almost the entire evening of September 2 is rendered unreadable, but the handwritten manuscript clearly recounts rumors of Korean arson and rape as well as Kume's own fears of being mistaken for a Korean.[30] In each case where editors replaced words or lines with XX or OO, the handwritten manuscripts contained a reference to Koreans. It is safe to say that the most commonly censored word after the disaster was "Korean."

25. The confiscation of this issue made newspaper headlines: "*Engeki shinchō* Banned due to Akita Ujaku's One-Act Play," *Yomiuri shinbun*, April 4, 1924, 5.
26. Akita Ujaku, "Gaikotsu no buchō," in *Shinkō bungaku zenshū Nihon hen*, vol. 1 (1928): 473–89.
27. Hosoda Tamiki, "Unmei no minikusa," *Bunshō kurabu* 8, no. 10 (October 1923): 82.
28. These manuscripts are available on DVD-ROM from Yūshōdō. Kōno Toshirō and Hidaka Shōji, "Kaizō jikihitsu genkō gazō dētabēsu" (2007). See also Kōno Kensuke's discussion of the entire series in his book *Ken'etsu to bungaku: 1920-nendai no kōbō*, (Kawade Shobō Shinsha, 2009).
29. Kōno Toshirō and Hidaka Shōji, "Kaizō jikihitsu genkō gazō dētabēsu. Kaizō genkō dētabēsu"; original article, Takehisa Yumeji, "Hensai zakki," *Kaizō* 5, no. 10 (October 1923): 124–30.
30. Kōno Toshirō and Hidaka Shōji, "Kaizō jikihitsu genkō gazō dētabēsu. Kaizō genkō dētabēsu"; original article, Kume Masao, "Kamakura shinsai nikki," *Kaizō* 5, no. 10 (October 1923): 246–53.

AMBIGUITY, IRONY, AND ALLEGORY AMID CENSORSHIP

The goal of political censorship is often to maintain order by removing any critique of the current regime or the status quo. The rumors of the Korean Massacre troubled the government because they showed its lack of control over both the population and the military. In many cases the censored passages in *Kaizō* that we can reconstruct by looking at the manuscripts were tame references to rumors that were readily available in contemporary newspapers. In contrast, one line cut from Mushanokōji Saneatsu's essay in *Kaizō* was particularly controversial: "Even supposing that a few Koreans did act as the rumors said, the ultimate reason for those actions is nothing more than that the Japanese have not respected our Korean brothers and sisters."[31] Though he allows that some rumors could have been true, Mushanokōji, like Nakanishi, cites Japanese prejudice as the root cause. This critique is omitted in the essay as published, which leaves only the impression that Mushanokōji mentioned something about Koreans. Thankfully, other authors found ways around the censorship, providing critiques through irony and allegory. In one creative example, Sasaki Mitsuzō replaced the word "Korean" with "Eskimo" in his essay "Self-Protection Group Dreams" ("Jikeidan yume monogatari"). The story opens wryly with the line "There were stories going around my neighborhood of Eskimos causing all sorts of trouble."[32] Sasaki was able to avoid censorship by merely changing the word, but the referent was clear to all who read it.

There is no use of the word "Korean" or indication of censorship in Ogawa Mimei's "Immeasurable Things" ("Hakarazaru koto"), published in the November 1923 issue of *Kaizō* (and discussed at the end of Chapter 7). Rather, Mimei takes the understanding that *jikeidan* acted out against Koreans as a way to discuss the panic without elaborating on the specifics. The protagonist of the story, K, takes refuge with his friend Y in western Tokyo. That night, Y must stay out for night watch in his community, and K sits with him on their assigned street corner. The experience of participating in a neighborhood watch was a common one mentioned by several authors, usually without incident. In this case, K and Y hear a commotion in the dark—the sound of whistles and people running—and go to find the cause. They encounter one of Y's neighbors, who asks if they have seen anyone. According to the neighbor, an unknown man (assumed to be a Korean) had run away from a checkpoint down the road. Neither Y nor K had seen the

31. Kōno Toshirō and Hidaka Shōji, "Kaizō jikihitsu genkō gazō dētabēsu. Kaizō genkō dētabēsu"; original article, Mushanokōji Saneatsu, "Zakkan," *Kaizō* 5, no. 10 (1923): 229–33. There are echoes of Nakanishi in Mushanokōji's essay, or at least a willingness to blame Japanese treatment of Koreans as part of the problem.

32. Sasaki Mitsuzō (as Iwatani Shirō), "Jikeidan yumemonogatari," *Kaizō* 5, no. 11 (November 1923): 214–24.

man, but soon another member of the *jikeidan* spots the fugitive, and the frantic shouting begins again:

> "Ah! He's here! He's here!" someone suddenly shouted.
> "He's there? Kill him!"
> "Beat him!"
> "Where? Where are you?"
> Half were watching outside a hedge. The other half came waving weapons in their hands. But it seemed like whoever had found the man had lost him again.
> "Where did he go?"
> "Where is he hiding? Hey! Careful everyone. I'm sure he's got a dagger or a pistol."[33]

The fugitive escapes, and the members of the *jikeidan* go back to their posts to wait out the remainder of the otherwise uneventful night. One man wielding a Japanese sword is familiar to the narrator. He is the same man who was spouting heavenly punishment rhetoric a few pages earlier: "'I wanted to at least cut off one head.' The tall man in the white shirt drew the *katana* he was carrying from its black scabbard. Even in the dark, the naked blade gleamed hideously, as if wet. He cut through the air a few times in protest at the missed opportunity and returned the blade to the scabbard."[34] Though this is only one short scene in the story, Mimei ably conjures up the fearful confusion in post-quake Tokyo and the deadly ease with which the group calls for killing a person whose only crime had been to flee when challenged. Without mentioning the word "Korean," Mimei calls attention to the panic and the way people responded to the unfounded rumors with violence and threats. The ambiguity of his writing allowed for "Immeasurable Things" to be published, but its condemnation of rumor-fueled violence based on ignorance remains clear.

One of the most interesting critiques of the rumors comes from Akutagawa Ryūnosuke in his essay "Earthquake Miscellany" ("Taishin zakki").[35] There, Akutagawa depicts a conversation in which Kikuchi Kan chides Akutagawa for his belief in the rumors. This section of his essay, worth quoting in full, is replete with what Kūm Pyōng-dong calls Akutagawa's "sarcasm toward a society in which authority reigns supreme":[36]

> I am a good citizen. But in my opinion, Kikuchi Kan is lacking in this respect.

33. Ogawa Mimei, "Hakarazaru koto," 16–17.

34. Ibid., 18.

35. Akutagawa Ryūnosuke, "Taishin zakki," *Chūō kōron* 38, no. 10 (October 1923): 133–37; reprinted in *Akutagawa Ryūnosuke zenshū* vol. 10 (1995): 142–47.

36. Kūm Pyōng-dong, *Chōsenjin gyakusatsu ni kansuru chishikijin no hannō*, 1.

> After martial law was imposed I was conversing with Kikuchi Kan, a cigarette dangling from my mouth. Though I say conversing, we spoke of nothing but the earthquake. As we were talking I said that I heard the cause of the fires was OOOOOOOOO. Upon hearing this, Kikuchi raised his eyebrows and exclaimed, "What a lie!" When put to me this way, I could do nothing but agree, "Hmm, so it's not true." But I still said again that it seemed that the OOOO (*futei senjin*) were the fingers of the Bolsheviks. Kikuchi again raised his eyebrows and scolded, "It's not true, you know, what they say." Again I said "Oh, so that's not true either," and immediately withdrew my explanation.
>
> Nevertheless, in my opinion, a good citizen believes in the existence of conspiracies (*inbō*) between Bolsheviks and OOOO (*futei senjin*).[37] If, by chance, one could not believe, one should at least put on a show of believing. But that barbaric Kikuchi Kan didn't even make a show of believing, let alone *believe*. This should be seen as a complete renunciation of the qualifications of being a good citizen. I—the good citizen and courageous member of a self-protection group (*jikeidan*) that I am—could not help but feel pity for Kikuchi.
>
> But then, becoming a good citizen requires a lot of hard work.[38]

In this passage Akutagawa portrays himself as a simpleton duped by the rumors, which were largely discredited in the press by September 8, 1923. In the essay, this simplistic unquestioning belief qualifies one as good citizen. The irony is clearest in the final line: "becoming a good citizen requires a lot of work." Here Akutagawa preposterously asserts that believing the rumors, or at least putting on a show of doing so, is actually harder than doubting them.

There is a stark contrast between the ironic image of Akutagawa here and that found in his diaryesque account published the same month in the magazine *Josei* (*Women*). In that version of his experiences, Akutagawa mentions having a fever and sending a student to stand watch in his stead, a far cry from action one might expect of the "courageous member of a self-protection group" depicted in "Earthquake Miscellany."[39] Though he does not go so far as to suggest that the

37. Here Akutagawa uses the word *inbō,* which was common in alarmist media reports about Koreans before the earthquake.

38. Akutagawa Ryūnosuke, "Taishin zakki," 136. The series of circles is probably a reference to rampaging Koreans. The "*futei senjin*" in parentheses is a likely candidate for the four censored characters in the original. Andre Haag brought to my attention that Kudō Miyoko uses this passage as an example in her revisionist history of the massacre, willfully ignoring the irony. Kudō, *Kantō daishinsai Chōsenjin gyakusatsu no shinjitsu* (Sankei Shinbun Shuppan, 2009), 31–32. Incidentally, despite the apparent skepticism in Akutagawa's essay, Kikuchi Kan talks of taking up a bamboo spear to stand guard in his neighborhood in his famous essay, "Post-Quake Impressions." He, too, was apparently a "good citizen." Kikuchi, "Saigo zakkan," 119.

39. The student whom Akutagawa sent in his stead was Watanabe Kurasuke (1901–1963), a writer from Nagasaki who lived in Akutagawa's neighborhood. The final line of the diary slightly pokes fun at Watanabe for looking like the prototypical *jikeidan* member with a wooden sword and

government was responsible for the rumors, Akutagawa critiques both the gullibility of citizens and a government that demands such a mindset.

One approach to discussing the panic and the massacre without raising the ire of the censors was to use allegory. Robert Tierney and other scholars have shown how Sato Haruo's short story "Demon Bird" ("Machō") recasts the massacre as an instance of scapegoating in a Taiwanese native village.[40] In the story, villagers attempt to kill a young woman and her family because of rumors that she made evil sprits kill villagers. At the end of the story the narrator clarifies the allegorical connection between the story he recounted as taking place among "barbarians" to the violence in "civilized" Japan: "The civilized resemble barbarians since they arbitrarily deem evil everything they do not understand and strive to exterminate people who wear an incomprehensible facial expression."[41] Allegory allowed the story to be published with its critique of the violence intact.

Tokuda Shūsei, a naturalist writer from Katai's generation, wrote a similarly allegorical exploration of the Korean Panic for the November 1923 issue of *Chūō kōron*. Shūsei sets his story "Fire-Gun" ("Fuaiyagan") in a police station a few days after the earthquake. In so doing he makes the context clear, but is unable to explore the violent consequences of rumor as fully as Satō Haruo. Nevertheless, even under the constraints of censorship Shūsei is able to highlight the mechanisms by which bias leads to rumor and to violence.

The story begins with several officers relaxing and talking about recent events in a brief respite from the chaos outside. As the narrator relates, "The policemen discussed the various things they saw and heard about the way the Koreans were feared by everyone and the brutality that came from misunderstanding. Every single report that made its way to the police was proven to be completely baseless upon further investigation."[42] This opening explicitly ties the story to the

dagger. In contrast to his public persona revealed in this diary and elsewhere, the Akutagawa depicted in "Post-Quake Miscellany" is a hopeless believer in the rumors despite evidence to the contrary, a model citizen. Akutagawa Ryūnosuke, "Daishin zengo," *Josei* 4, no. 4 (October 1923): 13.

40. See, for example, Robert Tierney, "Ethnography, Borders and Violence: Reading between the Lines in Sato Haruo's 'Demon Bird,'" *Japan Forum* 19, no. 1 (2007): 89–110; Kimura Kazuaki, "Kieta 'Hae': Satō Haruo no kantō daishinsai," in *Haikyo no kanōsei: gendai bungaku no tanjō*, ed. Kurihara Yukio, Bungakushi wo yomikaeru (Inpakuto Shuppankai and Izara Shobō, 1997); and Faye Yuan Kleeman, *Under an Imperial Sun: Japanese Colonial Literature of Taiwan and the South* (University of Hawai'i Press, 2003).

41. Quoted and translated in Robert Tierney, "Ethnography, Borders and Violence," 100. Tierney notes how the "incomprehensible facial expression was one way of identifying those who had the power to manipulate the 'Demon Birds.'"

42. Tokuda Shūsei, "Fuaiyagan," *Chūō kōron* 38, no. 12 (November 1923): 107. The word "Korean" remains in the text. Self-censorship was practiced inconsistently. Nevertheless, had this story appeared in the October rather than the November issue, the word would have most certainly been censored.

rumors. Though it mentions Koreans being feared without reason, the text is less explicit about "the brutality that comes from misunderstanding." Nevertheless, juxtaposed with the rumors about Koreans, a contemporary audience would have easily made the connection to the massacre.

The officers are called away from this discussion to a briefing on a new weapon. What follows is a comedy of mistranslation, assumption, and hubris. In the meeting the police chief introduces the officers to a professor and a strange-looking device: a shiny cylindrical object a little over a foot long and twice the diameter of a beer bottle, with an odd nozzle at one end. The professor claims that the object is a kind of firebomb, or a "Fire-Gun," as the label on the object states, that was used to spread the flames in the disaster. This "weapon," the professor says, is an American version of a German firebomb developed in the First World War, capable of sending 3,000-degree flames as far as 300 meters. On the object are instructions in English such as "Aim at the base of the fire," which the professor interprets as "Aim where you want the fire to go."[43]

The professor's prejudice is made explicit in the ending of the story. After the professor and the police chief leave, the officers talk among themselves about the object and begin questioning the professor's explanation. One officer recalls a similar-looking device at a neighboring house and goes to fetch it, finally revealing that the mysterious object is actually a fire extinguisher. "Fire-Gun" was actually a trademark for a fire extinguisher made in the first part of the twentieth century by the American La France Foamite Corporation. Shūsei had likely encountered one and saw the potential for humor and irony in the brand name. When confronted with the truth, the professor realizes his mistake: "This is definitely a fire extinguisher. A group of people came to me with this, saying that a Korean dropped it while fleeing. I thought it meant trouble and so I came right away to make a report. . . . Now I realize the problem here. It's all because I was biased."[44] After this revelation the professor leaves dejectedly, upset by the gravity of his mistake, and the policemen smile sheepishly at their gullibility.

On the surface, the story pokes fun at the professor's confidence in his clearly mistaken explanation and at the willingness of the police chief to believe him. The focus on how a small and completely harmless object became vilified suggests an allegorical interpretation. There are no ill consequences in this case of mistaken identity, but the implication is that such errors and biases became the root of the massacre. Other instances of vilification, the story implies, might not be so benign. By describing the process whereby mistakes by those in power spiral out of control, Shūsei shows how ignorance led to unsubstantiated rumors that resulted in the deaths of thousands of Koreans.

43. Ibid., 111.
44. Ibid., 117. Again the word "Korean" was left intact.

There is a limit to Shūsei's critique, however, imposed by the constraints of publication in a time of close government scrutiny: His allegory forecloses any possibility of police involvement in the massacre. Here the police, and particularly the lower-ranking officers who question the received wisdom, are the heroes of the story. Every rumor they investigate is found to be baseless, and it is they who ultimately discover the truth behind the "Fire-Gun." This sympathetic view of police officers is supported by some *jitsuwa* and personal accounts that show police officers saving Koreans.[45] At the same time, other accounts show that at least some segments of the police force participated in the massacre. For example, a picture scroll by Kayahara Hakudō depicts a police officer watching people killing Koreans.[46] By making the police officers heroes instead of villains, Shūsei appears to have created a work that was publishable, albeit by absolving the government of blame.

Reading between the lines of Shūsei's "Fire-Gun" nevertheless does reveal a critique of the police at the same time that it releases them from responsibility. This is possible because the setting of the story calls attention to the role of police in the massacre by its very focus on the officers themselves. The setting encourages the reader to imagine an alternate scenario, one in which the officers do not discover the truth and instead set off to capture and kill the Korean who dropped the "fire-gun" while fleeing. Regardless of the intent behind the story it retains a strong antiauthoritarian voice that critiques the gullibility of people in power. How far that critique extends is debatable, and that range of interpretations shows the power of the allegory as well as its limitations.

EMA SHŪ'S MORAL DILEMMA

Most of the work depicting the panic used broad strokes to either criminalize the Koreans or present simplistic ethical dilemmas. Ema Shū was unusual, in that he provided a more nuanced view of the panic. Ema's account of the disaster, the book *When Sheep Rise in Anger* (*Hitsuji no ikaru toki*), was originally serialized in the *Taiwan nichinichi* newspaper from 1924 to 1925.[47] Ema had sympathized

45. The *Yomiuri shinbun* reported on September 15, 1923 that a police officer saved four Koreans from *jikeidan* violence. Jinhee Lee recounts the experiences of a Korean labor activist, Kim T'ae-yŏp, who was taken into police custody for protection. Kim recalled that on his way to the station several *jikeidan* wanted to punish him themselves. Jinhee Lee, "Instability of Empire," 45–46. Takeuchi Shigeo's sketches of post-quake Tokyo include one of a Korean taken to a police officer, who recognized the Korean from his neighborhood. Based on his explanatory notes, this police officer probably rescued the Korean man from the angry mob. Takeuchi Shigeo, *Tokyo arekore: Taishō fuzoku sukecchi* (Tōa Insatsu, 1987), 107.

46. Kitahara Itoko and Oyobe Katsuhito, eds., *Kantō daishinsai wo egaku: emaki, manga, kodomo no e* (Yokohama: Kanagawa Daigaku Himoji Shiryō Kenkyū Sentā, 2010), 10.

47. Ema Shū, *Hitsuji*, reprinted by Kage shobō in 1989. It is interesting that one of the most telling explorations of the Korean panic and the subsequent massacre was published in one of Japan's colonies.

with the plight of resident Koreans for several years prior the quake. He had mentored an aspiring Korean author and done some work for resident Koreans at the local government level. This history is recounted in an analepsis in the first part of the book, covering the day of the quake. Ema's account is interesting because, though the text emphasizes his Korean friends—many of whom visit him and tell their own stories—Ema is also drawn into believing the rumors and admits as much in his book. Ema does not fault the media as directly as Nakanishi Inosuke and Hasegawa Nyozekan do, but his text does shows how the media-produced image of the "shadowy Korean" can corrupt even the most sympathetic of minds.

According to his memoir, Ema first heard the rumors of the Korean uprising on September 2, 1923. Soon afterward, Ema sees a Korean student and thinks, though briefly, that the inconspicuous object the student has in his hands is a bomb or some other device. Ema immediately comes to his senses, but remarks on how frightening the mind can be amid the uncertainty following a disaster. Later, when he hears that a group of 300 Koreans have massed for an attack, he believes this as well. He knows that the mansion of a former governor of Korea, General T, is in his neighborhood, and it makes sense to him that Koreans would target it.[48] He spends the evening locked in his house with his frightened family. As he huddles in the dark with them amid the incessant aftershocks, his mind wavers between fearing the worst and wishfully dismissing the rumors as fantasy. The sounds of yelling in the distance suggest the rumors could be true, and he is preoccupied with imagining the worst:

> [I imagined] four or five of them breaking into the room. In their hands were pistols, swords, and bombs. I saw my wife's face turned pale with fear, the figure of my children trembling, and me standing amidst them. One member of the group, with vile lust in his eyes, moved toward my wife. With no thought for myself, I stand between them. I know I will die.
>
> I would call out to them. "Yes, if you are going to kill me, go ahead. But I tell you, you will lose an ally."
>
> I conjure up one of my [Korean] acquaintances. No telling whether one or two might be in the mob. If so, he might calm the mob and vouch for me, "Don't kill that man, he's our friend."
>
> . . .
>
> But in response they might reply, "If that is so, we won't kill you. But in return you must help us. Take this bomb and join us."
>
> This would be a major problem. From a moral standpoint, I wouldn't be able to join them. I'd have to refuse. Of course then they couldn't let me live. But at the end at least I'd be able to say, "I implore

48. This is probably referring to General Terauchi Masatake, governor of Korea during the annexation phase. General Terauchi had died in 1919, though perhaps Ema thought that the general's family might be targeted.

> you, whatever you do to me is fine, but please don't kill my wife and children."[49]

Ema's waking nightmare revolves around the media-produced figure of the outlaw Korean come to life in his mind. At the same time, the image of Koreans on a rampage in his neighborhood is informed by his intimate knowledge of Korean feelings toward their Japanese colonizers. After first hearing the rumors and his neighbor the elderly lieutenant general's explanation of why "those who hate the Japanese nation" might use the disaster for their own purposes, Ema writes: "His words made me think. As I have said before, I have several (Korean) friends. And I know well what they think and feel about the government that represents Japan. And I have no small sympathy for them. Therefore, when I heard this rumor that (Koreans) were starting fires, I thought that it was not beyond the realm of possibility."[50]

The rumors of an attack on his neighborhood lead Ema to consider people who might deserve the resentment of Koreans, people such as his neighbor General T. Furthermore, this train of thought leads Ema to think of actual people whom he knows to be involved in Korean independence. The person he imagines leading the attack was a Mr. B, identified in the text as an anarchist Ema had met but was not on familiar terms with. This Mr. B would have been understood to refer to Boku Retsu (Kr. Park Yeol or Bak Yeol), a Korean anarchist who was falsely arrested on September 2 for plotting the uprising.[51] What Ema reveals in this vision is his torn loyalties between his sympathy for the Korean cause and his devotion to those who represent his country, including his family and neighbors. Given the choice he imagines in his vision, he finds that he could not join the mob in their attack but hopes that his sympathies would be enough to save his children.

Eventually, Ema and his family gather together at a neighbor's house until they hear word that the threat has subsided. At the end of the second day, he remarks that the rumored Korean uprising they so feared had no basis. For Ema and his family, these rumors meant they spent a night fearing for their lives, though as he puts it: "I cannot complain about what happened to us, with everything coming to naught as if in a comedy. Our fear was caused by our own ignorance. But the thing that we cannot console ourselves about was that because of this panic, the

49. Ema Shū, *Hitsuji no ikaru toki*, 114–15. The word "Korean" was excised from the original but reinserted by the editors of the reprint.

50. Ibid., 82.

51. Bak Yeol, along with his lover Kaneko Fumiko, were eventually convicted of planning to murder the emperor and the crown prince at the latter's wedding. Both were sentenced to death, but later given life sentences in an imperial amnesty. Kaneko Fumiko committed suicide in 1926, but Bak survived twenty-two years in prison to be released after the war in 1945. For a more detailed exploration of this incident, see Helene Bowen Raddeker, *Treacherous Women of Imperial Japan: Patriarchal Fictions, Patricidal Fantasies* (London; New York: Routledge, 1997).

cruel . . ."[52] The sentence is left unfinished, certainly a concession to censorship, but the word Ema ends us on—"cruel"—speaks of the killings that occurred elsewhere as he sat trembling in his home.

This hanging sentence is the limit of Ema's critique. Surprisingly, Ema does not further discuss his vision of the shadowy Koreans breaking into his home and threatening his family. Nevertheless, by drawing on tropes of the "outlaw Korean" familiar in the media at the time, this potent apparition stands as a testament to the influence of the media on the Korean panic and the massacre. As a whole, Ema Shū's *When Sheep Rise in Anger* is a bleak look at the unfounded rumors and their all-too-real consequences. Along with Ema's own experiences, the book includes the accounts of several Korean friends who recall their harrowing attempts to cross the city after the disaster and their concern over a friend who never returned.[53]

Though he does not go into details of the massacre, Ema's portrayal of the fear and the frenzy, and particularly the void left by the missing friend, speaks to the horrors he was unable to convey. At the end of the book Ema tells a friend that, unlike the earthquake, which was a natural event that could be ascribed to fate, "the Korean crisis was completely born from our ignorance and prejudice, so from a humanitarian standpoint, we must say that this is the larger issue." The friend wonders where the rumors began, and Ema replies, "I don't think we will ever know. What we can say for certain, though, is that they are the responsibility of every single Japanese."[54] Within the bounds of censorship, Ema shows the consequences of the rumors and blames the Japanese people themselves. Nevertheless, he has the courage to include himself among those responsible, and, by vividly recreating his foolish nightmare, acknowledges his own vulnerability to media persuasion, and expresses his personal remorse.

* * * * *

The Korean Panic was a large part of the earthquake experience and is ubiquitous in authors' accounts of the earthquake, be they reliable or not. The way the shadowy figure of the Korean appears in these stories reveals where the authors' sympathies lie. For Nagata Mikihiko, the Korean is every bit as scary as the media made him out to be—full of lust and cruelty. Akutagawa Ryūnosuke ironically

52. Ema Shū, *Hitsuji no ikaru toki*, 129.
53. One of these friends was likely Tei Zenkei (1899–1979, Kr. Cheong Yon'gyu), who was one of the few Korean voices discussing the massacre in the metropole afterward. See, for example, his series from November 28 to December 15, 1923 in the *Hōchi shinbun,* collected in Kūm Pyōng-dong, *Chōsenjin gyakusatsu ni kansuru shokuminchi Chōsen no hannō* (Ryokuin Shobō, 1996).
54. Ema Shū, *Hitsuji no ikaru toki*, 253–54.

called attention to the way the rumors functioned in the interest of the state, and Tokuda Shūsei's story can be read as either a mild critique of intellectual posturing by authorities or a daring association linking the police to the massacre. In the case of Ema Shū, however, the contrast between the phantoms in his vision and the kind Koreans he interacts with helps call attention to the disconnect between media and reality. Those authors who tried to critique the panic, or even mention it to any degree, helped call attention to the massacre it caused. It was this massacre that made discussing the panic both more difficult and more necessary. To critique the panic was a courageous act, but the more courageous act was to deal with the massacre directly, an event more distant from authors' actual experiences. Some rose to the challenge, and it is their work that is the subject of the next chapter.

Chapter 9

The Masses and the Massacre: Responsibility and the Korea Question in Representations of the Massacre

The real tragedy of the Korean Panic (*Chōsenjin sawagi*), as Ema Shū pointed out (see Chapter 8), was the subsequent massacre. In the days following the earthquake, Koreans—vilified by the rumors and the media—were targeted and killed by members of *jikeidan* (neighborhood self-protection groups), the police, and the military. This massacre was a major component of newspaper earthquake coverage, especially following the official lifting of the ban on reporting on October 20, 1923. A key issue in the ensuing discussion was the question of responsibility: Who started the rumors? Who did the killing? According to contemporary newspapers and official documents, the answer to both of these questions was the *jikeidan*, the masses. The truth is more complicated, and subsequent research has shown that the police and the military were also heavily involved.[1] Fiction that depicted the massacre worked to untangle the complicated web of responsibility.

The Korean *Panic* is ubiquitous in essays by established writers, but the *massacre*—the actual murder of Koreans—appears only rarely. Nevertheless, there were a few writers who used the massacre to offer up a critique of contemporary Japanese society and, to a lesser extent, the government. Many of the writers who dealt explicitly with the massacre were affiliated with the proletarian literary movement; these writers were no strangers to controversy, censorship, and government oppression. Yet the Korean Massacre posed difficult questions for the movement, especially because it illustrated the distance between the current ideological mood of the public and the socialist ideal. Critics such as Aono Suekichi (1890–1961) saw widespread participation in the massacre as an indication of reactionary tendencies in the population as a whole, including the laboring masses. Sano Kesami (1886–1945), Etchūya Riichi (1901–70), and Akita Ujaku all produced controversial fictional work that dealt with the massacre.

1. The documents collected by Kang Tōk-sang and Kūm Pyōng-dong in their edited volume clearly implicate police and military in the killing. See Kang and Kūm, *Kantō daishinsai to Chōsenjin*. Subsequent research has provided further evidence. See, for example, Yamada Shōji, *Kantō daishinsaiji no chōsenjin gyakusatsu*. Despite Kūm's assertions, there is no smoking gun implicating the government in the rumors themselves.

Their works remain the most explicit contemporary literary explorations of the massacre, yet they only confront the issue of the Korean Massacre as it relates to Japan, leaving aside crucial questions of ethnic difference and colonial oppression. There is some reference to government culpability, but most blame the *jikeidan*, following contemporary media coverage. What these texts reveal, however, is a clear attempt to come to terms with the massacre and what might need to change to ensure that it would never happen again.

THE MASSACRE

Koreans living in the disaster zone were in a heightened state of vulnerability when the earthquake struck. Many were impoverished and exploited. Apart from some students, most Koreans in Japan were laborers who had immigrated first during the rapid industrial expansion during World War I, and later due to growing rural poverty on the Korean peninsula under Japanese colonial rule. Once in Japan, Koreans suffered from discrimination in housing and work and chronic unemployment.[2] Though the majority of immigrant workers were based in factories and mines far from the capital, approximately 14,000–20,000 Koreans lived in the greater Kantō area before the quake, over half in Tokyo prefecture.[3] Circumstantial evidence suggests that the majority of Tokyo-centered Koreans were living in the devastated *shitamachi* wards of Asakusa, Honjo, and Fukagawa as well as the industrialized Minami Katsushika area to the east.[4] This fact alone made them more susceptible to the fires following the earthquake than residents in substantial housing in the *yamanote*. In addition, the popular association between Koreans and criminality (discussed in Chapter 8) led to the rumors, the Korean Panic, and finally the massacre. Thus the Koreans were subject to secondary and tertiary disasters instigated by the shift in tectonic plates.

The actual total number of Koreans killed in the massacre across Japan remains uncertain. After citing several examples of numbers, lawyer and editor Yamazaki Kesaya (1877–1954) wrote in 1924 with characteristic wit, "Well, in any case there were more than two and less than 10,000."[5] Adding up the numbers

2. For a detailed look at Korean labor recruitment and immigration in interwar Japan, see Ken C. Kawashima, *The Proletarian Gamble*. Ema Shū explicitly discusses discrimination against Koreans in his book *Hitsuji no ikaru toki*, 250.
3. These numbers include those residing in Kanagawa (including Yokohama) and surrounding prefectures. The total Korean population in Japan at this time was approximately 90,000–120,000. Yamada Shōji, *Kantō daishinsaiji no chōsenjin gyakusatsu*, 46–47. See also Kūm Pyōng-dong, *Chōsenjin gyakusatsu ni kansuru chishikijin no hannō*, 8.
4. Yamada Shōji, *Kantō daishinsaiji no chōsenjin gyakusatsu*, 188.
5. This is from Yamazaki's extended essay "Earthquakes, Soldiers, Fires, and Police," first published in 1924. The title references a Japanese expression about various destructive forces of nature: earthquakes, lightning, fires, and fathers. Yamazaki Kesaya, *Jishin, kempei, kaji, junsa* (Iwanami, 1982), 232.

found in newspaper reports results in about 1,500.[6] In contrast, the government listed 230 deaths.[7] Most scholars agree that the total was in the thousands, with the upper limit at about 6,600—the number arrived at by the Korean independence movement's post-quake survey.[8] According to this survey, about 1,780 deaths occurred in the Tokyo area, and about 4,000 from Kanagawa prefecture, including Yokohama. The remaining thousand deaths were recorded mostly in Saitama and Chiba prefectures. Though these numbers were perhaps slightly overstated, they function as a baseline by which to gauge the distribution of the massacre. Of the Tokyo deaths for which locations were given (about 1,000), only 140 deaths were from the wards of the city itself—primarily Honjo and Asakusa; about 675 were from Minami Katsushika, an industrial area east of Honjo and Fukagawa.

Most reporting on the massacre accused the *jikeidan*—in other words, ordinary citizens—of being perpetrators. Braving censorship, the *Hōchi shinbun* printed more than thirty articles on *jikeidan* violence and arrests during the time that such articles were forbidden.[9] After the ban was lifted, journalistic attention turned to the trials, which exposed new revelations about the massacre. There were a total of 139 cases involving 735 people accused of murdering Koreans—and Japanese mistaken for Koreans—in the aftermath of the quake.[10] While there was considerable coverage from both the right and the left condemning the actions of the *jikeidan*, there were also some voices that sympathized with those on trial.[11] These supporters argued that an overabundance of patriotism had led the killers to what was universally regarded as excessive force.[12] Such reasoning ultimately led to lighter sentences. While members of *jikeidan* who had killed Japanese because they mistook them for Koreans were given jail sentences, no one accused of killing "only" Koreans ended up having to serve time.[13]

Some defendants in these trials used police and military sanctioning of the

6. See Jin-hee Lee, "Instability of Empire," 2, footnote 3.

7. See, for example, Yamada Shōji, *Kantō daishinsaiji no chōsenjin gyakusatsu*, 186.

8. This survey was published on December 5, 1923 in the official newspaper of the Korean independence movement's government in exile, *Dokuritsu shinbun* (*Independence News*), based in Shanghai. For a full discussion of the numbers from various institutions, see Yamada Shōji, *Kantō daishinsaiji no chōsenjin gyakusatsu*, 164-211.

9. See the list of articles collected in Yamada Shōji, *Chōsenjin gyakusatsu hōdō shiryō*.

10. Jin-hee Lee, "Instability of Empire," 77–78. These prosecutions were likely show trials staged to prove to the international community that action was being taken. As Yamada Shōji has argued, these trials were also part of a concerted effort to blame *jikeidan* rather than the government for the massacre. Yamada Shōji, *Kantō daishinsaiji no chōsenjin gyakusatsu*, 89–106.

11. For criticism on from the right, see Masuda Giichi, who claimed that the *jikeidan* violence showed "A Defect in National Discipline," the title of his essay in the November 15, 1923 issue of *Jitsugyō no Nihon*, collected in Kūm Pyōng-dong, *Chōsenjin gyakusatsu ni kansuru chishikijin no hannō*, 104.

12. For a full discussion of support for *jikeidan*, see Jin-hee Lee, "Instability of Empire," 90–97.

13. Ibid., 92.

violence as part of their defense, thus implicating the authorities.[14] This was one of the few venues in which such insinuations were possible. Later eyewitness accounts show not only that certain officials sanctioned the violence, but that they were often major instigators. One horrific example took place in the Kameido police station on the west side of Minami Katsushika, where 86 Koreans were reportedly killed by military personnel.[15] Ultimately, no members of the military were court-martialed on account of their participation.

Explicit accusations of direct police and military involvement were extremely rare, due in no small part to concerted governmental efforts to conceal participation by organs of the state.[16] A notice in the *Hōchi shinbun* on October 26 reported that an earlier edition had been banned because of an article it ran on police misconduct.[17] Though it does not indicate what type of misconduct, swift reaction from the Home Ministry suggests the difficulty of reporting on police or military involvement in the massacre. Nevertheless, there are some examples of contemporary critics hinting at police participation. Korean-born writer Tei Zenkei (1899–1979, Kr. Cheong Yon'gyu) was quoted in the *Hōchi shinbun* as saying, "The *jikeidan* were given the blame, but weren't the police and military also at fault?"[18] Lawyer and activist Fuse Tatsuji (1880–1953) was a little more explicit. After blaming the military and police for spreading the rumors and for telling *jikedan* that it was permissible to kill Koreans—information that was reported in coverage of the trials—Fuse wrote, "Some say that no small number of police and soldiers cut down or shot Koreans themselves."[19]

The facts surrounding the massacre of Koreans after the earthquake have remained obscure. It is clear that those who participated included civilians organized into "self-protection groups" as well as military and police personnel, though the *jikeidan* bore the brunt of the blame in the media. But delving into why

14. See, for example, the *Hōchi shinbun*, October 27 (and 26 evening edition), 1923, collected in Yamada Shōji, *Chōsenjin gyakusatsu hōdō shiryō*, 62.
15. Yamada Shōji, *Kantō daishinsaiji no chōsenjin gyakusatsu*, 189–92.
16. This is particularly clear in government surveys of Koreans killed, and in efforts to hide bodies, as pointed out by Yamada Shōji. Ibid., 180–85.
17. Collected in Yamada Shōji, *Chōsenjin gyakusatsu hōdō shiryō*, 61.
18. Article published in the *Hōchi shinbun,* October 21, 1923 (and October 20, evening edition). Collected in Yamada Shōji, *Chōsenjin gyakusatsu hōdō shiryō*, 49. Diplomat Yanagisawa Takeshi also put at least some blame on the military and police in his article "The Cruel Actions of the *Jikeidan*," published in the November/December 1923 issue of *Fujin kōron* and collected in Kūm Pyōng-dong, *Chōsenjin gyakusatsu ni kansuru chishikijin no hannō*, 210.
19. Fuse Tatsuji, "Senjin sawagi no chōsa," collected in Kūm Pyōng-dong, *Chōsenjin gyakusatsu ni kansuru chishikijin no hannō*, vol. 1 (Ryokuin Shobō, 1996), 336. Jinhee Lee also mentions a teacher from Akita prefecture who published an article in a local newsletter condemning the actions of the *jikeidan*, along with those of the police and military, for giving Japan a bad name: "The lowly and uncivilized behavior of the soldiers, police officers, and vigilantes ruined the reputation of imperial Japan even more than the earthquake itself." Lee, "Instability of Empire," 68–69.

these people killed others extends into murkier territory. The massacre seems to have been sparked by an incendiary combination of civilians and military personnel conditioned by the media to suspect "shadowy" Koreans and indoctrinated to protect the nation from threats, rumors that seemed to confirm preexisting suspicions about Koreans, and the opportunity provided by the chaotic aftermath of a large-scale disaster.

The Proletarian Movement and the Massacre

The Japanese proletarian movement was profoundly affected by state repression following the earthquake, for major figures in leftist thought and art were killed by police and military officials. In the Kameido Incident, poet, playwright, and labor activist Hirasawa Keishichi, along with nine others involved in the labor movement, were killed after being taken to the Kameido jail. The Amakasu Incident was even more infamous. More than two weeks after the earthquake, anarchist Ōsugi Sakae, his lover Itō Noe, and his young nephew were killed by a military squad under the command of lieutenant Amakasu Masahiko. These incidents, while horrific, fit within the worldview of the proletarian movement: the government was the enemy and the oppressor. As such, these murders were considered to be the culmination of a history of persecution by police and military forces, and were treated as particular egregious examples of state oppression in sympathetic media outlets.

The death of Ōsugi Sakae and, to a lesser extent, that of Hirasawa Keishichi became major stories in newspapers and magazines. Some of the most vehement reactions against the murders came from progressive intellectuals who published pieces in middle-class general-interest journals such as *Chūō kōron* and *Kaizō,* and those involved in *Tanemaku hito* (*The Sower*). *Kaizō* devoted a special edition to Ōsugi in November 1923. The Kameido Incident was slightly less well publicized, but articles did appear in general-interest magazines. The proletarian literary magazine *Tanemaku hito* devoted its swan-song edition to exposing the facts and the personal tragedies surrounding the Kameido Incident.[20] Nevertheless, the media was not unanimous in its condemnation of military personnel overstepping their mandate to protect the country. And there were instances of government censors banning newspapers because columnists wrote *in support* of Amakasu killing Ōsugi.[21]

20. This edition of *Tanemaku hito* (*The Sower*), published in January 1924, was given a slightly different name, *Tanemaku zakki* (*Sowing Miscellany*).

21. This was mostly due to Arita Otomatsu's article praising Amakasu Masahiko, which ran in nearly thirty newspapers. See Matsuo Shōichi et al., *Kantō daishinsai seifu, riku-kaigun kankei shiryō*, 272.

Significant reactionary support for Amakasu suggested to proletarian thinkers, such as Aono Suekichi, that the masses were far from an ideal proto-revolutionary force. Rumors asserted that socialists were behind the supposed Korean riots, and thus known socialists were also targeted by *jikeidan*. Though no *jikeidan* killed leftists, many socialists active at the time reported being harassed.[22] Morito Tatsuo—the professor famously imprisoned in 1920 for his writings on Kropotkin—wrote a few months after the earthquake: "Socialists were persecuted from the top by the government and from the bottom by the masses, such that we were seen for a time as complete outlaws."[23] As another writer put it, "After the quake, we socialists deeply felt our isolation."[24]

The massacre of Koreans furthered the sense of distance felt by Morito and others. According to the media, this was not government versus the proletariat, but people verses people. Newspaper and court records on the people arrested for murdering Koreans reported that perpetrators included construction workers, bucket-makers, cart drivers, rickshaw-pullers, peddlers and day laborers.[25] Writers and critics of all political persuasions were troubled by the seemingly widespread participation in the massacre by ordinary citizens, but the unease was particularly acute for those sympathetic to the proletarian cause. In those construction workers, bucket-makers, and rickshaw-pullers accused of the murders, proletarian writers saw the very people they set out to save. This concern is manifest in Aono Suekichi's post-quake discussion of the relationship between "the masses" and the intellectuals who made up the vanguard of the movement.

The distance between the masses and the intellectual vanguard was a particular concern before the earthquake, and remained a point of debate throughout the life of the movement.[26] In 1921 the Japanese communist movement adopted the slogan "Closer to the masses" to help address the issue.[27] In early essays, critics articulated the need for the masses to be educated by the vanguard to help bring

22. Maeda Kakuzō, *Kyokō no naka no aidentiti* (Hosei Daigaku Shuppankyoku, 1989), 182.
23. Morito Tatsuo gives an overview of what he saw as persecution of socialists from both the government and the masses after the quake, in his article "The Earthquake, Socialist Thought, and Reactionary Power," in the January 1924 issue of *Warera*, collected in Kūm Pyōng-dong, *Chōsenjin gyakusatsu ni kansuru chishikijin no hannō*, vol. 1, 275–78.
24. Kitahara Yasuo, "Jishin to shakai shugi," collected in Kūm Pyōng-dong, *Chōsenjin gyakusatsu ni kansuru chishikijin no hannō*, vol. 1 (Ryokuin Shobō, 1996), 405.
25. Kang Tōk-sang, *Kantō daishinsai*. For more information on these trials, see Jin-hee Lee, "Instability of Empire." The absence of wealthier persons, as well as military personnel, also implies selective policing.
26. For a discussion of this argument later in the decade, see Heather Bowen-Struyk, "Rethinking Japanese Proletarian Literature" (Ph.D. dissertation, University of Michigan, 2001), especially chapter 4.
27. See Robert A. Scalapino, *The Japanese Communist Movement, 1920–1966* (Berkeley: University of California Press, 1967), 20–21; and George M. Beckmann and Genji Okubo, *The Japanese Communist Party, 1922–1945* (Stanford, CA: Stanford University Press, 1969), 50–53.

about revolution. But the Korean Massacre revealed a populace ready to believe imperial fear mongering and direct its anger toward fellow workers of a different ethnicity rather than against the government and the capitalists who oppressed them.

In an article published three months after the earthquake, "The Masses: From Abstraction to Reality" ("Gen'ei no taishū kara taishū no jittai e"), Aono Suekichi revisited the 1921 slogan. Aono claimed that, despite two years of discussion, there had been little progress in bridging the gap between the vanguard and the masses. He explicitly connected the lack of progress to the earthquake and the subsequent "events." He wrote: "This [distance between the vanguard and the masses] is evident from the events surrounding the recent earthquake disaster. The various events of that time painfully attest to the backward thought of Japanese masses (*Nihon no taishū*) today and the impossibility of finding even the slightest understanding of socialist ideas among them."[28] The word "events" is intentionally ambiguous to avoid censorship, though the referent is clear in context: the persecution of socialists and the massacre of Koreans.[29]

In part, it was the definition of "the masses" that was at stake in Aono's essay. He argued that the masses had been seen abstractly prior to the earthquake, and that now they must be seen as the concrete and diverse group they were. In other words, intellectuals in the vanguard must understand the masses as much more than just laborers and farmers. Rather, Aono asserted that the masses were a complex collection of people who included factory workers, but also shopkeepers, rickshaw-pullers, tinsmiths and so on—both the petite bourgeoisie and the laborer. All were complicit in some way with the events following the quake, either by directly participating or spreading rumors. Yet by acknowledging the complexity of the masses, Aono argued that proletarian writers could address them in more specific terms so that they might be better educated in socialist ideals. Aono ultimately maintained that education in class consciousness should not be limited to laborers. Many people from different class backgrounds were at fault in the massacre, and education thus needed to be directed to the masses as a whole.

Aono's loss of faith in the masses and his awareness of the great divide between the masses and the vanguard were echoed by other proletarian writers as well. In an overview of proletarian literature published in the magazine *Gakan*

28. Aono Suekichi, "Gen'ei no taishū kara taishū no jittai e," in idem, *Musan seitō to shakai undō* (Hakuyōsha, 1925), 144–45.

29. In some contemporary articles, Aono wrote about the "events" as "violent events" that make him lose faith in the masses. In other cases, he is more explicit. See, for example, his essay "Shakai no genjitsu to shisō to," *Shinkō* 1, no. 1 (February 1924), reprinted in Kūm Pyōng-dong, *Chōsenjin gyakusatsu ni kansuru chishikijin no hannō*, 9–12. This essay helps interpret the "events" with certainty as the Kameido Incident, the Amakasu Incident, and the Korean Massacre. See also Maeda Kakuzō, *Kyokō no naka no aidentiti*, 178.

(*Our Views*), Eguchi Kan wrote: "It is just as Aono Suekichi says—the recent earthquake gave proof of the great distance between the vanguard of the socialist movement and the masses. And I believe that literature is a valid means of bringing the masses and the vanguard closer together."[30] For Eguchi as well, education was the answer to solving the problem, and he posited literature as the ideal method. Eguchi continued in the article to rate recent literature in terms of its ability to educate about socialist ideals, and found much of it lacking.

Sano Kesami took the idea further in a 1925 essay, "The Massification of Literature" ("Bungei no taishūka"). In this essay Sano argued that in order to win the hearts of the masses in the post-quake reactionary milieu, proletarian literature must target its tastes specifically. Here Sano was reacting to the phenomenal success of mass-circulation magazines such as Kōdansha's *King*, which debuted in 1924 with a run of 740,000. To succeed at its goals, proletarian literature must have the same kind of reach, and to do so would mean couching its ideals in literature written for mass consumption. Proletarian literature would not achieve this kind of popular success until Tokunaga Sadao's *Sunless Street* (*Taiyō no nai machi*) in 1929. Nevertheless Sano's post-quake play about the Korean Massacre uses familiar melodramatic tropes to redeem one segment of the masses while blaming another. The black-and-white morality of the play would win him no converts from beyond the narrowly defined definition of the masses as workers. For Sano, however, they were the only ones worth convincing.

REDEEMING THE LABORER IN SANO KESAMI'S *THE HARBOR OF MAYHEM*

Sano Kesami's play *The Harbor of Mayhem* (*Konran no minato*) was published in the proletarian literary journal *Bungei sensen* (*Literary Front*) exactly one year after the earthquake. The play revolves around the actions and internal clashes of a *jikeidan* vigilante group a few days after the disaster. The primary conflict emerges when a local professor is asked to join the group, whereupon he speaks out against the rumors and the massacre to the mostly unsympathetic group. In the interaction between the professor and the crowd, we see the relationship between the vanguard and the masses dramatized in the midst of the "events" that troubled Aono Suekichi. Unlike Aono's pessimistic view of the masses as a whole, *The Harbor of Mayhem* redeems some segments of the population while condemning others. Sano blamed the petite bourgeoisie for the massacre and crafted his laborer character as one of the most levelheaded in his play. Sano pokes fun at the imperialist discourse and rationale for believing the rumors, but ultimately his critique is weakened by its oversimplifying the issue through crude class divisions that make the petite bourgeoisie evil and the laborers virtuous.

30. Eguchi Kan, "Bungei jihyō," *Gakan* 2, no. 2 (February 1924): 185.

The Harbor of Mayhem is in all respects a melodrama. It has the high emotions of post-earthquake tension, the sensationalism of vigilante violence, the pathos of innocent victims murdered, and a very clear moral polarity, one drawn strictly along class lines. Each member of the cast is identified solely by occupation; the central characters include the professor, a series of shopkeepers (a grocer, rice-seller, fishmonger, barber, and so on), a student, an office-worker, and a laborer. The play includes representatives from a range of class positions in the writings of Marx and Weber: the intelligentsia (the professor), the new middle class (office-worker), the petite bourgeoisie or "old middle class"(the shopkeepers), and the working class (the laborer). The only character who does not stand for a class is the student. Rather, he represents youth who have had, in the words of the play, "militaristic ideology beaten into them from childhood."[31] The student is the result of a misguided national education system that must be replaced with a proper education in socialist ideals.

When the play opens, neighborhood residents have gathered on the streets as a *jikeidan*. The office-worker speaks the first line: "They say that Koreans are setting fires, throwing bombs, and poisoning wells, but I wonder if they really did such terrible things."[32] His expression of doubt is met by vehement opposition from the shopkeepers and the student. The others cite the rumors as proof enough. In one humorous example of circular logic, the rice-seller asserts that the rumors must be true because the Koreans would not be killed without reason, and, as he puts it, "They are being captured and killed all over."[33] By his very doubt the office-worker is characterized as an intelligent, reasonable, and moral figure set in contrast to the irrational rice-seller.

The laborer is similarly established as moral. As the discussion continues, the shopkeepers wonder why the Koreans would turn on a country that helps them, parroting right-wing rationalizations of colonialism. In response to their questions the barber says: "They should be grateful to us Japanese. I mean, we're ruling their country for them. Their country was just a big mess, and they weren't able to do a thing about it, were they? And since we came along and peacefully took it over from them, they've been so much happier. . . . They don't have the power to rule themselves. They're happier ruled peacefully by Japan. Since we took over, they've grown more civilized. You can tell just by looking." The laborer takes the Korean point of view in response: "But how could Koreans think of that as 'civilization'? They are not happy that the Japanese are ruling over them."[34]

31. Sano Kesami, "Konran no minato," in *Hennentai Taishō bungaku zenshū*, vol. 13 (2003): 257. All citations are from this edition.

32. Ibid., 251.

33. Ibid., 252.

34. Ibid.

These initial interactions within the group establish the moral divide. The characters representing the petite bourgeoisie repeat the rumors and colonial discourse on Korea without self-reflection. The rice-seller's circular logic asserting that the Koreans must be guilty if they are being killed, and the barber's caricatured imperialistic rhetoric, are meant to look ridiculous. In contrast, the office-worker and the laborer are portrayed as moderates, people who do not rush to judgment but rather use logic to search for the truth. It is these very qualities that allow for redemption. Nothing in the play alters this dynamic.

When asked where he heard that the rumors were baseless, the office-worker identifies the professor who lives in the neighborhood. Incensed, the *jikeidan* call the professor to shoulder his share of the responsibility and join them. He does so reluctantly. From that point on, a series of events reinforce the moral gulf between the shopkeepers and the student on the one hand and the laborer, office-worker, and professor on the other. Rumors come and go, and various people wandering onto the stage are mistaken for Koreans. The worst agitator in the group is the student, who consistently accuses the professor of propagating "dangerous thoughts" that threaten the nation. The shopkeepers are not far behind him. They almost kill an artist because he looks Korean, and sexually harass a nurse. The office-worker and the laborer continue to express their reservations in every encounter, their hesitancy emphasizing their morality and rationality.

When a youth-group member tells the *jikeidan* that socialists have been killed in the Kameido area, the student can hardly hide his glee. Using characteristic circular logic, he asserts that if socialists are being killed, they must be guilty, and the group decides to seek them out for vengeance. The laborer tries to reason with them—he tells the group that the socialists want to bring about a society based on equality and have no reason to provoke Koreans to attack. His protestations go unheeded, and the *jikeidan* only abandons this effort when distracted.

The professor is the obvious hero throughout these interactions. He takes it upon himself to educate the group in socialist thought, and he also shows the folly and danger in trying to teach the masses the error of their ways. After one rumor is shown to be false, the office-worker comments on the "frightful" mob psychology he sees in the group, echoing a common critique of *jikeidan* at the time.[35] In response to this comment, the professor goes on a tirade against the ignorant masses. After complaining about the simplicity of the masses (*minshū*) and their self-destructive practices, the professor says: "I had put a lot of trust in the masses, and now feel as though I have been betrayed. . . . We must place the blame at the feet of the education system that has left the masses in their ig-

35. See, for example, the essays by Hasegawa Nyozekan, collected in Kūm Pyōng-dong, *Chōsenjin gyakusatsu ni kansuru chishikijin no hannō*, 139–44.

norance and not brought them to self-realization. . . . Oh, when will the masses awaken?"[36] In this lament, the professor echoes Aono Suekichi in his feelings of betrayal. His hope that people can be redeemed through education is dampened by the overwhelming counterrevolutionary education of the state that is embodied by the student.

As readers and viewers might suspect, the professor's direct condemnation is not well received by the members of the *jikeidan*, who increasingly see the professor as a purveyor of "dangerous ideas." At the climax of the play, two "real" Koreans enter from stage left and are immediately accosted by the group. The student and shopkeepers harass the couple until the professor steps in and chides them in another righteously indignant speech. He calls them no worse than animals and says he will defend the Koreans for as long as he has life left in him. This speech provokes rather than persuades the crowd, and the student calls to mob: "Let's take care of this guy first. Okay, everyone, get him! . . . Traitor!" The mob descends; the professor's wife screams; and the office worker frees the Koreans in the confusion. Finally the laborer is able to forcefully break up the mob. He takes the limp and bleeding body of the professor in his arms and pronounces in despair: "Ah! It's too late." The professor's wife wails as the curtain falls.

There is some precedent for this depiction of violence against those speaking out in favor of Koreans in accounts of the disaster. In the post-quake issue of *Tanemaku hito,* one writer recalled that Kondō Kōzō, one of those killed in the Kameido Incident, was at one point attacked by a *jikeidan* after expressing compassion for Koreans killed in the massacre.[37] In an essay published in the magazine *Bunka undō* (*Literary Movement*), in the same month Sano's play appeared, the social activist and critic Shimanaka Yūzō gave an account of his confrontation with his neighborhood *jikeidan*.[38] Shimanaka's rhetoric was far from the confrontational stance adopted by Sano's professor character, yet he was attacked.

Given Sano's argument in "The Massification of Literature" that proletarian literature must cater to the tastes of the masses, the example of the professor is a cautionary one. These shopkeepers are not ready to acknowledge their own ignorance, or for an outsider to tell them they are wrong. In *The Harbor of Mayhem*, only the laborer and the office-worker are receptive to the professor's lectures. Yet, like the rhetoric of the professor, Sano's play as a whole can be directed only toward those who already subscribe to the ideas expressed. Converting the masses

36. Sano Kesami, "Konran no minato," 257.

37. Sasaki Takamaru, "Chōsenjin e dōjō shite," *Tanemaku zakki* 1, no. 1 (January 1924): 22.

38. This article by Shimanaka Yūzō is collected in Kūm Pyōng-dong, *Chōsenjin gyakusatsu ni kansuru chishikijin no hannō*, 408–11.

as a whole would require considerably more finesse.

In the end, Sano does show the "masses" to be a complex entity by including people of different class backgrounds, as Aono suggested. But in *The Harbor of Mayhem* Sano divides the "masses" into those who can be persuaded by socialist arguments and those who cannot. The former include those who are important to the movement: namely, the new middle class of educated white-collar workers (who were one part of the audience of the proletarian journal *Bungei sensen*), and the laborers. There is even a hint that with a different educational environment the impressionable student might not have become a killer. There is little indication that the same might be true of the petite bourgeoisie. The way they harass the innocent and readily accept nationalist rhetoric implies a deeply ingrained fear of others and an insurmountable ignorance.

Despite the fact that the professor mimics Aono's words, Sano's simplistic division of the masses into the good and the bad betrays Aono's original point: namely, that a variety of people from different class backgrounds participated in the massacre, both laborer and shopkeeper, and that education needs to extend to all. There are implied criticisms of the state in *The Harbor of Mayhem*; the barber caricatures the absurdity of official colonial rationalization, and the indoctrinated student embodies the excesses of militarized education. Nevertheless, the brunt of the criticism is leveled at the bloodthirsty petite bourgeoisie. There is no direct reference to the wealthy capitalists or to the state—two categories that fall outside any definition of "the masses." More importantly, there is nothing that addresses the fact that laborers, along with the petite bourgeoisie, overwhelmingly supported Japan's imperial expansion, or that laborers and other marginal people were often at the forefront of those colonizing the Korean peninsula. It is common in proletarian literature to structure moral polarity in conflicts between capitalists and laborers along class divisions. Those boundaries are clear. But when the problem is mass ethnic violence, it becomes difficult to create unambiguous ethical boundaries based on class alone.

The clear class divisions in *The Harbor of Mayhem* fail to describe the realities of Japanese laborers' ambiguous position in relation to colonial policy. Sano Kesami tried to erase those problems by dividing the masses involved in the Korean Massacre into categories that fit the proletarian worldview. However, in showing only the petite bourgeoisie to be the evil actors in the Korean Massacre, Sano is blatantly rewriting history. The laborers *were* involved in the massacre. And, as the trials of the *jikeidan* show, the brand of anti-Korean rhetoric spoken in the play came from the mouths of laborers as often as it came from the petite bourgeoisie. The real conundrum of the Korean massacre is left unarticulated: namely, that the Japanese worker was complicit in ethnic and colonial oppression. By leaving out questions of ethnicity and colonialism as he redeems the laborer, Sano attempts to translate ethnic tension into class tension.

Critique of the State in Etchūya Riichi's "One Soldier's Record of the Quake"

Three years after Sano wrote his play, a young proletarian writer named Etchūya Riichi debuted on the literary scene with a striking work about the massacre, "One Soldier's Record of the Earthquake" ("Ippeisotsu no shinsai shuki").[39] Like Sano Kesami, Etchūya was a writer fully involved in the proletarian literary movement, and his work fits squarely within that paradigm.[40] It is the story of a soldier's growing class-consciousness, set amid the chaos after the earthquake. The plot then moves to a depiction of the Korean Massacre, which serves to illustrate the way soldiers are manipulated by the state. By 1927 the complicated relationship between the masses and the massacre was no longer a pressing issue for the proletarian movement. Rather, "One Soldier's Record of the Earthquake" displaces the responsibility for the massacre from the worker/soldier onto the capitalist state, freeing them from blame as Sano did, even though in this case soldiers are clearly shown to have participated in the massacre.

The first half of "One Soldier's Record of the Earthquake" works to create a sense of solidarity among soldiers, sufferers, and workers. As such it is a fictionalized representation of Etchūya's argument in his first published essay, "Socialism and the Army" ("Guntai to shakaishugi," 1921), written the year he entered the military.[41] The essay stresses the need to win over the conscripted troops to the socialist cause and then work toward resistance from within the ranks. Similarly, "One Soldier's Record of the Earthquake" establishes the soldier as a worker and then points out, through an internal monologue, the deficiencies within that system, finally coming to the climactic class awakening.

Etchūya begins "One Soldier's Record of the Earthquake" by situating his protagonist first as a person suffering from the disaster, and second as a worker oppressed by those above him. The story opens ten days after the disaster, as the unnamed soldier-protagonist finally receives word from his parents confirming his worst fears—his younger brothers and his older brother's entire family are missing and presumed dead. This chain of events places the protagonist among

39. Etchūya Riichi's story must have been popular because it was reprinted several times in the next few years. "One Soldier's Record of the Earthquake" also spawned a small revival in proletarian works dealing with the earthquake. In addition to "One Soldier's Record of the Earthquake," Etchūya published another short work in *Senki* (*Battle Flag*) on the fifth anniversary of the quake in September 1928. In that same issue, Tsuboi Shigeji published "Fifteen Yen, Fifty Sen" ("Jūgoen, gojūsen"), and in November 1928 Yanase Masamu published "Bitten by a Mad Dog" ("Kyōken ni kamareru") in the same magazine.

40. Etchūya was involved in a different faction. Sano published in *Bungei sensen* (*Literary Front*), whereas Etchūya published in its rival *Kaihō* (*Emancipation*).

41. Etchūya Riichi, "Guntai to shakaishugi," *Rōdōsha,* September 1921; reprinted in *Etchūya Riichi chosakushū* (Gifu: Tōkai keizai shinbunsha, 1971), 501–2.

the hundreds of thousands who lost family in the earthquake, emphasizing that he is one of the suffering masses and not merely a soldier. At the same time, his status as a soldier establishes him as a member of the oppressed proletariat. Within the story, soldiers are put in the service of the capitalists, with blatant disregard for the welfare of the soldiers and their families. Typical of the heartless employer, the protagonist's commanding officer does not allow him to take leave to check on his family. Etchūya's protagonist is doubly affected by the earthquake disaster, making him an object of sympathy, a sympathy intended to lead toward solidarity.

By introducing his protagonist as someone oppressed by both the natural disaster and the elites, Etchūya attempts to create a discursive solidarity between the protagonist and the reader, presumed to be a worker or someone sympathetic to their cause. While the imperial rescripts stress unity based on nationality, Etchūya stresses unity based on the shared conditions of suffering and oppression. This unity is then set in opposition to the forces that create the suffering: not the natural disaster, but the human choices that exacerbated it. With his pedigree as a sufferer and worker established, the protagonist engages in an interior monologue focusing first on the uneven distribution of the damage and second on the misuse of state power, not to aid the people but to persecute them.

Deeply saddened by the news of his brothers and frustrated by his confinement to his duties, the protagonist cries out in his mind against the injustice, foregrounding the class divisions emphasized by the earthquake: "Oh, the idiotic irony of forcing soldiers who lost their homes and families to stand sentry over the safe of a merchant."[42] The merchant referred to here has been affected by the quake and has presumably lost his store. But merchants were able to take refuge, while the soldiers/workers were forced to guard their money. Unlike the soldiers, this merchant's difficulties are being alleviated by the government and its military. The soldiers have been dispatched not to protect their own interests or those of their class, but instead to protect those of the capitalists. By dwelling on these differences, Etchūya challenges the unity proclaimed by the state, illustrating the discrepancy between the classes in both the earthquake damage and the distribution of aid.

In depicting the soldier-protagonist protecting capitalist wealth, Etchūya suggests that the primary role of the troops enforcing martial law was protecting property rather than distribution of aid. This critique of misplaced priorities was being circulated in Etchūya's circle at the time, notably by Yamazaki Kesaya, the

42. Etchūya Riichi, "Ippeisotsu no shinsai shuki," in *Nihon puroretaria bungaku shū*, vol. 14 (1984): 179. I am using the version reprinted in the *Nihon puroretaria bungakushū* as the basis for my translations. This version is based on the *Shinkō bungaku zenshū* version and includes some of the words previously censored. A similar complaint by a soldier was published anonymously in the *Hōchi shinbun* on October 2, 1923. That soldier was forced to stand watch outside a bank for a month after the quake. Yamada Shōji, *Chōsenjin gyakusatsu hōdō shiryō*, 24–25.

outspoken lawyer and editor of *Kaihō* (*Emancipation*), in which "One Soldier's Record of the Earthquake" was published. In his book *Earthquake, Soldier, Fire, Officer* (*Jishin, kempei, kaji, junsa*), published the year following the earthquake, Yamazaki wrote about the difference between the San Francisco Earthquake and the Kanto Earthquake in these terms. According to Yamazaki, the deployment of the troops in the San Francisco earthquake was to help the victims, whereas in the Kanto earthquake the focus was on maintaining control.[43] Yamazaki argues that this difference contributed to the excesses of martial law—namely, the Korean Massacre and the persecution (and murder) of socialists. Though he mentions the role of the military in these atrocities, Yamazaki further argues that the martial law itself created an atmosphere of fear that fueled the crazed attacks on Koreans. As he puts it, "In truth, martial law was the equivalent of pouring oil on fire."[44]

In "One Soldier's Record of the Earthquake," Etchūya is more concerned with the excesses of martial law and the military itself than with how martial law provoked the masses. In the internal monologues of the protagonist, he exclaims that martial law was nothing more than persecution of the people, specifically, the socialists and Koreans: "What does the military do each day? Uphold martial law. In other words, it seems to be nothing other than the *** (Imperial Army persecuting and murdering Koreans) and socialists."[45] According to the protagonist, martial law was actually part of the disaster itself, despite the pressing need to alleviate suffering. And among the targets of military persecution were socialists, like the soldier-protagonist himself. This accusation identifies the state as the enemy of the protagonist, and by extension the enemy of the workers and the people.

The protagonist's resentment at being forced to play a part in the persecution—if only by association—leads to a stronger class-consciousness and desire to fight oppression. His thoughts about the misuse of state power in a time of need prevent him from sleeping, and he tosses and turns in his bunk. The climactic conclusion to this section depicts him waking up, both literally and figuratively: "Within his head a frightening but strangely bright, historical idea burst open like a firework. Struck by his own realization, he felt as if a bolt of lightning pulsed

43. Yamazaki Kesaya, *Jishin, kempei, kaji, junsa*, 223–24. Etchūya was a frequent contributor to Yamazaki's magazine. Scholars of the San Francisco earthquake refute Yamazaki's overly rosy impression of the differences. See, for example, the mayor's order to kill looters on sight, found in the online exhibit "The Great 1906 Earthquake and Fire" by the Museum of San Francicsco. <http://www.sfmuseum.org/1906.2/killproc.html> (accessed August 5, 2013). See also Andrea Davies, *Saving San Francisco: Relief and Recovery after the 1906 Disaster* (Philadelphia: Temple University Press, 2012). For a discussion of military looting of Chinatown, see Walter Ko, "1906 San Francisco Chinatown Burning and Rebuilding," *Chinese American Forum* 22, no. 3 (January 2007): 34–37.

44. Yamazaki Kesaya, *Jishin, kempei, kaji, junsa*, 223.

45. Etchūya Riichi, "Ippeisotsu," 179. The *** indicate unknown characters removed from the text to help it pass the censors. The words in parentheses have been reinserted by the editors based on context. The editorial notes say that the words are educated guesses.

throughout his whole body. . . . He could feel the power entering him as he lay on his bunk. 'Yes that's it, joining hands between the soldiers and the masses. What wonderful "solidarity."'"[46] There is a power in this awakening, conveyed by Etchūya's metaphorical use of lightning and fireworks, and a sense that this power will be put toward creating that "wonderful 'solidarity.'"

If this soldier-as-oppressed-worker attaining class-consciousness were the entire story, there would be little to distinguish "One Soldier's Record of the Earthquake" from other proletarian works, especially those portraying life in the military. After this point, however, the story begins to explore how the state employs violence against its people—a people that includes Koreans. The protagonist's vision at the end of the first part is of the soldiers and the people joining hands in solidarity to oppose the excesses of the state, excesses in which he, as a soldier, is expected to play a role.

The soldiers are called out of their slumber to respond to claims of an indeterminate number of Koreans advancing on a neighborhood in the suburbs. When they arrive in battle formation, the *jikeidan* have already sounded the warning and groups of locals are running about in fear of the attack. The soldiers take control and set up a perimeter to force the Koreans to the river. Etchūya goes on to describe in vivid detail the suspenseful lead-up to the battle. The morning fog rolls in as the protagonist and his squad wait for the Koreans to be driven toward them. When the Koreans approach, the protagonist's commanding officer announces that the enemy is armed and gives orders to kill any who resist. Soon the Koreans emerge and confusion reigns as shots are exchanged. Eventually the "enemy" realizes they are surrounded and surrender. After the squad leader and others kill a few of the captured and unarmed Koreans, the rest are forced to march back to the military base. This depiction is rare in that it references a specific instance of state involvement in the Korean Massacre rather than portraying it as involving only the usual perpetrators: the *jikeidan*. Within the story, the state is to blame for the excessive application of martial law violence, and for forcing the soldiers to fight against an enemy that is not their own.

Among the dead from the firefight are two Koreans who have died with pistols in hand: "Two (Koreans) who had probably given cover fire for those trying to cross the river were lying on top of one another grasping their (pistols) firmly in their hands until the end."[47] By their act of sacrifice, futile though it was, these two Koreans are portrayed in the story as martyrs, the heroes of the battle. Though there is pity for the defenseless Koreans who were massacred after surrendering, these two are depicted with a sense of awe.

46. Ibid., 180.
47. Ibid., 184. Again the words in parentheses were added by the editors.

If these martyred Koreans are the heroes of this battle, who are the villains? The protagonist seems to ask this question, though both the question and the answer are obscured by censors: "**** those who gave this order ****? The squad leader, the platoon leader, or (the soldier)? No, no, he whispered. It is something greater than all of them, something that can use them as its arms and legs to further its designs***************,*********** and looking at this fact he was unable to hide his resentment."[48] The protagonist questions the culpability of the regular soldier, but does so only to deny it. Just as Sano Kesami found it necessary to redeem the worker in his play, so Etchūya preserves the soldier as an ethical character. As a worker, the soldier becomes part of the resistance in the thoughts of the protagonist, even though some soldiers participated in the massacre. The real villain is something much larger, larger even than the officers—something that uses the soldiers and their leaders as "its arms and legs to further its designs."

The true guise of this evil force manipulating the soldiers is obscured by censorship, its immorality confirmed by its shadowy machinations. Perhaps the censored passage implicates the state, the emperor system, imperialism, or capitalism. Nevertheless, readers would fill in the gaps with forbidden ideas, perhaps more damning than the original. The most likely reading of the censored words is suggested by the complaints of the soldier earlier in the story, the source of his original resentment: the combination of the government and the capitalists that forced soldiers to stand guard over the safes of the wealthy.

The move toward blaming the state for the massacre can be seen in other examples of proletarian literature published after Etchūya's work. The year following "One Soldier's Record of the Earthquake" saw three more works that dealt with the Korean Massacre. One of these, Tsuboi Shigeji's 1928 short story "Fifteen Yen, Fifty Sen" ("Jūgo en gojū sen"), recounts the author's experience of the Korean Panic. The title refers to a phrase that was particularly difficult for native Korean speakers to pronounce. As a soldier compels a worker to repeat these words, the narrator muses on the cause behind the soldier's demand: "Behind these odd words spoken through the borrowed mouthpiece of this soldier, we cannot help but see the crazed form of the ruling classes." He blames the ruling classes for deflecting "the enmity of the oppressed classes" onto an innocent scapegoat instead of those who oppress them.[49] In the conclusion to the story Tsuboi claims that the reactionary mood following the earthquake—symbolized by the Korean Massacre, the Amakasu Incident, and the Kameido Incident—has only become stronger, and that it has led to events such as the mass arrests of communist sympathizers in the March 15 Incident of 1928, in which over 1,600

48. Ibid., 185. The word in parentheses was added by the editors, although the long censored passages remain.

49. Tsuboi Shigeji, "Jūgoen, gojūsen," *Senki* 1, no. 5 (1928): 82.

communist activists and sympathizers were arrested across the country.[50] In other words, Tsuboi links what he considers to be a state-sanctioned massacre of Koreans to state persecution of socialists and communists and not to the general injustices of imperial rule.

In his story, Etchūya sees state-sponsored violence in the massacre as an extension of imperial violence in occupying Korea. Regarding his choice to abstain from killing, the protagonist muses on the plight of the Koreans: "Oh, how would I have been able to kill them? These people kneeling before me with their hands clasped together, with their country (stolen), driven from their homeland, enduring the iron rods of (exploitation), contempt, and abuse, their very existence denied them. They wander without food to eat or homes in which to sleep—How could I have struck them (heartlessly with this bayonet)?"[51] The violent military response against the Koreans is an extension of preexisting oppression. The protagonist does not fault the Koreans for defending themselves in this skirmish, and even valorizes their resistance in the form of the two martyrs. Indeed, Etchūya draws out the reasons behind this battle by focusing first on the immediate causes of the Koreans' desperation—the loss of home, food, and livelihood—as well as the larger causes for their misery—the cruelties of imperial rule and the harsh reality of life as an outsider in Japan. The story shows rumors and martial law to have further exacerbated their troubles by creating popular antagonism against all Koreans, forcing some to arm themselves for self-protection.[52] By drawing out these reasons behind what is a fictional encounter, Etchūya gives sanction to the Korean resistance as a whole.

Etchūya examines a natural disaster to show the human disaster that follows. The use of state-sponsored violence against the most oppressed speaks to the need for unity that will ultimately work toward resistance against that state. There is little opportunity for soldiers to resist in this story besides refusing to kill, the path taken by the protagonist. Though his options are limited, the protagonist feels guilty for not more actively opposing the massacre and calls himself a coward. It is on this negative note that the original story in *Kaihō* ended, but the 1928 *Shinkō bungaku zenshū* edition of "One Soldier's Record of the Earthquake" ends with hope for some form of resistance. In that version the protagonist decides upon action: "He firmly resolved to ********." Perhaps he will finally fight the military system from within.[53] Perhaps the censored passage reveals a decision to leave

50. Ibid.

51. Etchūya Riichi, "Ippeisotsu," 185. The words in parentheses were added by the editors.

52. There is little credible evidence that such armed resistance after the earthquake actually happened.

53. This was a fight that Etchūya promised to wage at the end of his essay on the army and socialism in *Rōdōsha* in 1921: "If I decide to enlist, I will attempt vehement resistance in the manner mentioned above, a resistance which will certainly take some physical form." Etchūya Riichi, "Guntai to shakaishugi," 502.

the army, as Etchūya did after the earthquake. Etchūya observed firsthand the cruelties of martial law and the horrors perpetrated by the soldiers, and this may have crushed his hopes of internal resistance. Etchūya thus turned to literature to fight against the evils of the imperial state. Yet for proletarian literature to succeed against the state, it was imperative for it to win the ideological war and gain the hearts of the masses it wanted to save.

Critique of Nationalism in Akita Ujaku's *Dance of the Skeletons*

Akita Ujaku's play *Dance of the Skeletons* (*Gaikotsu no buchō*) is one of the earliest and best-known literary responses to the Korean Massacre.[54] It was published in April 1924 in the dramatic journal *Engeki shinchō*, a companion magazine to the general-interest literary journal *Shinchō*. Despite the fact that *Dance of the Skeletons* appeared in a magazine not associated with the proletarian movement, it was controversial enough to warrant a ban immediately after it appeared.[55] The Korean Massacre was still a sensitive issue six months after the quake, yet mention of the massacre alone was an unlikely reason for censorship. In addition to the portrayal of the massacre, *Dance of the Skeletons* contains an explicit critique, based not on class divisions but on national ones. Ujaku condemns national and ethnic divisions as outmoded, and advances universal humanity as the ideal. Contemporary censors certainly saw this anti-nationalist critique as the larger threat to civic order.

As with Sano Kesami's *The Harbor of Mayhem*, *Dance of the Skeletons* includes an encounter between a character who criticizes the massacre and a *jikeidan*. In this case, however, the characters are given no clear class identity. In Ujaku's play the moral character is identified only as a young man and the *jikeidan* is similarly unidentified. By refusing to label his characters in the way Sano did, Ujaku raises the possibility that anyone could have been in a *jikeidan* and anyone could have opposed them. Referring to the play in his postwar autobiography, he wrote: "In *Dance of the Skeletons* I tried to express my great anger at the ignorant people of this country (*kokumin*)."[56] At first glance this appears similar to the rhetoric of Aono Suekichi or even Sano Kesami. But the word Ujaku uses here is different. He chooses *kokumin*—citizens or Japanese nationals—rather

54. Akita Ujaku, "Gaikotsu no buchō," *Engeki shinchō* 1, no. 4 (April 1924): 28–49. For an English translation and brief explanation of the play, see Cody Poulton, *A Beggar's Art: Scripting Modernity in Japanese Drama, 1900–1930* (Honolulu: University of Hawai'i Press, 2010), 134–52.

55. As mentioned in Chapter 8, note 25, the banning of this April 1924 issue of *Engeki shinchō* made headlines. It was later released as part of the 1928 *Shinkō bungaku zenshū*. This version was heavily censored to avoid a similar situation.

56. Akita Ujaku, *Akatsuki e no tabi* (Shinchōsha, 1950); quoted in Maeda Kakuzō, *Kyokō no naka no aidentiti*, 183.

than the words *minshū* or *taishū*, meaning "masses." This difference is crucial in understanding Ujaku's play. Though Ujaku did occasionally participate in *Tanemaku hito* and other proletarian journals and literary associations, he cannot be considered a proletarian writer like Sano Kesami. The criticism in the play, as Ujaku suggests in his postwar commentary, is directed toward the nation as a whole and not toward a particular class. Specifically, Ujaku criticizes nationalism as outdated, but he refuses to navigate the difficult minefield of class and ethnicity that is inherent in the Korean Massacre.

The play is set in a temporary shelter for refugees established in a small town somewhere in northeastern Japan. Most of the dialogue is between an old man who recently arrived in the shelter and the young man. Both have fled the fires in Tokyo and are on their way to take refuge with relatives. At first the two commiserate about their suffering, but the conversation soon turns to the rumors about Koreans. The old man relays the rumors as though they were fact. In response, the young man explains that the rumors were baseless. After talking about the massacre, the young man expresses his loss of faith in the Japanese people. "I have come to despise the Japanese. I had thought we were a nation of calmer people, but that has been undercut by these recent events. My loss of faith runs deep."[57] His words here are strikingly similar to those of Aono Suekichi and Sano Kesami. There is, however, an important difference. In this quote, the boy avoids the key word "*minshū*," or "the masses." Rather, his loss of faith is in the Japanese in general, and he uses broad descriptions, just as Ujaku did in talking about the play in his autobiography. In other words, his critique is classless.

The rhetoric in *Dance of the Skeletons* is thus derived less from the proletarian literature movement or socialism than from a more general humanism. This is apparent in other essays and poetry that Ujaku wrote prior to *Dance of the Skeletons*. In an article published in the December 1923 edition of *Kaizō*, for example, Ujaku mentions encountering people who were proud of killing Koreans, and then sarcastically remarks: "Everyone accepted the actions of these 'brave warriors' [meaning the *jikeidan*]. Not one person entertained the slightest doubt. It made me sad. . . . What sort of education have we Japanese had that we don't think of fellow 'humans' as 'human'?"[58] Here Ujaku particularly faults the education system, which he sees as emphasizing national difference over international similarity, and thus reinforcing arbitrary ethnic and national division.

Dance of the Skeletons criticizes any ideology that divides people. In the play, these outdated ideas take a particular material form: that of feudal Japanese

57. Akita Ujaku, "Gaikotsu no buchō," in *Puroretaria gikyoku shu* (Shin Nihon Shuppansha, 1988), 100; all cited page numbers are from this edition.

58. Akita Ujaku, "Tanan no kōhanki: nikki no naka kara," *Kaizō* 5, no. 12 (December 1923): 250–51; reprinted in Kūm Pyōng-dong, *Chōsenjin gyakusatsu ni kansuru chishikijin no hannō*, 21–22.

costumes. Midway through the plot, a *jikeidan* enters the tent searching for a Korean. The production notes are very clear about costuming: "At that point a *jikeidan* group enters the tent. The leader is wearing samurai armor with a drawn sword. Other members are wearing similar garb: a samurai battle overcoat (*jinbaori*), the uniform of a veteran militia group (*zaigō gunjin*), a headband (*hachimaki*) and a student's uniform, respectively. They are all carrying swords and spears."[59] In line with their clothing, these *jikeidan* members are remnants of a past that is incompatible with the modern age.

The importance of clothing is suggested early in the play. When the young man and the old man are first discussing the massacre, the young man says of the perpetrators: "I have no faith in them. They are gladly wearing the clothes that others have put upon them. I have lost faith in the Japanese as *citizens* (*kokumin*), but not in Japanese as human beings (*ningen*). People of all nations are, as human beings, good and innocent."[60] In this passage clothing is a metaphor for ideas. The term he uses for "wearing the clothes that others have put upon them" is *kiseta ifuku*, an idiom referring to ill-fitting ideas imposed from elsewhere. The use of this idiom early in the play sets the stage for the later appearance of symbolic clothing. In this context the unnatural "clothing" is imposed on the people by the state. The humanity that lies beneath the clothing goes beyond national boundaries.

The costumes in the play are absurd, but they were only a slight exaggeration of reality. *Jikeidan* were often depicted carrying old samurai weapons such as swords or spears. When spears were not readily available, people made spears from bamboo, something often mentioned in contemporary accounts.[61] In his essay "Saigo zakkan," Kikuchi Kan commented on the anachronistic appearance of the *jikeidan*: "I thought that carrying an XX[62] and using passwords was not something befitting the Taisho era, but in the few days after the quake, I too carried an XX in my hand, used passwords and took my turn watching the neighborhood."[63] Though he, too, participated in the efforts by standing guard in his neighborhood, these *jikeidan*, according to Kikuchi Kan, were "not something befitting the Taishō era." Critic Chiba Kameo was even more specific: "Men in feudal times would cut off a person's head the way we would chop potatoes. But

59. Akita Ujaku, "Gaikotsu no buchō," 106.

60. Ibid., 100.

61. In the short story "Amid the Uncertainty," Tokuda Shūsei referred to the Korean Panic as the "bamboo spear panic." Tokuda Shūsei, "Fuan no naka ni," 200.

62. This XX is in the original, a sign of self-censorship, but given the context it was likely a bamboo spear, a common tool of the *jikeidan*. The specific reason for its omission is unclear, but perhaps even at this early date, publishers were aware that even a slight reference to the massacre of Koreans could cause problems.

63. Kikuchi Kan, "Saigo zakkan," 119. Miyake Gaikotsu similarly saw the reintroduction of passwords as a restoration of the Sengoku era. Miyake Gaikotsu, "Kyūjibutsu no fukkō," *Shinsai gahō* 3 (November 1923): 45.

this is the twentieth century. I thought that surely this sort of murderous barbarism no longer existed."[64]

Sinister remnants of the past are also apparent in *Dance of the Skeletons.* Despite the protests of the nurse supervising the shelter, the *jikeidan* enter the tent dressed in their spectacular armor. They walk among those in the tent, harass the refugees, and eventually find someone they think looks Korean. The *jikeidan* members start to interrogate this man and, on account of his inability to pronounce certain words or state the Japanese year of his birth, declare him to be a Korean. At this point the young refugee protagonist stands up in defiance to challenge the *jikeidan.* The ensuing interaction is the moral center of the play:

> *Armored leader* [of the *jikeidan*] (Looking at the young man): "Who do you think you are?"
> *Young man* (Quietly): I am a human. . . .
> *Armored leader*: Of course you're a human. I'm not asking whether you're a human or a beast; I'm asking what *kind* of human you are.[65]

In his reply, the young man rejects categories of nation and ethnicity that were the central issue in the massacre. This assertion of a shared humanity continues in the way the young man introduces the Korean also as a human:

> *Young man* [To the *jikeidan*]: We already have an army, a police force. Why are you dressed like that, wearing armor, battle coats, judo uniforms? Don't you have your own clothes? (Looking at the man [who was accused of being a Korean]:) Why don't you get up? Stand firm. [To the *jikeidan*:] This man may be, as you say, a Korean. But Koreans aren't your enemy. . . . The Koreans haven't hurt you. Other Japanese have. Don't you understand that?
> (He holds the hand of the Korean.)
> *Young man*: Look at this man. He is a human being. Look at this face. Could this man kill innocent people and put poison in wells? This man has enemies too, but you are not his enemies. You don't understand. You don't know anything. You haven't been told anything. And you don't try to find out anything. People like you have thoughtlessly killed innocent friends of this man, innocent people who had no weapons. Look at this man. All he has is the life that nature gave him. He is a true human. What are you? What do you have? Just dead and dusty morals. Sure, the armor and the

64. Chiba Kameo, "Kokuminseijō no futa gimon," *Josei Kaizō* 2 no. 11 (November 1923), 13; reprinted in Kūm Pyōng-dong, *Chōsenjin gyakusatsu ni kansuru chishikijin no hannō*, 201. Miyake Gaikotsu made a similar point, claiming that the earthquake brought back "*kirisute gomen*," the law that made it possible for samurai to kill members of the lower classes without fear of repercussions. Miyake Gaikotsu, "Kyūjibutsu no fukkō," 44.

65. Akita Ujaku, "Gaikotsu no buchō," 108.

> battle overcoat have value as antiques. But what are they good for? If you have blood running through your veins, you need your own clothing. Take off that armor. Take off that battle coat. You are marionettes without life! Wax figures! Mummies! Skeletons!
>
> *Headband-[wearing* jikeidan *member]*: Traitorous Japanese (*futei Nihonjin*)[66] . . .
>
> *Battle overcoat*: Socialist . . .
>
> *Student*: Agitator [literally, "dangerous person"] . . .
>
> *Armored leader*: Kill them both![67]

The Korean had only "the life that nature gave him." He is unadorned by the trappings of nationalism, possessing only his life and his humanity. The passage associates life with the Korean and death and antiquity with the *jikeidan.*

Early in the confrontation, the young man compares the improvised costumes of the *jikeidan* with those of the military and police: "We already have an army, a police force. Why are you dressed like that, wearing armor, battle coats, judo uniforms? Don't you have your own clothes?" The youth asserts that the police and the army are the legitimate organs of control in modern times, not a vigilante group with makeshift uniforms. But the anachronistic outfits of the *jikeidan* symbolize more than their lack of authority to legitimize violence. Recalling the reference earlier in the play to "wearing the clothes that others have put upon them," the *jikeidan* not only lack authority but lack ideas they can call their own. They are clothed in an outdated nationalism that has been imposed on them. The antique costumes are juxtaposed with "dead and dusty morals," suggesting that both are useless remnants of a bygone era. It is the "dead and dusty" ideas that ultimately make the *jikeidan* lifeless.

This climactic confrontation marks the beginning of the expressionist phase of the play. The dramatic notes in the text specify a change in tone. The young man stands with the Korean as the mob surrounds them with weapons raised, but his final speech literally stops them in their tracks:

> *Young man*: Oh, new mysticism! Oh, new mysticism that has been born to bond a new race with power and friendship! Rise up and destroy this ugly, soulless mold! Tear off the masks of the false ancestor worship, of hero worship, of ethnic nationalism (*minzoku shugi*), and make them dance the dance of the hideous skeletons! Wait a moment, orchestra; turn to stone, you hideous skeletons! Turn to stone, you hideous skeletons! Turn to stone, you hideous skeletons! . . .

66. The term "*futei Nihonjin*" is particularly interesting because of the way *futei* was often used in conjunction with the Koreans involved in rebellious actions against the Japanese occupiers. See Chapter 8 for more information on the term.

67. Ibid., 108–9.

> [All characters freeze, including the director of the field hospital, who has just rushed in.]
>
> Skeletons, Dance!
>
> [Lights out, and the tent goes dark. Phosphorescent lights return, showing ten skeletons in the same poses as the members of the *jikeidan*.][68]

With these words the young man explicitly reveals the antiquated ideas imposed on the people of Japan: ancestor worship, hero worship, and nationalism. In its place there should arise a "new mysticism" of international unity and humanism, a system that unites people with bonds of friendship.

The phosphorescent lights present an alternative space or dreamscape in which the *jikeidan* has been transformed into a group of skeletons. The young man orders them to dance in order to placate those they have killed, to dance until they collapse—the text specifies a waltz, a fantasia, and a round dance. The lights go out again and gradually come back in full realistic force. A refugee woman is crying and the nurse says: "How terrible, but what else could we expect. . . ."[69] With this last line, it is revealed that the young man's magical choreography was a fantasy; he and the Korean were killed by the *jikeidan*.[70]

By the end of the play, the *jikeidan* have become hideous skeletons dancing absurdly. This transformation underscores both their lifelessness and the ridiculous anachronism of their appearance in modern Japan. But at the same time it is important to explore what they represent in larger terms. Their costuming suggests that they are asserting a strong national identity associated with the past. They represent the feudal tradition that has continued into modern Japan. This is emphasized by the first two evils mentioned by the young man in his final speech: "Tear off the masks of the false ancestor worship, of hero worship." Here the evils that the "new mysticism" of humanism must confront are: first, false ancestor worship, which is the explicit link to the past; and second, hero worship, a reference to the way of the warrior, or *bushidō*.[71]

The final target of the young man's speech is nationalism. In contrast to the costuming, nationalism is a modern construct and could hardly be considered

68. Ibid., 110–11.

69. Ibid., 112.

70. Tsukui Takeshi suggests an alternate reading of the ending in which a sick child who made an earlier appearance dies at the end, but the disjunction makes such a reading difficult. He does note that the first performance of the play in the 1980s used the interpretation of the ending that I present here. Tsukui Takeshi, "Kantō daishinsai wo egaku to iu koto: Akita Ujaku no 'Gaikotsu no buchō' wo yomu," *Kokubungaku kenkyū* 150 (October 2006): 88.

71. Nitobe Inazō and his Meiji-era work on *bushidō* molded the old warrior codes into new ideas of national character. See Inazō Nitobe, *Bushido: The Soul of Japan* (Philadelphia: The Leeds & Biddle Co., 1900). See also Michele Mason, "Empowering the Would-Be Warrior: Bushidō and the Gendered Bodies of the Japanese Nation," in *Recreating Japanese Men*, ed. Sabine Fruhstuck and Anne Walthall (Berkeley: University of California Press, 2011).

anachronistic. Yet, by placing nationalism alongside the antiquated ideas linked to the *jikeidan*, Ujaku is showing them to be part of a past that must be cast off in favor of a new international humanism. This is consistent with Ujaku's other work and his interest in Esperanto. The new "race" that the young man invokes in his speech is one that elides ethnic difference. It is a universal ideal that transcends national, ethnic, and class boundaries. By asserting his humanity against his nationality, the young man paints an idealized view of the future in contrast to the dead and dusty ideas of the *jikeidan*. In his martyrdom, the bright future is destroyed by remnants of the past.

Erasing Colonization in Depictions of the Korean Massacre

Each of these authors assigns blame for the massacre, but for the most part they do not address the crucial questions of colonization and empire. Though Sano Kesami criticizes the idea that Koreans appreciated Japanese "assistance" by colonizing them, and Etchūya Riichi points out the injustices carried out against Koreans, there is little exploration of ethnic violence except to show the "ignorance" of the masses or the manipulation of a shadowy state. Sano uses stereotypical characterizations of class to redeem the worker. Etchūya links the massacre to the state—a necessarily ambiguous entity here—and in so doing exonerates the individual soldier. But to redeem the worker or the soldier rewrites history to allow the Korean massacre to be compatible with socialist ideology. Aono Suekichi and Akita Ujaku placed the blame more broadly, on the public at large. Aono supposes that socialist thought will help alleviate ethnic tension. Ujaku claims that shaking off the trappings of nationalism in favor of a universal humanity will do the same. Nevertheless, in all these cases, the Koreans who were being killed were not the main issue the writers were addressing. Rather, Koreans were tools to discuss other concerns: the gap between the masses and the vanguard, the reactionary thought of the petite bourgeoisie, the oppression of soldier-workers by the capitalist state, and the backward nationalism of the Japanese.

The proletarian movement had difficulty defining its position on the "Korean question"—the Japanese colonial relationship with Korea—even before the earthquake. Its proponents did not know how to incorporate the colonial endeavors of Japan or ethnic tensions among the working class into their conception of society. Proletarian writers and critics saw oppression as inherently grounded in class, without national or ethnic boundaries. As Ishizaka Kōichi argues, "the Japanese communists should have been the most able to perceive the structure [of colonial oppression], but in reality they refused to recognize the ethnic subjectivity that went along with the search for ethnic freedom inherent in the Korean question."[72]

72. Ishizaka Kōichi, "Nihon no shakaishugisha no Chōsen-kan," *Sanzenri* 34 (1983): 83.

In other words, ethnic identity was an illusion and a distraction from the true systems of capitalist oppression based on modes of production. As such, any oppression based on ethnicity would be erased after a proletarian revolution.

This faith in the liberating powers of class revolution can be found in an early interaction between Japanese and Korean representatives at a Soviet-sponsored conference in Moscow. During the 1922 "Far Eastern Peoples Conference," one Korean participant asserted: "The Japanese working classes are among those who persecute the Korean working classes." In response, the Japanese delegation replied that the awakening of the Japanese proletariat "would bring about the complete liberation of Korea from the rule of the Japanese capitalists."[73] When pressed for specifics, however, the delegation was unable to elaborate. The Japanese proletarian movement was focused on class liberation of Japanese workers and refused to address the ethnically motivated persecution of Koreans among Japanese laborers.

Proletarian critics, following orthodox Marxist thought from the Comintern, saw ethnic identity as a capitalist construct. In a special issue devoted to issues of ethnicity, the communist journal *Senki* ran an article by Takahashi Sadaki entitled "The Proletarian Revolution and the Ethnic Question" ("Musansha kakumei to minzoku mondai," April 1923). There, Takahashi argued that "ethnic conflicts are nothing other than ignorant nationals caught up in the propaganda of capitalists to continue these beastly wars."[74] In this quote, Takahashi appears to not recognize ethnic identity as separate from nationalist propaganda. The only real form of conflict, Takahashi implies, is the class conflict between the capitalist ruling class and the proletariat. In one sense, Takahashi is right. National and ethnic identities are constructs that do, at times, serve the purposes of rallying people to fight for a capitalist cause, perhaps to protect domestic products from imports or to secure natural and human resources for growing industries. Yet, as is the case with class identity, national and ethnic identities also serve to unify people to resist subjugation.

* * * * *

Aono Suekichi, Sano Kesami, and Etchūya Riichi all focused on class within the Japanese *naichi* (homeland) in their explorations of the Korean Massacre.[75] Aono and Sano both showed the importance of educating the masses to help liberate the workers from capitalist domination. Etchūya called for a class-based soli-

73. The "Far Eastern Peoples Conference" (also known as "The Congress of the Toilers of the Far East") was a conference held by the Comintern in Moscow and Petrograd to encourage the spread of communism in Asia. Quoted in ibid.

74. Quoted in ibid., 84.

75. *Naichi* referred to the Japanese homeland, as opposed to *gaichi,* which referred to the colonies. These terms require some flexibility at the borders.

darity that could mimic Korean resistance in a similar fight against the collusion between capitalists and the state. Akita Ujaku, as the only writer among them not ideologically wed to the proletarian movement, used the massacre to criticize nationalism. Like Takahashi Sadaki, Ujaku saw nationalism as a construct, as ill-fitting clothes forced upon people from above. For Ujaku, with his ideals of universal humanity, ethnic and national differences created systems of oppression. It is true that eliminating nationalism in favor of a universalizing humanism would advance world peace, but far from being anachronistic, nationalism has proved to be a tenacious construct that has survived well into the twenty-first century. Akita Ujaku did not recognize the potential of ethnic and national identity in the fight against oppression. Nationalism, for all its faults, helped bring about the decline of overt colonial domination during the twentieth century. Erasing ethnic differences would have erased the force behind the Korean independence movement.

Thus, along with censorship, ideology also constrained possibilities for critique in each case. Nevertheless, within those confines, each of these writers shed light on the brutality of the massacre and the inequalities inherent in the colonization of Korea. Although Koreans themselves play a minor role in Sano Kesami's play *The Harbor of Mayhem*, their plight is the focus of the drama. His play calls attention to both the massacre and the conditions of colonialism that made it possible. Etchūya's critique is almost completely masked by censorship, but his valorization of armed resistance by Koreans displays his sympathy with their cause. Even more crucially, he revealed the role of the military in the massacre, which had been omitted from newspaper reports and other representations. While Ujaku's humanism may have been proven overly idealistic, his intervention remains relevant. It is essential to see the shared humanity underneath the clothing of national, ethnic, and even class identity.

Conclusion

Japanese Literature after the Quake

When people set out to describe the Great Kanto Earthquake, one metaphor they often turned to was war. The *shitamachi* did look like a war zone in the immediate aftermath; there were burnt-out buildings, piles of rubble, and dead bodies strewn throughout the streets. Ema Shū described what he saw in the devastated districts thus: "The acrid stench of burning assaulted my senses, and I could hardly open my eyes due to the ash that was blown about by the wind. I hurried forward through the chaos of the war zone, without even glancing sideways."[1] Though Ema had no real war experience, he was familiar with what warfare looked like from images provided by newspapers and newsreels.

The devastation was not the only connection. After martial law was proclaimed, about 35,000 troops descended on the city.[2] Noting the troops alongside the devastation, Tayama Katai remarked, "I felt as though I was in the middle of a war zone."[3] Katai had witnessed the Russo-Japanese War (1904–5) as a correspondent and was probably recalling that experience. Most commentators looked to the more recent war, the Great War in Europe, which had ended five years earlier. Okutani Fumitomo, a Tenrikyō priest, wrote that the Great Kanto Earthquake was "comparable to the major disturbance that occurred in Europe."[4] With the scope of destruction, the presence of the martial-law garrisons, and the overall state mobilization, the comparison to a war zone was inevitable.

1. Ema Shū, *Hitsuji no ikaru toki*, 133.
2. Fujisawa Morihiko and Bureau of Social Affairs Home Office, *Great Earthquake of 1923*, 19.
3. In addition to Tayama Katai, Ema Shū and Etchūya Riichi, among others, described the disaster as similar to a war. Tayama Katai, *Tōkyō shinsaiki*, 108.
4. The full quote ends with Okutani saying that the Great War occurred ten years ago. Okutani, writing in 1923, was referring to when World War I began (1914) rather than when it ended. Quoted in J. Charles Schencking, "1923 Tokyo as a Devastated War and Occupation Zone: The Catastrophe One Confronted in Post Earthquake Japan," *Japanese Studies* 29, no. 1 (May 2009): 126. In his article, Schencking argues that war was an apt metaphor not only because of the scope of the destruction and the martial law, but also because of how the disaster was presented the public and the way the state mobilized itself for reconstruction. This massive government effort at both propaganda and rebuilding suggested a strong correlation with the wars Japan had engaged in over the previous three decades.

The widely shared comparison to war eventually suggested that the earthquake had the same effect on Japan as the Great War had on Europe. Ten years after the disaster, Yokomitsu Riichi wrote, "Looking back on it now, to the citizens of Japan, the Great Kantō Earthquake Disaster of 1923 had a profound influence equal to that of the Great World War."[5] This idea was taken up by many postwar literary historians, for whom the disaster appeared as a ready-made division between literary movements and seemed to usher in an age of modernism. Despite such claims, the earthquake did not did not have the kind of impact on Japanese culture that Paul Fussell describes World War I having on European culture in his groundbreaking work on literature of the Great War.[6] Previous chapters in this book have outlined the immediate response to the earthquake in representation; this conclusion explores the more lasting effects, especially in the realm of literature.

One of the first critics to make an explicit link between Japanese literature after the earthquake and European literature after the Great War was Chiba Kameo, in an essay entitled "War Literature and Post-Quake Literature" ("Sensō bungei to shingo no bungaku"). In this essay, published in *Waseda bungaku* in January 1924, Chiba writes that there was little to compare the two events qualitatively, yet he expresses hope that a new literature will be born from the disaster as it was in Europe.[7] As he puts it, "The misguided art [of the past] will be buried in the burnt earth, and only that which is new, that with everlasting life, will be born again renewed."[8] For Chiba, the post-quake art must be strong and vibrant. And it must particularly look beyond the self: "[Authors] must turn their attention away from themselves and toward the society that surrounds the self, and from that society they must turn their discerning eyes toward the age."[9] As discussed in Chapter 2, many critics yearned for a change in literature after the disaster. Like Chiba, several of these critics sought a kind of literature that looked outside the self. It is possible to see in the literature following the disaster a redirection of the literary gaze toward the outside world. One form this took was in the work of experimental modernists who looked to the city for inspiration.

Chiba found authors dealing with the modern age in the way he had hoped for not long after he wrote his essay. In October 1924, a year after the earthquake,

5. Yokomitsu Riichi, "Oboegaki 8," in *Yokomitsu Riichi zenshū*, vol. 13 (1982): 225.

6. Fussell argues that the Great War brought about the advent of irony to describe the modern condition. He writes, "I am saying that there seems to be one dominating form of modern understanding; that it is essentially ironic; and that it originates largely in the application of mind and memory to the events of the Great War." Paul Fussell, *The Great War and Modern Memory* (New York: Oxford University Press, 1975), 35.

7. Reprinted as Chiba Kameo, "Sensō bungei to shingo no bungaku," in *Hennentai Taishō bungaku zenshū* vol. 12 (2003): 318–25.

8. Ibid., 320.

9. Ibid., 322.

Kawabata Yasunari, Yokomitsu Riichi, and several other young writers established a literary magazine to showcase their experimentations. Its title, *Bungei jidai* (*Literary Age*), reflected a concern with the modern age and the work included indicated that literary experimentation was required to address it. Collectively, these writers were given the name "Neo-Perceptionists" (*shinkankaku-ha*) by Chiba himself, signaling the new modes of perceiving the modern world discernable in their work.[10] Though the earthquake did not figure in their literary theory when the magazine was founded, not long after the disaster Kawabata wrote, "It is a fact that the earthquake was the endpoint for established literature and the origin of new literature."[11] If modernism can be defined as a break from the past, then the earthquake symbolized just such a rupture.

Several postwar critics emphasized the connection between the "new perception" heralded by contemporary critics discussing the *shinkankaku-ha* and the earthquake. The most important proponents of this idea were Takami Jun, Senuma Shigeki, Yoshida Seiichi, and Odagiri Susumu.[12] Odagiri portrayed the earthquake as a defining line in his history of Shōwa literature: "After having endured the earthquake, Japanese literature welcomed Taishō 13 (1924). The urban literature of the past was changed into something different in the *shinkankaku-ha*. The avant-garde, with Dadaism at its center, continued its audacious experimentation with renewed vigor, and proletarian literature began a new era of development. From 1924 to 1925 the state of Japanese letters (the *bundan*) changed completely."[13] Odagiri's causal link between the earthquake and modernism has now become one standard narrative in the development of Japanese modernism. More recently Iwata Mitsuko characterized the literature of the *shinkankaku-ha* as "Late Taishō earthquake literature."[14] With the earthquake, Odagiri and the others were able to create a trajectory of Japanese literary development that equated it with European literary history through a narrative of trauma followed by literary experimentation. Through their use of the disaster these critics could say that Japan was not merely copying the surface trappings of European modernism, but

10. In addition to naming the group in the magazine *Seiki* (*The Age*) in November 1924, Chiba Kameo was one of the primary champions of the new magazine *Bungei jidai* (*Literary Age*) and the literature it represented.

11. Kawabata Yasunari, "Yojin bungei no sakuhin," in *Kawabata Yasunari zenshū*, vol. 30 (1982): 60; originally in the *Jiji shinpō* on October 21, 1923.

12. Takami Jun, *Shōwa bungaku seisuishi* (Bungei Shunjū Shinsha, 1958); Senuma Shigeki, *Kindai Nihon bungaku no kōzō*, vol. 2 (Shūeisha, 1963), 269; Yoshida Seiichi, *Gendai Nihon bungaku shi* (Ōfūsha, 1980), 130; Odagiri Susumu, *Shōwa bungaku no seiritsu*. See Thomas Woolsey's final chapter in his M.A. thesis, "Rumblings in Modernism," for a good overview of what Odagiri, Yoshida, and several other literary historians had to say about the earthquake. Woolsey, "Rumblings in Modernism" (M.A. thesis, University of Washington, 1991), 49–69.

13. Odagiri Susumu, *Shōwa bungaku no seiritsu*, 46.

14. Iwata Mitsuko, *Kawabata Yasunari: Ushirosugata e no dokuhaku* (Yumani Shobō, 1992), 19.

that the underlying trauma was also felt. As Thomas Woolsey has argued in his thesis on the earthquake and modernism, Japanese critics used the earthquake as a means of lending an "air of legitimacy" to avant-garde arts in Japan.[15]

Nevertheless, a clear causal relationship between the earthquake and modernism is problematic. In his seminal 1983 study of urban literature, Unno Hiroshi clearly disavowed the connection.[16] As was true of proletarian literature, there was "modernism" before the disaster. Odagiri also pointed out that Futurism and Dadaism emerged onto the poetry scene in the late 1910s and early 1920s, respectively.[17] Even *shinkankaku-ha*-like writing predates the earthquake. A few months before the disaster Yokomitsu Riichi wrote a short story entitled "The Fly" ("Hae") in which he rejects realism and the supremacy of the individual human subject by writing from the point of view of the fly.[18] In reviewing this work two months before the earthquake, Kawabata Yasunari noted that Yokomitsu wrote with a "fresh perception" (*shinsen na kankaku*).[19] Yokomitsu's personification of the non-human was also seen in his *shinkankaku-ha* story "Heads and Bellies" ("Atama narabini hara"), which debuted in the inaugural issue of *Bungei jidai*.[20]

It is clear that the disaster, in and of itself, did not provoke a new mode of "perceptionist" modernism. Nevertheless, the quake did show some limits to the prior systems of representation, particularly the solipsistic realism of Japanese Naturalism that had dominated Japanese letters since the publication of Katai's *Futon* in 1907. The earthquake forced writers outside and encouraged them to deal with the world they saw. Karatani Kōjin has written that the response to modernity by Meiji-era writers was to look inward through the discovery of landscape, which he sees paradoxically as an aestheticization of the external world:

15. Thomas Woolsey, "Rumblings in Modernism," 69.
16. Unno Hiroshi, *Modan toshi Tōkyō: Nihon no 1920-nendai* (Chūō kōron-sha, 1983), 11. This point is echoed by William Tyler in *Modanizumu: Modernist Fiction from Japan, 1913–1938* (Honolulu: University of Hawai'i Press, 2008), 21.
17. Miryam Sas covers the modernist poetry of this time in her book *Fault Lines: Cultural Memory and Japanese Surrealism* (Stanford, CA: Stanford University Press, 1999).
18. This story was first published in *Bungei shunjū* in May 1923. See Yokomitsu Riichi, "Hae," in *Yokomitsu Riichi shū* (Shūeisha, 1966). The story begins with a fly in a stable that recuperates on a horse's back after becoming entangled in a spider's web. Throughout the next few scenes, various characters enter the narrative and wait for the carriage to depart: a mother worried about her son, a mother and child, a country gentleman. Eventually they all depart for a nearby town, but the driver falls asleep and the carriage plummets off the road onto the riverbank below. The only survivor is the fly.
19. Kawabata Yasunari, "Shichigatsu no shōsetsu," in *Kawabata Yasunari zenshū*, vol. 30 (1982): 46; originally in *Kokumin shinbun*, July 14, 1923.
20. This story and other works by Yokomitsu Riichi are discussed by Arthur Mitchell in his dissertation. Mitchell sees *shinkankaku-ha* texts by Yokomitsu as reacting not to the devastation of the disaster, but the self-improvement discourse that arose in the aftermath. See Arthur M. Mitchell, IV, "Subverting Language: Japanese Modernism, Modernity, and Linguistic Critique" (Ph.D. dissertation, Yale University, 2012), Chapter 2.

"It is only within the 'inner man,' who appears to be indifferent to his external surroundings, that landscape is discovered. It is perceived by those who do not look 'outside.'"[21] Karatani takes Kunikida Doppo as his prime example, but the same thing could be said of other Naturalists such as Tayama Katai. Eventually, the *bundan* came to be characterized by even more inwardly focused writers whose primary subject was the landscape of their minds. While there were some iconoclasts writing in different genres, notably Tanizaki and Akutagawa, Taishō Japan saw the zenith of the I-novel.

Thus although new modes had begun before the earthquake and were not an immediate result of it, the kinds of writing sanctioned by the cultural gatekeepers following the disaster did encompass approaches to the outside world that were more varied than before. I-novels did not disappear, but they were increasingly published alongside modernist fiction and socially aware works influenced by the proletarian movement. Outside of the *bundan*, popular fiction was gathering a larger audience, further prompting debates to differentiate high and low literature. This study differs from previous efforts to include the earthquake in literary history because it does not retroactively place the earthquake within the development of literary modernism, narrowly defined as the *shinkankaku-ha* and its descendants. Rather, the texts discussed herein show the pressures on members of the literary world to move beyond the confines of the self and engage with the world around them.

In discussing Japanese experimental modernism, Seiji Lippit has pointed out a shift in topography concomitant with the transition to the Shōwa period: "Against the dominant topographies of Taishō-period fiction, which tended to be focused on enclosed, interior spaces, modernism moves out onto the streets, beyond the boundaries of the private and domestic worlds and onto the fluidity of city space."[22] The experimental modernism Lippit explored was but one mode that authors adopted to represent the changes of the age. The others were popular fiction and proletarian literature. Each was present before the quake, but also grew in prominence and prestige afterward. And each dealt with urban modernity by moving "onto the fluidity of city space."

Recent scholarship on Japanese modernism, or *modanizumu*, has tended to define the term expansively. In the introduction to his edited volume on the topic, Roy Starrs declared that modernists share "a desire to break with the past and make something radically new."[23] This definition allows Starrs to see both the proletarian literature movement and the experimental *shinkankaku-ha* as modernist: "The so called neo-sensory school (*shinkankaku-ha*) tended to be aesthetically

21. Kōjin Karatani, *Origins*, 25.

22. Seiji M. Lippit, *Topographies of Japanese Modernism*, 7.

23. Roy Starrs, ed., *Rethinking Japanese Modernism* (Leiden; Boston: Global Oriental, 2012), 3.

modernist while politically conservative, while the other, the Marxist-influenced proletarian literature (*puroretaria bungaku*) movement, was quite the reverse. Thus, although both were 'modernist' in the widest sense of the term, in that they believed that the conditions of modernity called for radical change, politically they were very much at odds with each other." Starrs continues to explain that political radicalism did not always translate into artistic conservatism: "not all artists on the left subscribed to 'proletarian realism'—there were even some surrealists among them."[24]

Following Unno Hiroshi and others, William Tyler sees the city as central to his definition of *modanizumu*, yet the aesthetically conservative proletarian movement with its rigid ideology falls outside the boundaries he sets.[25] For Tyler, some degree of formal experimentation is crucial, but so, too, is a flexible cosmopolitanism that opposes strict ideology. This latter aspect allows for the inclusion of popular literature under his rubric.[26] Tyler's examples of popular modernism do not extend to melodrama, but melodrama also dealt with the radical changes of urban modernity. Ben Singer situates Western melodrama in relation to the changes wrought by urban modernity "as a product and a reflection of modernity—of modernity's experiential qualities, its ideological fluctuations, its cultural anxieties, its intertextual cross-currents, its social demographics, and its commercial practices."[27] Melodrama may have the spectacle of modernism and its concern with urban life, but rarely the formal experimentation.

While the term "modernism" may not be broad enough to encompass all popular melodrama and proletarian fiction from this era, Lippet, Starrs and Tyler show a turn toward engagement with the city in Japanese literature occurring through the Taishō era and culminating in early Shōwa literature. Experimental literary modernism, proletarian literature, and popular fiction all had roots predating the disaster, but the larger cultural shift took place afterward. Of the twenty-five short stories Tyler includes in his anthology of *modanizumu*, all but four appeared after September 1923. By examining how authors were forced to deal with the disaster, this book has suggested that the earthquake was an impetus for authors to move into the city space. As such, the disaster marks a key moment, though not the only one, in the cultural transition from the interiority that Karatani Kojin sees in Meiji literature to the exteriority that Seiji Lippit sees in early Shōwa-era experimental modernism.

24. Ibid., 8–9.

25. William J. Tyler, *Modanizumu: Modernist Fiction from Japan, 1913–1938*, 17.

26. Ibid., 4; see also 26–32 for more on popular modernism.

27. Ben Singer, *Melodrama and Modernity*, 1. See also William J. Tyler, *Modanizumu: Modernist Fiction from Japan, 1913–1938*, 26–32.

The Scarlet Gang of Asakusa as a Post-Quake Text

The work that best shows the possibilities of post-earthquake literature is Kawabata Yasunari's *The Scarlet Gang of Asakusa* (*Asakusa kurenaidan*, 1930). This novel can be connected to the disaster in two ways. First, the earthquake is explicitly invoked as integral to the creation of the contemporary Asakusa world, and to the lives of the beggars, thieves, prostitutes, and entrepreneurs who inhabited it. The second connection is more abstract. *The Scarlet Gang of Asakusa* is a conglomeration of texts and genres that creates a collage of literary trends following the disaster: reportage, popular melodramas, proletarian literature, and, of course, experimental modernism. Although the novel cannot be reduced to its connection with the disaster, the traces of the earthquake run throughout.[28]

The Scarlet Gang of Asakusa centers on a young writer who relates to an imagined audience his observations of the post-earthquake cityscape. Those observations focus on the "Scarlet Gang" of the title—especially the young waif Yumiko—and its turf, the *shitamachi* entertainment district of Asakusa. The novel is set just before Tokyo was officially declared rebuilt in 1930, and reflects many of the changes brought about in the district through reconstruction. Early on in the novel, the narrator defines his book as a "map" of the post-quake city: "Here, let me unfold it before you, dear readers, the newly revised 'Showa Map' drawn following the reorganization of the city after the shake up of the 1923 Great Kanto Earthquake."[29]

The novel's connection to the earthquake runs deep; the very concept can be said to have germinated in the ashes. Kawabata Yasunari was fascinated by the destruction wrought by the 1923 disaster. His desire to explore the spectacular ruins is reflected in a short piece he wrote for the first post-quake issue of *Bungei shunjū* called "Viewing the Fires" ("Taika kenbutsu").[30] In this essay, Kawabata describes some of the bodies he sees and some actresses walking through the ruins. Taking these actresses as a starting point, he begins to discuss the White Russian refugee dancers in Asakusa, and from there hints at a work he might want to write later: "Sometime I want to write a long, strange novel, with Asakusa Park

28. Arthur Mitchell discusses *The Scarlet Gang of Asakusa* as a reaction to the progressive discourse of reconstruction that erased the trauma of the earthquake in a celebration of the modern, rational metropolis of Tokyo. See Arthur M. Mitchell, IV, "Subverting Language: Japanese Modernism, Modernity, and Linguistic Critique," Chapter 3.

29. The quote here is from Alisa Freedman's translation. Kawabata Yasunari, *The Scarlet Gang of Asakusa,* trans. Alisa Freedman (Berkeley, CA: University of California Press, 2005), 4; for the original text, see Kawabata Yasunari, *Asakusa kurenaidan* (Senshin-sha, 1930), 8.

30. Kawabata Yasunari, "Taika kenbutsu," *Bungei shunjū* 1, no. 11 (November 1923): 66–68. In a short autobiographical essay in 1934 Kawabata mentions walking around the ruins of the city for weeks, showing both that he spent considerable time in the ruins and that the experience remained etched in memory a decade later. Kawabata Yasunari, "Bungakuteki jijoden," in *Kawabata Yasunari zenshū*, vol. 33 (1982): 84–99; originally published in *Shinchō* in May 1934.

as the backdrop and featuring the lowly women of the area: the factory girls of the Monopoly Bureau in Kuramae, the girls in the movie houses, and the girls on horseback or doing acrobatics in the circus."[31] The novel Kawabata was planning became *The Scarlet Gang of Asakusa.*[32] As the latter work shows, Kawabata was even more enamored with the modern metropolis that emerged from the ashes than he was with the destruction.

Kawabata's fascination with Asakusa translates into *The Scarlet Gang of Asakusa* taking the form of a travelogue at times. These qualities have led Seiji Lippit to characterize the novel as a "cartographic text."[33] In this respect there are several similarities between Tayama Katai's travelogue-like writing in *Record of the Tokyo Earthquake* and Kawabata's *The Scarlet Gang of Asakusa*. In both instances the descriptions of the journey and the observations of the narrator threaten to upstage the plot. For example, Kawabata describes the location of the gang's hideout with precision, but only up to a point:

> Walking north from the bus stop in back of the Sensō, the Asakusa Kannon Temple, you see Umamichi-machi is on the right and Senzoku-machi is on the left. Go on a bit, passing the Kisakata Police Station on the left and the Fuji Elementary School on the right. Then after the Sengen Shrine, you come to a crossroads. Walk along the stone wall of the shrine, and you pass the public market, the Kamiarai Bridge, spanning the banks of the Yoshiwara canal. But before reaching the bridge, there is a certain alley. . . . Well, to say "a certain alley" sounds like I am beginning an old-fashioned novel.[34]

In this passage, Kawabata playfully blurs the distinction between fact and fiction by drawing attention to novelistic use of the phrase, "a certain alley." This is done throughout the work, starting with the epigraph in which Kawabata apologizes for the trouble that the publication of the novel might cause for the fictional Scarlet Gang, only to undermine it with the dismissal that what follows is "mere fiction." Kawabata's combination of precision and ambiguity lends an air of authenticity to his fictional world and undercuts it at the same time. In contrast, the prose styles of Tayama Katai and Nagata Mikihiko, discussed in Chapters 3 and 6 respectively, endeavor to convince audiences of their transparent connection to reality.

31. Kawabata Yasunari, "Taika kenbutsu," 67; also collected in Kawabata Yasunari, "Taika kenbutsu," in *Kawabata Yasunari zenshū*, vol. 26 (1980): 9. The "Monopoly Bureau" was a tobacco factory. Tobacco was monopolized by the state in 1898 and remained so until 1985.
32. Kawabata quotes extensively from his 1923 work "Taika kenbutsu" in chapter 44 of *The Scarlet Gang of Asakusa.* After so doing he writes, "I tossed around the idea of writing a long strange novel. And, dear reader, in these pages, after ten years, I have finally begun to do just that." Kawabata Yasunari, *The Scarlet Gang of Asakusa*, 133.
33. Seiji M. Lippit, *Topographies of Japanese Modernism*, 135.
34. Kawabata Yasunari, trans. Alisa Freedman, *The Scarlet Gang of Asakusa*, 4–5; for the original text, see Kawabata, *Asakusa kurenaidan*, 8–9.

Kawabata's "real" descriptions of Asakusa did serve as guides to the area. The Casino Follies show became more popular after he mentioned it in his novel, and many of the dancers and performers he described were real people. To a certain extent, his novel could have served as a guide to the district just as other, more clearly nonfictional works had done.[35] The narrator, led by the fictional gang member Yumiko, guides the readers through the landscape of post-earthquake Asakusa. Despite depicting a fairly close relationship with the street urchins he describes, the narrator maintains a detached position vis-à-vis the object of his observations. This was even more true of the author himself. According to a later essay about the novel, Kawabata remained aloof from the crowd throughout his journeys into Asakusa. As he wrote in 1934, "Although I spent the night in the park a number of times, all I did was walk. I never became acquainted with any of the young delinquents. I never addressed a word to vagrants either."[36]

In this way Kawabata was very much a *flâneur*. As Donald Richie observes in his introduction to Alisa Freedman's English translation of *The Scarlet Gang of Asakusa*, "An often ironic observer, [Kawabata] turned perception itself into a kind of judgment. Like Baudelaire on the boulevard, Kawabata in Asakusa was a literary dandy whose gaze was his only comment."[37] Kawabata retains the detached gaze that Walter Benjamin attributed to Baudelaire's *flâneur*, and that is also seen in Tayama Katai's post-disaster work (see Chapter 3).[38]

Kawabata's own description of *The Scarlet Gang of Asakusa* highlights the role his observations played in its creation. He recognized that his account could not possibly serve as a "record of life and customs in Asakusa" along the lines of Gonda Yasunosuke's reportage, Kon Wajirō's *Modernology* (*Kōgengaku*), or Soeda Azenbō's *Record of the Asakusa Underworld* (*Asakusa teiryūki*), each of which influenced Kawabata's depiction of Asakusa, as Miriam Silverberg and others have pointed out.[39] For Kawabata, *The Scarlet Gang of Asakusa* is rather

35. Here I am referencing nonfiction works by Gonda Yasunosuke and Soeda Azenbō. See Miriam Silverberg, *Erotic Grotesque Nonsense: The Mass Culture of Japanese Modern Times* (Berkeley, CA: University of California Press, 2006), 177–202.

36. Donald Keene, *Dawn to the West*, 795. For the original essay, see Kawabata Yasunari, "Bungakuteki jijoden," 92.

37. Donald Richie, "Foreword," in Kawabata, trans. Freedman, *The Scarlet Gang of Asakusa*, xxviii.

38. Unno Hiroshi also mentions the connection with Baudelaire and Benjamin. Unno, *Modan toshi Tōkyō: Nihon no 1920-nendai*, 32–33, 46.

39. Kawabata Yasunari, "*Asakusa kurenaidan* zokkō yokoku," in *Kawabata Yasunari zenshū* vol. 33 (1982): 102. Translated by Seiji Lippit in Seiji M. Lippit, *Topographies of Japanese Modernism*, 127. For the influence of these authors on Kawabata, see Miriam Silverberg, *Erotic Grotesque Nonsense*, 188–89, and Alisa Freedman, "Translator's Preface," in Kawabata, *The Scarlet Gang of Asakusa*, xl–xli and note 13. See also Kon Wajirō et al., *Moderunorojio: kōgengaku*, Fukkokuban edition (Gakuyō Shobō, 1986), and Soeda Azenbō, *Asakusa teiryūki*, vol. 2, Soeda Azenbō, Soeda Tomomichi chosakushū (Tōsui Shobō, 1982).

"an account of my observations (*kenbunki*) and impressions (*inshōki*) of Asakusa."[40] The focus on his subjective observations, rather than the more "objective" gaze of Soeda and others, points to the similarity between Kawabata's perspective here and Katai's *heimen byōsha* (surface portrayal) style.

Despite the surface similarity, Kawabata's *flâneur* is qualitatively different from Katai's. Though the descriptions of the city are filtered through the narrator's observations, Kawabata's subject is always Asakusa and never himself. The fragmented city in fact undermines the notion of the bounded, self-contained subject. Several scholars have shown how the narrator is actually split into three in this text. One is the character of the narrator who interacts with the other characters in the book, the character who sees Yumiko and talks with her. Another is the narrator/author who speaks directly to the reader throughout the work in passages that begin with the phrase, "Dear reader." Finally, there is the omniscient narrator who describes events the other two would not be privy to (for example, those transpiring inside the boat where Yumiko has trapped a man).[41] Rather than looking outside and seeing only "the ruin within," as Katai did, Kawabata turns this idea on its head. The process of observing and describing the chaos in the city outside fractures the subjectivity of the narrator until the self and the outside are dissolved into almost indistinguishable fragments of modernity.

This is one crucial difference between Tayama Katai's *Record of the Tokyo Earthquake*—especially the "Burnt Remains" chapter—and Kawabata's *The Scarlet Gang of Asakusa.* The former is an I-novel taken outside, with little effect on the narrator and the narrative style, whereas the latter undercuts the stability of the narrator in the swirling chaos of the city. This difference can be attributed to changes occurring over the six years between the two works, and to the generational difference between the two authors: Katai was a member of the *bundan* establishment and a key figure in the development of the I-novel, while Kawabata was a rising avant-garde star. *The Scarlet Gang of Asakusa* registers those changes.

Whereas Kawabata's experimentation here clearly reflects his background in modernism, the influence of the proletarian movement is harder to find. In addition to the bright urban spectacles of Asakusa, Kawabata documents its darker side, with particular attention to the impoverished lives of vagrants. Miriam Silverberg has discussed this element of the novel in her survey of interwar grotesquerie: "Kawabata's work speaks of historic ruptures caused by the earthquake in 1923 and the depression in 1930."[42] The changes wrought by the depression are

40. Kawabata Yasunari, "*Asakusa kurenaidan* zokkō yokoku," 102. Translated by Seiji Lippit in Seiji M. Lippit, *Topographies of Japanese Modernism*, 127.

41. Seiji Lippit discusses this point, giving credit to Ōta Suzuko.

42. Miriam Silverberg, *Erotic Grotesque Nonsense*, 220. Part III, chapter 2 in particular, explores various responses to the lower levels of society in Asakusa.

clear; an out-of-work beggar in a pond scoops up food meant for the carp, and day laborers, unable to make ends meet, buy food scraps from beggars.

In the second half of the book, Kawabata links the depression to both the proletarian labor movement and the proliferation of beggars, delinquents, and prostitutes in Asakusa. He quotes from a newspaper headline a few months earlier, "End of the Shinshū Silk Filatures," and notes how the price of silk collapsed, leading to over 300 factories closing and almost 100,000 unemployed factory girls.[43] Kawabata follows this by drawing a link between the economy and Asakusa: "Where do they go? Probably some of them go back to their hometowns in the hinterlands or up in the mountains. Others join the fight against the capitalists—but this isn't all of them. The others are welcomed with open arms by the Asakusa regiment of underhanded pimps."[44] There is no question that Kawabata is more concerned with those who end up in the hands of pimps than he is with those fighting capitalism. Nevertheless, though he is a detached *flâneur* and an aesthete, he cannot ignore the inequalities protested by the proletarian movement.

The Korean Massacre does figure in the work, although tangentially. In reminiscing about the earthquake, Yumiko recalls the massacre by saying, "It was a time you thought it was perfectly normal to see people beaten to death with iron bars."[45] Wider-ranging discussions of foreigners are more prevalent. There are Koreans in the novel, and Asakusa is portrayed as an area populated by characters from a variety of backgrounds. It is a world that celebrates difference, particularly among the performers. As Kawabata puts it, "In general, the Asakusa masses are kind to foreign performers." Chinese, Russian and Finnish dancing girls (many of whom are recognizable as real women known to have been there at the time) all make an appearance.

At the same time, this is not an idealized world where ethnic and racial differences no longer matter, and there are elements of xenophobia that filter in. One of the young male gang members rejects the advances of an Indian pedophile, yelling, "If you want to make out with a Japanese you better go bleach your skin."[46] He thus questions the man's race rather than the differences in their ages. On another occasion the narrator says of a pair of Russian dancers, "these foreign bitches (*furyōshōjo*) act like they own the place." To this Haruko, another female

43. Kawabata Yasunari, *Asakusa kurenaidan*, 155; idem, trans. Freedman, *The Scarlet Gang of Asakusa*, 124. This segment appeared in the September 1930 issue of *Kaizō* and it referenced a headline in mid-July.

44. Kawabata Yasunari, *Asakusa kurenaidan*, 155–56; idem, trans. Freedman, *The Scarlet Gang of Asakusa*, 125.

45. Kawabata Yasunari, *Asakusa kurenaidan*, 81; idem, trans. Freedman, *The Scarlet Gang of Asakusa*, 63.

46. Kawabata Yasunari, *Asakusa kurenaidan*, 60; idem, trans. Freedman, *The Scarlet Gang of Asakusa*, 47.

gang leader, replies, "Don't know about that, but, lately, in the park, there are so many more of these foreigners [*ketō*, a derogatory term meaning hairy foreigners, specifically Europeans]. I heard someone say that sooner or later this place might turn into some international gangland."[47] Though the shadowy figure of the outlaw Korean is absent, an undercurrent of ethnic prejudice and fear of unruly foreigners is implied in this passage.

The Scarlet Gang of Asakusa shows the impact of literary modernism along with hints of the social consciousness found in proletarian literature, but the work also reflects another major change in the literary world after the earthquake: the rise of popular literature. This is not to say that popular literature did not exist before the quake, but merely that the distinction between popular and "pure" literature was more clearly drawn afterward. This was particularly true as the *bundan* responded to the ascent of mass-circulation magazines such as *King*, which competed with the more highbrow *Chūō kōron* and *Kaizō.*

The Scarlet Gang of Asakusa is a borderline text that is stylistically avant-garde, but its content celebrates the popular culture of Asakusa and includes quotations from songs, revues, and performances.[48] Its publication history bears out its hybridity, for it was serialized in both the evening edition of the *Tokyo Asahi shinbun* and in highbrow magazines such as *Shinchō* and *Kaizō.* Despite its fragmented, experimental style, *The Scarlet Gang of Asakusa* was itself a popular text. As Kawabata himself claimed, the popularity of the novel brought the Casino Follies revue to fame.[49] Perhaps more revealing, *The Scarlet Gang of Asakusa* was made into a film while still being serialized.[50] This film focused on a short episode of the mostly plotless work, a melodrama in which the earthquake plays a central role.[51] In this crucial episode we see that the core of Kawabata's work is connected to the disaster.

In this episode, the protagonist Yumiko, who is the narrator's guide to Asakusa, conspires against the man who drove her sister mad. This revenge plot is re-

47. Kawabata Yasunari, *Asakusa kurenaidan*, 147; idem, trans. Freedman, *The Scarlet Gang of Asakusa*, 118. Alisa Freedman's translation of *furyōshōjo* as "bitches" seems a bit strong; perhaps "bad girls from overseas" might be more accurate, if not as colorful.

48. As Seiji Lippit has written, "Through its rejection of linear plot, the frequent use of interruption in both language and narrative, and the deployment of multiple interweaving points of view, the work resists easy consumption by the reader." Seiji M. Lippit, *Topographies of Japanese Modernism*, 129.

49. This is from Kawabata's own assessment, but it is often repeated in scholarship on the book. As he puts it, "That *The Scarlet Gang of Asakusa* brought about the 'Asakusa fad' of the time was an unexpected result for the author." Kawabata Yasunari, "*Asakusa kurenaidan* ni tsuite," in *Kawabata Yasunari zenshū*, vol. 33 (1982): 141.

50. The film was produced by the Teikoku Kinema company and directed by Takami Sadae. It premiered on September 5, 1930, almost precisely seven years after the quake.

51. See the descriptions in *Kinema Junpo*, no. 369 (June 21, 1930): 69, and no. 378 (September 21, 1930): 77.

vealed gradually. At first Yumiko flirts with her target, Akagi, at a carousel where she is working. At this point neither Akagi nor the reader is aware of the significance of the flirtation. After leading him along, Yumiko plans an assignation on a boat in the Sumida River. Once Akagi arrives and the boat is unmoored, Yumiko tells him the story of her sister, Ochiyo, who has been introduced several chapters earlier as a "lovely lunatic." According to her narration, Yumiko and her sister had taken refuge in the Asakusa Elementary School after being burnt out of their home by the fires. There, they were crammed in among the refugees, with each family divided by makeshift partitions. One night, Akagi woke Ochiyo and she disappeared into the night with him. Upon her return, Yumiko notes, "She was trembling all over. She was looking for something. Then she felt for the ends of my braids with her hands. She jammed those braids into her mouth and quietly sobbed."[52] Kawabata makes it perfectly clear what happened. This was a rape.

In the story of Ochiyo, we have the pathos of lost innocence; the clear moral polarity between the predator, Akagi, and his prey; and the strong emotions displayed by Ochiyo's stifled sobbing. These elements resonate with several earthquake-era texts. The melodramatic mode is taken farther when we learn that Ochiyo has been driven mad after the incident, rendering her even more pitiable. Nothing here would be out of place in an earthquake melodrama. The earthquake forced Yumiko and Ochiyo from their home and made them vulnerable to the designs of Akagi and his ilk. The disaster functioned similarly for the character of the miner's daughter, Ohatsu, in Ōkubo Tadamoto's film *Facing Death* (see Chapter 4). That film also featured a subplot with a woman driven to hysterics by the disaster, as did several *jitsuwa* published shortly after the earthquake. Another element of the story can be found in Nagata Mikihiko's sensational story "Red Moon" (see Chapter 8), with its implied rape, though the Korean ethnic element is absent in *The Scarlet Gang of Asakusa*. Kawabata did not necessarily overtly copy these features from previous texts, but they were part of the cultural milieu of post-quake Japan.

Though Ochiyo's story in *The Scarlet Gang of Asakusa* is melodramatic, Yumiko's is less so. Yumiko cannot be considered innocent or defenseless. She has lived on the streets since the earthquake and has become a leader of a gang of dispossessed youths. She fends for herself, and takes care of the younger members of the gang and her older sister. She remains in complete control over Akagi. She lures him to the boat using her charms, prevents his escape, and eventually kills him with an arsenic-laced kiss. With Yumiko, Kawabata draws a contrast between the women before the earthquake, who were innocent and susceptible to the wiles of men like Akagi, and post-quake women such as Yumiko, who are aware of

52. Kawabata Yasunari, *The Scarlet Gang of Asakusa*, 70. For the original text, see *Asakusa kurenaidan*, 88.

the threats of the world and can combat them. Yumiko's story is sensational and thrilling, and her vengeance is morally ambiguous.

* * * * *

The Scarlet Gang of Asakusa is a complicated text that cannot be reduced to a single interpretation. Nevertheless, it incorporates many of the literary trends that rose to prominence after the Great Kanto Earthquake. It is clearly a modernist work, although the influences of proletarian literature and mass literature and culture are evident as well. At the same time, it is explicitly linked to the earthquake on the levels of both narrative and concept. The crucial plot of Yumiko's revenge on Akagi is set in motion by the disaster and the way it makes Yumiko and Ochiyo vulnerable.

Even more significant, however, is how the novel serves as a "map" of post-quake Tokyo. This is not an example of earthquake culture as explored in this book. Rather, *The Scarlet Gang of Asakusa* celebrates the "charm of asphalt and concrete" and the "eroticism, and nonsense and speed" that was spawned amid the newly rebuilt metropolis. The old brick Asakusa "Twelve Story" tower collapsed in the disaster, and the new architectural symbol of Asakusa modernity became the reinforced concrete Asakusa Subway Restaurant tower. The novel is fascinated with the latter. Cosmopolitan and hybrid, *The Scarlet Gang of Asakusa* displays the new style of urban literature that replaced the staid modernity of I-novel individualism. But this urban literature in its various forms—experimental, political, and popular—also faded. By the late 1930s, the ecstasy of the new and the cosmopolitan was exchanged for the veneration of the nation and its traditions. The proletarian literature movement was crushed, the experimental modernism of *The Scarlet Gang of Asakusa* all but disappeared, and Japanese literature once again turned inward. Yet during those heady years following the earthquake, Japanese literature engaged with the world and basked in cosmopolitan modernity, with all its complications.

Bibliography

Akagi Kōhei. "Yūtō bungaku no bokumetsu." *Kindai bungaku hyōron taikei*, vol. 4, 260–66. Kadokawa Shoten, 1971.

———. "Yūtō bungaku no bokumetsu." *Yomiuri shinbun*, August 6–8, 1916.

Akita Ujaku. *Akatsuki e no tabi*. Shinchōsha, 1950.

———. "Gaikotsu no buchō." *Engeki shinchō* 1, no. 4 (April 1924): 28–49.

———. "Gaikotsu no buchō." In *Puroretaria gikyoku shū*, vol. 1, 98–112. Shin Nihon Shuppansha, 1988.

———. "Gaikotsu no buchō." *Shinkō bungaku zenshū Nihon hen*, vol. 1, 473–89. Heibonsha, 1928.

———. "Shi no miyako." *Bunshō kurabu* 8, no. 10 (October 1923): 37.

———. "Tanan no kōhanki: nikki no naka kara." *Kaizō* 5, no. 12 (December 1923): 244–51.

Akutagawa Ryūnosuke. "Daishin ni saiseru kansō." *Akutagawa Ryūnosuke zenshū*, vol. 10, 152–54. Iwanami Shoten, 1995.

———. "Daishin ni saiseru kansō." *Kaizō* 5, no. 10 (October 1923): 194–95.

———. "Daishin zengo." *Josei* 4, no. 4 (October 1923): 11–13.

———. "Mōmon mōtō." *Akutagawa Ryūnosuke zenshū* vol. 10, 166–69. Iwanami Shoten, 1995.

———. "Mōmon mōtō." *Kaizō* 5, no. 11 (November 1923): 282–84.

———. "Taishin zakki." *Akutagawa Ryūnosuke zenshū* vol. 10, 142–47. Iwanami Shoten, 1995.

———. "Taishin zakki." *Chūō kōron* 38, no. 10 (October 1923): 133–37.

Aldrich, Daniel P. *Building Resilience: Social Capital in Post-Disaster Recovery*. Chicago: University of Chicago Press, 2012.

Ambaras, David. "Social Knowledge, Cultural Capital, and the New Middle Class in Japan, 1895–1912." *Journal of Japanese Studies* 24, no. 1 (Winter 1998): 1–33.

Anderson, Benedict. *Imagined Communities: Reflections on the Origin and Spread of Nationalism*. London: Verso, 1991.

Andrew, Dudley, and Paul Andrew. *Kenji Mizoguchi: A Guide to References and Resources*. Boston: G. K. Hall, 1981.

Anonymous. "Daichi wa yuragu." *Katsudō zasshi* 10, no. 8 (August 1924): 139.

———. "Daichi wa yuragu." *Nikkatsu gahō* 1, no. 5 (November 1923): 40–42.

———. "Haikyo no naka." *Katsudō zasshi* 10, no. 8 (August 1924): 138.

———. "Jūichiji gojūhappun." *Katsudō zasshi* 10, no. 2 (February 1924): 95.

———. "Jūichiji gojūhappun." *Kinema junpō* 147 (January 1, 1924): 20.

———. "Shi ni men shite: daishingai ni kakawaru aiwa." *Kamata* 16 (October 1923): 26–27.

——— (probably Kikuchi Kan). "Shinsai no ato." *Bungei shunjū* 2, no. 1 (January 1924): 38–39.

———. "Shinsaigo no shisōkai." *Kikuchi Hiroshi zenshū* vol. 2, 170–71. Musashino Shobō, 2002.

Aono Suekichi. "Gen'ei no taishū kara taishū no jittai e." In *Musan seitō to shakai undō*, 143–51. Hakuyōsha, 1925.

———. "Shinsai to shisō, geijutsu." In *Tenkanki no bungaku*, 366-78. Shunjūsha, 1927.

———. "Shakai no genjitsu to shisō to." *Shinkō* 1, no. 1 (February 1924), reprinted in Kūm Pyōng-dong, ed. *Chōsenjin gyakusatsu ni kansuru chishikijin no hannō*. vol. 2, 9–12. Ryokuin Shobō, 1996.

Arano Kōhei. *Shinsai romansu*. Seishindō Shoten, 1923.

Araragi Hakkōsho, ed. *Kaijinshū: Taishō jūninen shinsai kashū*. Kokin Shoin, 1924.

Baudelaire, Charles. *The Painter of Modern Life, and Other Essays*. Translated and edited by Jonathan Mayne. London: Phaidon, 1964.

Beckmann, George M., and Genji Okubo. *The Japanese Communist Party 1922–1945*. Stanford, CA: Stanford University Press, 1969.

Benjamin, Walter. *Charles Baudelaire: A Lyric Poet in the Era of High Capitalism*. Translated by Harry Zohn. London: NLB, 1973.

Bestor, Theodore. "Tokyo's 'Traditional' Urbanism." In *The Cultural Meaning of Urban Space*, edited by Robert Rotenberg and Gary McDonogh, 47–60. Westport, CT: Bergin & Garvey, 1993.

Borland, Janet. "Capitalising on Catastrophe: Reinvigorating the Japanese State with Moral Values through Education Following the 1923 Great Kanto Earthquake." *Modern Asian Studies* 40, no. 4 (October 2006): 875–907.

———. "Stories of Ideal Japanese Subjects from the Great Kantō Earthquake of 1923." *Japanese Studies* 25, no. 1 (May 2005): 21–34.

Bottomore, Stephen. *The Titanic and Silent Cinema*. East Sussex, England: Projection Box, 2000.

Bourdieu, Pierre. *Distinction: A Social Critique of the Judgement of Taste*. Cambridge, MA: Harvard University Press, 1984.

———. "The Forms of Capital." In *Education: Culture, Economy, and Society*, edited by A. H. Halsey et al., 46–58. Oxford; New York: Oxford University Press, 1997.

Bowen-Struyk, Heather. "Rethinking Japanese Proleterian Literature." Ph.D. dissertation, University of Michigan, 2001.

Brooks, Barbara. "Peopling the Japanese Empire: The Koreans in Manchuria and the Rhetoric of Inclusion." In *Japan's Competing Modernities*, edited by Sharon Minichiello, 25–44. Honolulu: University of Hawai'i Press, 1998.

Brooks, Peter. *The Melodramatic Imagination: Balzac, Henry James, Melodrama, and the Mode of Excess*. New Haven, CT: Yale University Press, 1995.

Bungei nenkan, vol. 2. Bunsendō Shoten, 1974.

Chambers, Ross. *Untimely Interventions: AIDS Writing, Testimonial, and the Rhetoric of Haunting*. Ann Arbor: University of Michigan Press, 2004.

Chiba Kameo. "Kokuminseijō no futa gimon." *Josei Kaizō* 2, no. 11 (November 1923): 7–15.

———. "Sensō bungei to shingo no bungaku." *Hennentai Taishō bungaku zenshū*, vol. 12, 318–25. Yumani Shobō, 2003.

———. "Shinsaigo-ha no shisō to bungei." *Kaizō* 5, no. 11 (November 1923): 257–64.

Chikamatsu Shūkō. "Tensai ni arazu tenken to omoe." *Kaizō* 5, no. 10 (October 1923): 216–19.

Chūō bōsai kaigi saigai kyōkun no keishō ni kan suru senmon chōsakai. 2006. "1923 no Kantō dai jishin hōkokusho." http://www.bousai.go.jp/jishin/chubou/kyoukun/rep/1923--kantoDAISHINSAI/index.html (accessed November 16, 2011). Web.

Chūō Shōgyō Gakkō, ed. *Kugatsu tsuitachi: risai gakusei shuki*. Sankōsha, 1924.

Davies, Andrea. *Saving San Francisco: Relief and Recovery after the 1906 Disaster*. Philadelphia: Temple University Press, 2012.

Dodd, Stephen. *Writing Home: Representations of the Native Place in Modern Japanese Literature*. Cambridge, MA: Harvard University Press, 2004.

Doležel, Lubomìr. "Truth and Authenticity in Narrative." *Poetics Today* 1, no. 3 (Spring 1980): 7–25.

Duara, Prasenjit. *Rescuing History from the Nation*. Chicago: University of Chicago Press, 1995.

Dyson, Michael. *Come Hell or High Water: Hurricane Katrina and the Color of Disaster*. New York: Basic Civitas, 2006.

Eagleton, Terry. *Literary Theory: An Introduction*. Minneapolis: University of Minnesota Press, 1996.

Eberhard, Wolfram. "The Political Function of Astronomy and Astronomers in Han China." In *Chinese Thought and Institutions*, edited by John K. Fairbank, 33–70. Chicago: University of Chicago Press, 1957.

Ebrey, Patricia Buckley, ed. *Chinese Civilization: A Sourcebook*. New York: Free Press, 1993.

Edogawa Ranpo. "Osoroshiki sakugo." *Shin-seinen* 4, no. 13 (November 1923): 122–48.

Eguchi Kan. "Bungei jihyō." *Gakan* 2, no. 2 (February 1924): 183–86.

Ema Shū. *Hitsuji no ikaru toki*. Kage Shobō, 1989.

———. *Hitsuji no ikaru toki*. Shūhōkaku, 1925.

Etchūya Riichi. "Guntai to shakaishūgi." In *Etchūya Riichi chosakushū*. Gifu: Tōkai keizai shinbunsha, 1971.

———. "Ippeisotsu no shinsai shuki." *Nihon puroretaria bungaku shū*, vol. 14, 175–86. Shin Nihon Shuppansha, 1984.

Fowler, Edward. *The Rhetoric of Confession: Shishōsetsu in Early Twentieth-Century Japanese Fiction*. Berkeley: University of California Press, 1988.

Freedman, Alisa. "Translator's Preface." In Kawabata Yasunari, *The Scarlet Gang of Asakusa*. Berkeley: University of California Press, 2005.

Friedberg, Anne. *Window Shopping: Cinema and the Postmodern*. Berkeley: University of California Press, 1993.

Fujioka Hiroyasu and Akira Imafuji. "'Marunouchi shinshiroku' Taishō 11 nenban, Taishō 15 nenban, Shōwa 6 nenban ni keisai sareta kōkyū shain no kyojūchi bunpu ni mirareru tokuchō: Taishō makki kara Shōwa shoki ni okeru Tōkyō no chūsan kaikyū no kyojūchi ni kansuru kenkyū." *Nihon kenchiku gakkai keikakukei ronbunshū* 470 (1995): 235–42.

Fujisawa Morihiko and Bureau of Social Affairs Home Office. *The Great Earthquake of 1923 in Japan*. Naimushō-Shakaikyoku, 1926.

Fujisawa Morihiko and Naimushō-Shakaikyoku. *Taishō shinsaishi*. Iwanami, 1926.

Fujita Fujio and Ōwada Shigeru. *Hyōden Hirasawa Keishichi: Kameido Jiken de gisei to natta* rōdō engeki, seikyō, rōkin no senkusha. Kōbunsha, 1996.

Fukui Shirō. "Shi ni men shite." *Katsudō kurabu* 6, no. 10 (October 1923): 40–42.

Fuse Tatsuji. "Senjin sawagi no chōsa." In *Chōsenjin gyakusatsu ni kansuru chishikijin no hannō*, edited by Kūm Pyōng-dong, 335–37. Ryokuin Shobō, 1996.

Fussell, Paul. *The Great War and Modern Memory*. New York: Oxford University Press, 1975.
Gendaishi no Kai. *Dokyumento Kantō Daishinsai*. Sōfūkan, 1983.
Gluck, Carol. *Japan's Modern Myths: Ideology in the Late Meiji Period*. Princeton, NJ: Princeton University Press, 1985.
Goi Makoto. "Tetsudō, 'Nihon,' byōsha: Tayama Katai no kikōbun 'Kusa-makura' wo megutte." *Nishōgakusha* 43 (2000): 53–75.
Gordon, Andrew. *Labor and Imperial Democracy in Prewar Japan*. Berkeley: University of California Press, 1991.
Haag, Andre. "Nakanishi Inosuke to Taishōki Nihon no 'futei senjin' e no manazashi." *Gengobunka kenkyū* 22, no. 3 (January 2011): 81–98.
Hall, Stuart. "The Work of Representation." In *Representation: Cultural Representations and Signifying Practices*, edited by Stuart Hall, 13–74. London; Thousand Oaks, CA: Sage, 1997.
Hammond, Charles E. "The Interpretation of Thunder." *The Journal of Asian Studies* 53 (1994–05–01): 487–503.
Hasegawa Nyozekan. "Ryūgen higo wa dōshite okoru ka." In *Chōsenjin gyakusatsu ni kansuru chishikijin no hannō*, edited by Kūm Pyōng-dong, 143–44. Ryokuin Shobō, 1996.
Hastings, Sally A. *Neighborhood and Nation in Tokyo, 1905–1937*. Pittsburgh, PA: University of Pittsburgh Press, 1995.
Havens, Thomas. *Farm and Nation in Modern Japan: Agrarian Nationalism, 1870–1940*. Princeton, NJ: Princeton University Press, 1974.
Hazumi Tsuneo. *Eiga gojūnenshi*. Osaka: Sōgensha, 1951.
Hibiya, Junko. "Variationist Sociolinguistics." In *The Handbook of Japanese Linguistics*, edited by Natsuko Tsujimura, 101–20. Malden, MA: Blackwell Publishers, 1999.
High, Peter. "Japanese Film and the Great Kanto Earthquake of 1923." *Kokusai kankei gakubu kiyō* 31 (1985): 71–84.
Hirano Ken. "Kaisetsu." In *Gendai Nihon bungaku ronsō shi*. Miraisha, 2006.
Hiroi Osamu. *Saigai to Nihonjin: kyodai jishin no shakai shinri*. Jiji Tsūshinsha, 1986.
Hirotsu Kazuo. "Hinan to bengo." *Hennentai Taishō bungaku zenshū*, vol. 12, edited by Sone Hiroyoshi, 558–64. Yumani Shobō, 2002.
Hoffman, Susannah M., and Anthony Oliver-Smith, eds. *Catastrophe & Culture: The Anthropology of Disaster*. Santa Fe, NM; Oxford: School of American Research Press, 2002.
Hori Shin. "Kantō daishinsai to tenkenron: Shibusawa Eiichi wo chushin ni." In *Rekishi to bungaku, geijutsu: Kantō daishinsai*, 129–53. Kyōritsu Joshi Daigaku Sōgō Bunka Kenkyūjo Kanda Bunshitsu, 2004.
Hosoda Tamiki. "Unmei no minikusa." *Bunshō kurabu* 8, no. 10 (October 1923): 80–83.
Ikuta Hanayo. "Hinan no niya." *Bunshō kurabu* 8, no. 10 (October 1923): 57–59.
Inagaki Tatsurō. "Kantō daishinkasai to bundan." *Kokubungaku: kaishaku to kyōzai no kenkyū* 129 (1964): 42–47.
Ishiguro, Yoshiaki. "A Japanese National Crime: The Korean Massacre after the Great Kantō Earthquake of 1923." *Korea Journal* 38, no. 4 (Winter 1998): 331–54.
"Ishihara Chiji 'Tsunami wa tenbatsu, gayoku wo arai otosu hitsuyō.'" *Yomiuri shinbun*, March 15, 2011, <http://www.yomiuri.co.jp/politics/news/20110314-OYT1T00740.htm> (accessed August 1, 2013). Web.
Ishizaka Kōichi. "Nihon no shakaishugisha no Chōsen-kan." *Sanzenri* 34 (1983): 79–87.

Ishizuka, Hiromichi. "The Slum Dwellings and the Urban Renewal Scheme in Tokyo, 1868–1923." *The Developing Economies* 19, no. 2 (1981): 169–93.

Itami Saburō. "Shinsai aiwa 'Shi ni men shite' wo miru." *Shōchiku gahō* 1, no. 11 (November 1923): 18–19.

Ito, Ken K. *An Age of Melodrama: Family, Gender, and Social Hierarchy in the Turn-of-the-Century Japanese Novel.* Stanford, CA: Stanford University Press, 2008.

Itō Kazumi. "Shōnen no nageki." *Shōnen sekai* 29, no. 11 (November 1923): 50–56.

Iwamoto Keiji, and Makino Mamoru, eds. *Eiga nenkan Shōwa hen*, vol. 1. Nihon Tosho Sentā, 1994.

Iwasaki Katsumi. "Kaigenreika no besuto serā: *Taishō daishinsai daikasai* 70 nen go no shohyō." *Masukomi jyanarizumu ronshū* 4 (December 1995): 56–84.

Iwata Mitsuko. *Kawabata Yasunari: Ushirosugata e no dokuhaku.* Yumani Shobō, 1992.

Kanagawa-ken. *Taishō jūninen kugatsu ichinichi daishinsai shashinchō.* Yokohama: Kanagawa Shinbun-sha, 1923.

Kang Tōk-sang. *Kantō daishinsai.* Chūō Kōron-sha, 1975.

———. "Kantō daishinsai ka 'Chōsenjin bōdō ryūgen' ni tsuite." *Rekishi hyōron* 281 (October 1973): 21–30.

Kang Tōk-sang and Kūm Pyōng-dong. *Kantō daishinsai to Chōsenjin.* Misuzu Shobō, 1963.

Karatani, Kōjin. *Origins of Modern Japanese Literature.* Translated by Brett de Bary. Durham, NC: Duke University Press, 1993.

Kasai Zenzō. "Ugomekumono." *Kasai Zenzō zenshū*, vol. 2, 33–58. Hirosaki: Tsugaru Shobō, 1974.

Katagami Noboru. "Shinsaikasai to bungaku." *Shinkō bungaku zenshū*, vol. 9, 486–508. Heibonsha, 1930.

Katsuyama Kō. *Taishō shishōsetsu kenkyū.* Meiji Shoin, 1980.

Kawabata Yasunari. *Asakusa kurenaidan.* Senshin-sha, 1930.

———. "*Asakusa kurenaidan* ni tsuite." *Kawabata Yasunari zenshū*, vol. 33, 137–45. Shinchōsha, 1982.

———. "*Asakusa kurenaidan* zokkō yokoku." *Kawabata Yasunari zenshū*, vol. 33, 100–105. Shinchōsha, 1982.

———. "Bungakuteki jijoden." *Kawabata Yasunari zenshū*, vol. 33, 84–99. Shinchōsha, 1982.

———. *The Scarlet Gang of Asakusa.* Translated by Alisa Freedman. Berkeley, CA: University of California Press, 2005.

———. "Shichigatsu no shōsetsu." *Kawabata Yasunari zenshū*, vol. 30, 33–47. Shinchōsha, 1982.

———. "Shinshun bundan no shūkaku." *Kawabata Yasunari zenshū*, vol. 30, 89–94. Shinchōsha, 1982.

———. "Taika kenbutsu." *Bungei shunjū* 1, no. 11 (November 1923): 66–68.

———. "Taika kenbutsu." *Kawabata Yasunari zenshū*, vol. 26, 7–10. Shinchōsha, 1980.

———. "Yojin bungei no sakuhin." *Kawabata Yasunari zenshū*, vol. 30, 60–68. Shinchōsha, 1982.

Kawashima, Ken C. *The Proletarian Gamble: Korean Workers in Interwar Japan.* Durham, NC: Duke University Press, 2009.

Kawatake Shigetoshi.. "Honjo wo dasshutsu shite." *Josei* 4, no. 5 (November 1923): 110–18.

———. "Sōnan ki." In *Taishō daishin kasai shi.* Edited by Yamamoto Miyoshi, 22–31. Kaizō-sha, 1924.

Keene, Donald. *Dawn to the West: Japanese Literature of the Modern Era; Fiction*. New York: Columbia University Press, 1998.
Kendrick, Thomas D. *The Lisbon Earthquake*. Philadelphia: Lippincott, 1957.
Kikuchi Kan. "Bungei sakuhin no naiyōteki kachi." In *Gendai Nihon bungaku ronsō shi*, edited by Hirano Ken, 49–52. Miraisha, 1956.
———. "Bungei sakuhin no naiyōteki kachi." *Kindai bungaku hyōron taikei*, vol. 5, 269–72. Kadokawa Shoten, 1972.
———. "Bungei to jinsei." *Kikuchi Hiroshi zenshū*, vol. 14, 345–47. Chūō Kōron-sha, 1937.
———. "Bungei tōzachō: seisan." *Bungei shunjū* 2, no. 1 (January 1924): 51–53.
———. "Bungei tōzachō: seisan." *Kikuchi Hiroshi zenshū*, vol. 14, 339–41. Chūō Kōron-sha, 1937.
———. *Kikuchi Hiroshi zenshū*, 15 vols. Chūō Kōron-sha, 1937.
———. "Kuriyagawa Hakuson-shi no omoide." *Josei Kaizō* 2, no. 11 (November 1923): 105–6.
———. "Saigo zakkan." *Bungei shunjū* 1, no. 11 (November 1923): 71–72.
———. "Saigo zakkan." *Chūō kōron* 38, no. 11 (October 1923): 116–19.
———. "Saigo zakkan." *Kaizō* 5, no. 10 (October 1923): 228.
———. "Sairon bungei sakuhin no naiyōteki kachi." In *Gendai Nihon bungaku ronsō shi*, edited by Hirano Ken, 59–66. Miraisha, 1956.
Kimura Kazuaki. "Kieta 'Hae': Satō Haruo no kantō daishinsai." In *Haikyo no kanōsei: gendai bungaku no tanjō*, edited by Kurihara Yukio, 183–97. Inpakuto Shuppankai and Izara Shobō, 1997.
Kimura Matsuo and Ishii Toshio. *Ehagaki ga kataru Kantō daishinsai*. Tsuge Shobō, 1990.
Kitahara Itoko and Oyobe Katsuhito, eds. *Kantō daishinsai wo egaku: emaki, manga, kodomo no e*. Yokohama: Kanagawa Daigaku Himoji Shiryō Kenkyū Sentā, 2010.
Kitahara Yasuo. "Jishin to shakai shugi." In *Chōsenjin gyakusatsu ni kansuru chishikijin no hannō*, edited by Kūm Pyōng-dong, 401–5. Ryokuin Shobō, 1996.
Kleeman, Faye Yuan. *Under an Imperial Sun: Japanese Colonial Literature of Taiwan and the South*. University of Hawai'i Press, 2003.
Klinenberg, Eric. *Heat Wave: A Social Autopsy of Disaster in Chicago*. Chicago: University of Chicago Press, 2003.
Ko, Walter. "1906 San Francisco Chinatown Burning and Rebuilding." *Chinese American Forum* 22, no. 3 (January 2007): 34–37.
Kobayashi Ichirō. *Tayama Katai kenkyū*, vol. 8–9. Ōfūsha, 1984.
Kōdansha, Dai Nihon Yūbenkai, ed. *Taishō daishinsai daikasai*. Kōdansha, 1923.
Kōdansha Shashi Hensan Iinkai. *Kōdansha no ayunda gojūnen*. Kōdansha, 1959.
Kondo, Dorinne. *Crafting Selves: Power, Gender, and Discourses of Identity in a Japanese Workplace*. Chicago: University of Chicago Press, 1990.
Kōno Kensuke. *Ken'etsu to bungaku: 1920-nendai no kōbō*. Kawade Shobō Shinsha, 2009.
Kōno Toshirō and Hidaka Shōji. "Kaizō jikihitsu genkō gazō dētabēsu." Yūshōdō Shuppan, 2007. DVD-ROM.
Kon Wajirō et al. *Moderunorojio: kōgengaku*. Fukkokuban edition. Gakuyō Shobō, 1986.
Kudō Miyoko. *Kantō daishinsai Chōsenjin gyakusatsu no shinjitsu*. Sankei Shinbun Shuppan, 2009.
Kūm Pyōng-dong. *Chōsenjin gyakusatsu ni kansuru chishikijin no hannō*, vol. 1. Ryokuin Shobō, 1996.
———. *Chōsenjin gyakusatsu ni kansuru chishikijin no hannō*, vol. 2. Ryokuin Shobō, 1996.

———. *Chōsenjin gyakusatsu ni kansuru shokuminchi Chōsen no hannō*. Ryokuin Shobō, 1996.

Kume Masao. "Kamakura shinsai nikki." *Kaizō* 5, no. 10 (October 1923): 246–53.

———. "Watakushi shōsetsu to shinkyō shōsetsu." *Kindai bungaku hyōron taikei*, vol. 6, edited by Miyoshi Yukio and Sofue Shōji, 50–57. Kadokawa Shoten, 1973.

Kuriyagawa Chiyōko. "Kanashimi no tsuioku." *Josei Kaizō* 2, no. 11 (November 1923): 107–13.

———. "Kanashiki tsuikai–Kuriyagawa Hakuson hakase no shi." *Josei* 3, no. 6 (November 1923): 119–47.

Kurosawa, Akira. *Something Like an Autobiography*. New York: Vintage, 1983.

"Kusai to bundan shoka shōsoku ki." *Bunshō kurabu* 8, no. 10 (October 1923): 95–105.

Kyodo News. "Ishihara apologizes for 'divine punishment' remark." *Japan Times*, March 15, 2011, http://search.japantimes.co.jp/cgi-bin/nn20110315x7.html (accessed January 17, 2012). Web.

Lebra, Takie Sugiyama. *Above the Clouds: Status Culture of the Modern Japanese Nobility*. Berkeley: University of California Press, 1993.

Lee, Jinhee. "The Enemy Within: Earthquake, Rumours and Massacre in the Japanese Empire." In *Violence: Mercurial Gestalt*, edited by Tobe Levin, 187–211. Amsterdam; New York: Rodopi, 2008.

———. "Instability of Empire: Earthquake, Rumor, and the Massacre of Koreans in the Japanese Empire." Ph.D. dissertation, University of Illinois, 2004.

Lennon, J. John, and Malcolm Foley. *Dark Tourism*. London; New York: Continuum, 2000.

Levitt, Jeremy I., and Matthew C. Whitaker. *Hurricane Katrina: America's Unnatural Disaster*. Lincoln: University of Nebraska Press, 2009.

Lippit, Seiji M. *Topographies of Japanese Modernism*. New York: Columbia University Press, 2002.

Mack, Edward. *Manufacturing Modern Japanese Literature: Publishing, Prizes, and the Ascription of Literary Value*. Asia-Pacific: Culture, Politics, and Society. Durham, NC: Duke University Press, 2010.

———. "The Value of Literature: Cultural Authority in Interwar Japan." Ph.D. dissertation, Harvard University, 2002.

Maeda Kakuzō. *Kyokō no naka no aidentiti*. Hosei Daigaku Shuppankyoku, 1989.

Masamune Hakuchō. "Tanin no saigai." *Chūō kōron* 39, no. 1 (January 1924): 1–25.

———. "Tanin no saigai." *Hennentai Taishō bungaku zenshū*, vol. 13, 53–69. Yumani Shobō, 2003.

———. "Tsūzoku bungaku sono hoka." *Masamune Hakuchō zenshū*, vol. 7, 73–78. Shinchōsha, 1965.

Mason, Michele. "Empowering the Would-Be Warrior: Bushidō and the Gendered Bodies of the Japanese Nation." In *Recreating Japanese Men*, edited by Sabine Fruhstuck and Anne Walthall, 68–90. Berkeley: University of California Press, 2011.

Masuo Nobuyuki. *Mitsumura Risō den*. Mitsumura Genshokuban Insatsusho, 1964.

Mathy, Francis. *Shiga Naoya*. New York: Twayne Publishers, 1974.

Matsuo Shōichi et al. *Kantō daishinsai seifu, riku-kaigun kankei shiryō*. Nihon Keizai Hyōronsha, 1997.

Matsuo Takayoshi. "Kantō daishinsai ka no Chōsenjin gyakusatsu 1." *Shisō* 471 (1963): 44–61.

———. "Kantō daishinsai ka no Chōsenjin gyakusatsu 2." *Shisō* 476 (1964): 110–20.

Minami Hiroshi. *Taishō bunka*. Keisō Shobō, 1965.

Mitchell, Arthur M., IV. "Subverting Language: Japanese Modernism, Modernity, and Linguistic Critique." Ph.D. dissertation, Yale University, 2012.

Mitchell, Richard H. *Censorship in Imperial Japan*. Princeton, NJ: Princeton University Press, 1983.

Miyake Gaikotsu. "Bandai fukyū rokuhen genryō: Kōdansha no shinsaiki." *Shinsai gahō* 5 (January 1924): 96.

———. "Kyūjibutsu no fukkō." *Shinsai gahō* 3 (November 1923): 44–45.

———. "Tenpenchii wo dōtokuteki ni kaisuru wa yaban shisō nari." *Shinsai gahō* 3 (November 1923): 41.

Miyauchi Shunsuke. "Shoki Tayama Katai ron: kikōbun to shōsetsu to no tanima." *Geibun kenkyū* 36 (1977): 222–33.

Miyoshi Yukio. "Jishin to bungaku- Kantō daishinsai wo megutte." In *Jishin*, edited by Hayashi Kentarō, 291–307. Tōkyō University Press, 1980.

Mizuno Naoki and Horiuchi Minoru. "Senzen Nihon zaijū Chōsenjin kankei shinbun kiji kensaku (Database of prewar newspaper articles related to Koreans in Japan)." http://www.zinbun.kyoto-u.ac.jp/~mizna/shinbun/shinbun.html (accessed May 3, 2011). Web.

Monbushō Futsū Gakumu Kyoku. *Shinsai ni kan suru kyōiku shiryō*, vol. 3. Monbushō, 1923.

Moretti, Franco. "Kindergarten." Translated by David Forgacs in *Signs Taken for Wonders: Essays in the Sociology of Literary Forms*, 157–81. London; New York: Verso, 1988.

Moroi Takafumi and Takemura Masayuki. "Kantō jishin (1923–9–1) ni yoru higai yoin betsu shisha sū suitei." *Nihon jishin kōgakkai ronbun hōkoku shū* 4, no. 4 (September 2004): 21–45.

Munro, Donald J. *The Concept of Man in Early China*. Stanford, CA: Stanford University Press, 1969.

Murō Saisei. "Nichiroku." *Kaizō* 5, no. 10 (October 1923): 210–13.

Mushanokōji Saneatsu. "Zakkan." *Kaizō* 5, no. 10 (October 1923): 229–33.

Nagamine Shigetoshi. *Modan toshi no dokusho kūkan*. Nihon Edita Skūru Shuppanbu, 2001.

Nagata Mikihiko. *Daichi wa furū*. Shun'yōdō, 1923.

Nakamura Murao. "Bungei jihyō: bungakusha to shakai ishiki." *Shin-shōsetsu* 29, no. 1 (January 1924): 11–24.

———. "Honkaku shōsetsu to shinkyō shōsetsu to." *Kindai bungaku hyōron taikei*, vol. 6, 11–16. Kadokawa Shoten, 1973.

Nakanishi Inosuke. "Chōsenjin no tame ni benzu." *Fujin kōron* 8, no. 12 (December 1923): 53–56.

Narita Ryūichi. "Kantō daishinsai no metahisutori no tame ni: hōdō, aiwa, bidan." *Shisō* 866 (August 1996): 61–90.

———. *"Kokyō" to iu monogatari: toshi kūkan no rekishigaku*. Yoshikawa Kōbunkan, 1998.

Needham, Joseph. "Seismology." *Science and Civilisation in China*, vol. 3, 624–35. Cambridge, UK: Cambridge University Press, 1954.

Nihon gairaigo jiten. Sanseidō, 1916.

Nitobe, Inazō. *Bushido: The Soul of Japan*. Philadelphia: The Leeds & Biddle Co., 1900.

Odagiri Susumu. "Kindai bungaku to Kanto daishinsai." *Nihon kindai bungaku daijiten*, vol. 4, 81–83. Kōdansha, 1977.

———. *Shōwa bungaku no seiritsu*. Keisō Shobō, 1965.

Ogasawara, Haruno. "Living with Natural Disasters: Narratives of the Great Kanto and Great Hanshin Earthquakes." Ph.D. dissertation, Northwestern University, 1999.

Ogawa Mimei. "Hakarazaru koto." *Kaizō* 5, no. 11 (November 1923): 2–26.

Okada Kōyō. *Kantō daishin daika kinen shashin chō*. Tōkyō Zuan Insatsu, 1924.

Orihara, Minami, and Gregory Clancey. "The Nature of Emergency: The Great Kanto Earthquake and the Crisis of Reason in Late Imperial Japan." *Science in Context* 25, no. 1 (2012): 103–26.

Ōsugi Sakae. "Atarashiki sekai no tame no atarashiki geijutsu." *Waseda bungaku* 143 (October 1917): 232–51.

Otsuki Fumihiko. *Daigenkai*. Fuzanbō, 1935.

Poulton, Cody. *A Beggar's Art: Scripting Modernity in Japanese Drama, 1900–1930*. Honolulu: University of Hawai'i Press, 2010.

Raddeker, Helene Bowen. *Treacherous Women of Imperial Japan: Patriarchal Fictions, Patricidal Fantasies*. London; New York: Routledge, 1997.

Richie, Donald. "Foreword." In Kawabata Yasunari, *The Scarlet Gang of Asakusa*, Berkeley: University of California Press, 2005.

Robertson, Jennifer. *Native and Newcomer: Making and Remaking a Japanese City*. Berkeley: University of California Press, 1991.

Rodríguez, Havidán, and Russell Dynes. 2006. "Finding and Framing Katrina: The Social Construction of Disaster." http://understandingkatrina.ssrc.org/Dynes_Rodriguez/ (accessed November 15, 2010). Web.

Rojek, Chris. *Ways of Escape: Modern Transformation in Leisure and Travel*. Lanham, MD: Rowman & Littlefield, 1994.

Rubin, Jay. *Injurious to Public Morals: Writers and the Meiji State*. Seattle: University of Washington Press, 1984.

Ryang, Sonia. "The Great Kanto Earthquake and the Massacre of Koreans in 1923: Notes on Japan's Modern National Sovereignty." *Anthropological Quarterly* 76, no. 4 (2003): 731–48.

Sadamura Seihyō. *Taishō jūninen kugatsu tsuitachi daijishin daikasai sōnan hyakuwa*. Chiba: Tadaya Shoten, 1923.

———. *Yume no miyako: Daishin daikasai sōnan jikki*. Chiba: Tadaya Shoten, 1923.

Saitō Hideo. "Kantō daishinsai to chōsenjin sawagi: sanjūgo shūnen ni yosete." *Rekishi hyōron* 99 (November 1958): 25–39.

Sand, Jordan. *House and Home in Modern Japan: Architecture, Domestic Space, and Bourgeois Culture, 1880–1930*. Cambridge, MA: Harvard University Asia Center, 2005–09–06.

Sangai shashin chō: kyū Tōkyō meisho to Kantō no daishinsai. Naigai Shuppan Kyōkai, 1923.

Sano Kesami. "Konran no minato." *Hennentai Taishō bungaku zenshū*, vol. 13, 250–63. Yumani Shobō, 2003.

Sas, Miryam. *Fault Lines: Cultural Memory and Japanese Surrealism*. Stanford, CA: Stanford University Press, 1999.

Sasaki Kiichi and Tanida Shōhei. *Hori Tatsuo: sono shōgai to bungaku*. Kayōsha, 1983.

Sasaki Mitsuzō (as Iwatani Shirō). "Jikeidan yumemonogatari." *Kaizō* 5, no. 11 (November 1923): 214–24.

Sasaki Mitsuzō. "Sōsaku hihyō-san gatsu." In *Bungei nenkan*, 126–45. Nishodō Shoten, 1925.

Sasaki Takamaru. "Chōsenjin e dōjō shite." *Tanemaku zakki* 1, no. 1 (January 1924): 21–22.

Satomi Ton. "Bungei kanken." *Satomi Ton zenshū*, vol. 10, 105–76. Chikuma Shobō, 1979.

———. "Tama wa kudakezu." *Satomi Ton zenshū*, vol. 10, 102–4. Chikuma Shobō, 1979.

Sawa Toyohiko. "Kisei sakka no daishinsai: Tayama Katai to Nagata Mikihiko no ba'ai." *Shakai bungaku* 8 (July 1994): 69–72.

Scalapino, Robert A. *The Japanese Communist Movement, 1920–1966*. Berkeley: University of California Press, 1967.

Schencking, J. Charles. "1923 Tokyo as a Devastated War and Occupation Zone: The Catastrophe One Confronted in Post Earthquake Japan." *Japanese Studies* 29, no. 1 (May 2009): 111–29.

———. *The Great Kanto Earthquake and the Chimera of National Reconstruction in Japan*. New York: Columbia University Press, 2013.

———. "The Great Kanto Earthquake and the Culture of Catastrophe and Reconstruction in 1920s Japan." *The Journal of Japanese Studies* 34, no. 2 (2008): 295–331.

Seidensticker, Edward. *Kafū the Scribbler: The Life and Writings of Nagai Kafū, 1879–1959*. Ann Arbor: University of Michigan, Center for Japanese Studies, 1990.

———. *Low City, High City: Tokyo from Edo to the Earthquake*. New York: Knopf, 1983.

———. "Translator's Notes." In *Modern Japanese Stories: An Anthology*, edited by Ivan Morris, 138. Rutland, VT; Tokyo: Charles E. Tuttle Co., 1961.

Seki Tōfū. "Mōka wo okashite." *Shōnen sekai* 29, no. 11 (November 1923): 64–70.

Senuma Shigeki. *Kindai Nihon bungaku no kōzō*, vol. 2. Shūeisha, 1963.

Shiwakai, ed. *Saika no ue ni: shinsai shishū*. Shinchō-sha, 1923.

Silverberg, Miriam. *Erotic Grotesque Nonsense: The Mass Culture of Japanese Modern Times*. Berkeley: University of California Press, 2006.

Simmel, Georg. "The Ruin." In *Essays on Sociology, Philosophy, and Aesthetics*, edited by Kurt Wolff, 259–66. New York: Harper and Row, 1965.

Singer, Ben. *Melodrama and Modernity: Early Sensational Cinema and Its Contexts*. New York: Columbia University Press, 2001.

Smith, Henry D. "The Edo-Tokyo Transition: In Search of Common Ground." In *Japan in Transition, from Tokugawa to Meiji*, edited by Marius B. Jansen and Gilbert Rozman, 347–74. Princeton, NJ: Princeton University Press, 1986.

———. "Review: *Low City, High City: Tokyo from Edo to the Earthquake*." *Monumenta Nipponica* 39, no. 2 (1984–07–01): 206–10.

Soeda Azenbō. *Asakusa teiryūki. Soeda Azenbō, Soeda Tomomichi' chosakushū*, vol. 2. Tōsui Shobō, 1982.

Soma Tsuneo. "Tayama Katai no 'heimen byōsha.'" In *Nihon shizen shugi ron*, 67–83. Yagi Shoten, 1970.

Stanley, Thomas. Ōsugi Sakae, Anarchist in Taishō Japan: The Creativity of the Ego. Cambridge, MA: Council on East Asian Studies; Harvard University Press, 1982.

Starrs, Roy, ed. *Rethinking Japanese Modernism*. Leiden; Boston: Global Oriental, 2012.

Suzuki, Tomi. *Narrating the Self: Fictions of Japanese Modernity*. Stanford, CA: Stanford University Press, 1996.

Tachibana Sueo. *Honoo no yukue*. Osaka: Seibunkan Shoten, 1923.

Tadokoro Shigeyasu. "Tenken no moto ni hirefu shite." *Shin-seinen* 4, no. 12 (October 1923): 2–10.

Taishō daishin kasai shi. Edited by Yamamoto Miyoshi. Kaizō-sha, 1924.

Takami Jun. *Shōwa bungaku seisuishi*. Bungei Shunjū Shinsha, 1958.

Takao Mitsuko. "Koneko wo nihiki idaita mama." *Shōchiku gahō* 1, no. 11 (November 1924): 20–21.

Takegawa Shigetarō. "Yoshiwara." *Bungei shunjū* 2, no. 1 (January 1924): 39–40.
Takehisa Yumeji. "Hensai zakki." *Kaizō* 5, no. 10 (October 1923): 124–30.
Takehisa Yumeji et al. *Yumeji to Karyō, Kōka no kantō daishinsai rupo*. Kuresu Shuppan, 2003.
Takematsu Yoshiaki. "Metsubō suru teito: bungakushijo no kantō daishinsai." In *Haikyo no kanōsei: gendai bungaku no tanjō*, edited by Kurihara Yukio, 173–82. Inpakuto Shuppankai and Izara Shobō, 1997.
Takemura Masayuki. *Kantō daishinsai: Dai Tōkyō ken no yure wo shiru*. Kajima Shuppankai, 2003.
Takeuchi Shigeo. *Tokyo arekore: Taisho fuzoku sukecchi*. Tōa insatsu, 1987.
Tanaka Jun. "Bungei-Ran." *Yomiuri shinbun*, March 15, 1924, 7.
———. "Yurareteiru toki." *Bungei shunjū* 1, no. 11 (November 1923): 61–63.
Tanizaki Jun'ichirō. "'Kugatsu tsuitachi' zengo no koto." *Tanizaki Jun'ichirō zenshū*, vol. 22, 196–219. Chūō Kōron-sha, 1983.
———. "Tōkyō wo omofu." *Tanizaki Jun'ichirō zenshū*, vol. 21, 1–76. Chūō Kōron-sha, 1983. Originally ran in *Chūō kōron* 49:1–4 (January–April 1934).
Tayama Katai. "Byōsha-ron." *Kindai bungaku hyōron taikei*, vol. 3, 369–84. Kadokawa Shoten, 1971.
———. *Literary Life in Tōkyō, 1885–1915: Tayama Katai's Memoirs "Thirty Years in Tōkyō."* Translated by Kenneth G. Henshall. Leiden; New York: Brill, 1987.
———. *The Quilt and Other Stories*. Translated by Kenneth G. Henshall. University of Tokyo Press, 1981.
———. "Sei ni okeru kokoromi." *Kindai bungaku hyōron taikei*, vol. 3, 448–51. Kadokawa Shoten, 1971.
———. "Taikai no ichizoku." *Sandē Mainichi* 2, no. 46 (October 21, 1923): 3–5, 23.
———. *Tōkyō shinsaiki*. Hakubunkan, 1924.
———. "Yakeato." *Shin-shōsetsu* 29, no. 4 (March 1924): 68–80.
Tester, Keith. *The Flâneur*. London; New York: Routledge, 1994.
Tierney, Robert. "Ethnography, Borders and Violence: Reading between the Lines in Sato Haruo's 'Demon Bird.'" *Japan Forum* 19, no. 1 (2007): 89–110.
Tokuda Shūsei. "Fuaiyagan." *Chūō* kōron 38, no. 12 (November 1923): 106-17.
———. "Fuan no naka ni." *Chūō kōron* 39:1 (January 1924): 248–73.
———. "Fuan no naka ni." *Shūsei zenshū*, vol. 6, 171–205. Kyoto: Rinsen Shoten, 1991.
Toriumi Yasushi et al. *Nihon kin-gendaishi kenkyū jiten*. Tōkyōdō Shuppan, 1999.
Tsuboi Shigeji. "Jūgoen, gojūsen." *Senki* 1, no. 5 (1928): 78–82.
Tsuchida Mitsufumi. "Bungakusha no mita kantō daishinsai." *Nihon kosho tsūshin* August (1992): 2–5.
Tsuda Kōzō. "Daishin to geijutsu." *Gakan* 1, no. 1 (October 1923): 120–26.
Tsukui Takashi. "Kantō daishinsai wo egaku to iu koto: Akita Ujaku no 'Gaikotsu no buchō' wo yomu." *Kokubungaku kenkyū* 150 (October 2006): 81–91.
Twine, Nanette. *Language and the Modern State: The Reform of Written Japanese*. London; New York: Routledge, 1991.
Tyler, William J. *Modanizumu: Modernist Fiction from Japan, 1913–1938*. Honolulu: University of Hawai'i Press, 2008.
Uchida Roan. "Daihakai to fukkō." *Taiyō* 29, no. 12 (October 1923): 68–73.
Uchimura Kanzō. "Sodomu to Gomora no fukumetsu." *Uchimura Kanzō zenshū*, vol. 28, 38–55. Iwanami Shoten, 1983.
———. "Tensai to tenbatsu oyobi tenkei." *Uchimura Kanzō zenshū*, vol. 28, 18–20. Iwanami Shoten, 1983.

Unno Hiroshi. *Modan toshi Tōkyō: Nihon no 1920-nendai*. Chūō Kōron-sha, 1983.
Uno Kōji. "Shinsai bunshō." *Uno Kōji zenshū*, vol. 12, 7–33. Chūō Kōron-sha, 1969.
———. "Satomi Ton." In *Satomi Ton Kubota Mantarō shu*, 417–28. Chikuma Shobō, 1972.
———. "Sanbyakunen no yume." *Shinchō* 39, no. 4 (October 1923): 20–25.
Urry, John. *The Tourist Gaze: Leisure and Travel in Contemporary Societies*. London; Newbury Park, CA: Sage Publications, 1990.
Vlastos, Stephen. "Agrarianism without Tradition." In idem, *Mirror of Modernity: Invented Traditions of Modern Japan*, 79–94. Berkeley: University of California Press, 1998.
Voltaire. "Poem on the Lisbon Disaster: Or an Examination of the Axiom, 'All is Well.'" trans. by Joseph McCabe, originally published in *Toleration and Other Essays by Voltaire*. New York: G. P. Putnam & Sons, 1912, http://oll.libertyfund.org/title/349/28298 (accessed February 1, 2012). Web.
Waley, Paul. "Moving the Margins of Tokyo." *Urban Studies* 39 (August 2002): 1539–50.
Walkley, Arthur. *Drama and Life*. New York: Brentano's, 1908; http://books.google.com/books?id=zDjieJK1zGwC (accessed August 2, 2013). Web.
Weisenfeld, Gennifer. *Imaging Disaster: Tokyo and the Visual Culture of Japan's Great Earthquake of 1923*. Berkeley: University of California Press, 2012.
Williams, Linda. *Playing the Race Card: Melodramas of Black and White from Uncle Tom to O. J. Simpson*. Princeton, NJ: Princeton University Press, 2001.
Woolsey, Thomas. "Rumblings in Modernism." M.A. thesis, University of Washington, Seattle, 1991.
Yamada Shōji. *Kantō daishinsaiji no chōsenjin gyakusatsu*. Sōshisha, 2003.
Yamada Shōji, ed. *Chōsenjin gyakusatsu kanren shinbun hōdō shiryō*, vol. 1. Ryokuin Shobō, 2004.
———. "Kantō daishinsai to Chōsenjin gyakusatsu." *Sanzenri* 36 (November 1983): 39–55.
Yamamoto Kenkichi. "Masamune Hakuchō." *Nihon kindai bungaku daijiten*, vol. 3, 232–36. Kōdansha, 1977.
Yamazaki Kesaya. *Jishin, kempei, kaji, junsa*. Iwanami, 1982.
Yamazaki Shikō. "Yonin no hone wo hirō." *Fujin kōron* 8, no. 12 (1923): 57–64.
Yano, Christine. *Tears of Longing: Nostalgia and the Nation in Japanese Popular Song*. Cambridge, MA: Harvard University Press, 2002.
Yokomitsu Riichi. "Hae." In idem, *Yokomitsu Riichi shū*, 148–52. Shūeisha, 1966.
———. "Oboegaki 8." In idem, *Yokomitsu Riichi zenshū*, vol. 13, 225–29. Kawade Shobō, 1982.
Yoshida Seiichi. *Gendai Nihon bungaku shi*. Ōfūsha, 1980.
Young, James. "Interpreting Literary Testimony: A Preface to Reading Holocaust Diaries and Memoirs." *New Literary History* 218 (1987): 403–23.
Zwicker, Jonathan E. *Practices of the Sentimental Imagination: Melodrama, the Novel, and the Social Imaginary in Nineteenth-Century Japan*. Cambridge, MA: Harvard University Asia Center, distributed by Harvard University Press, 2006.

Index

About the Author

Alex Bates is an associate professor of Japanese language and literature at Dickinson College in Carlisle, Pennsylvania. He received his B.A. from Brigham Young University and his Ph.D. from the University of Michigan. His research interests include disasters, ecocriticism, urban modernism, and the early postwar period in literature and film.